THE FURTHEST GOAL

ENGELBERT KAEMPFER'S ENCOUNTER WITH TOKUGAWA JAPAN

THE FURTHEST GOAL

ENGELBERT KAEMPFER'S
ENCOUNTER WITH
TOKUGAWA JAPAN

BEATRICE M. BODART-BAILEY
DEREK MASSARELLA

JAPAN
LIBRARY

THE FURTHEST GOAL

JAPAN LIBRARY
Knoll House, 35 The Crescent
Sandgate, Folkestone, Kent CT20 3EE

Japan Library is an imprint of Curzon Press Ltd
St John's Studios, Church Road, Richmond, Surrey TW9 2QA

First published 1995
© Japan Library 1995

British Library Catalogue in Publication Data
A CIP entry for this book is available
from the British Library

ISBN 1-873410-37-9

Typeset by Bookman, Slough, in Garamond 12 0n 13 pt
Printed and bound in England by Bookcraft, Midsomer Norton, Avon

Contents

Acknowledgements

THIS BOOK has its origins in a symposium to mark the three-hundredth anniversary of Engelbert Kaempfer's arrival in Japan held in Tokyo in December 1990. The symposium was organized jointly by the Philip Franz-von-Siebold Institut für Japanstudien, Tokyo, and Beatrice Bodart-Bailey. Most of the chapters are much revised versions of papers given there.

While writing and editing we have received institutional support from the Department of East Asian Studies of Princeton University, the Institute of Social Science of the University of Tokyo, the International Research Center for Japanese Studies, Kyoto, the Japan Foundation, and the Research School of Pacific and Asian Studies of the Australian National University. A number of individuals have been most generous either with support and encouragement or in making a number of valuable suggestions for improvement. Most of these are mentioned in the footnotes, but in addition the editors would like to thank George Akita, Josef Bohaczeck, Michael Cooper and Marius B. Jansen.

Derek Massarella, Tokyo
Beatrice M. Bodart-Bailey, Canberra

List of Contributors

CARMEN BLACKER was a Lecturer in Japanese at Cambridge University from 1958 to 1991. Her books and articles on Japanese religion and folklore include *The Catalpa Bow: a Study in Shamanistic Practices in Japan*, 1975. She is a Fellow of the British Academy.

BEATRICE M. BODART-BAILEY is a Research Fellow in the Research School of Pacific and Asian Studies of the Australian National University. She is the author of *Kenperu to Tokugawa Tsunayoshi*, 1994, and numerous articles. She is preparing a new translation of Kaempfer's *History of Japan*.

DEREK MASSARELLA is a Professor in the Faculty of Economics of Chuo University, Tokyo. He is the author of *A World Elsewhere: Europe's Encounter with Japan in the Sixteenth and Seventeenth Centuries*, 1990, and numerous articles.

WOLFGANG MUNTSCHICK is an editor at the Deutscher Apotheker Verlag, Stuttgart. He is the translator and editor of Kaempfer's *Flora Japonica* and *Phoenix persicus*, and author of numerous articles.

JÖRG SCHMEIßER is Head of the Printmaking Workshop, Institute of the Arts, Australian National University, Canberra. He is an internationally renowned artist with many solo exhibitions to his credit.

PAUL VAN DER VELDE is the editor for the International Institute for Asian Studies, Leiden. He has edited six volumes of *Deshima Dagregisters: Their Original Tables of Contents* in the *Intercontinenta* series of Leiden University, and is the author of numerous articles on colonial history.

Abbreviations

Add.	British Library, London, Additional Manuscript.
Amoenitates Exoticae	Engelbert Kaempfer, *Amoenitatum exoticarum politico-physico-medicarum fasciculi V*, . . ., Lemgo, 1712.
ARA/VOC	Algemeen Rijksarchief, The Hague, 01.04.01, Het Archief van de Vereenigde Oostindische Compagnie,1602-1796.
BL	British Library, London.
Bodl.	Bodleian Library, Oxford.
Dohm	Engelbert Kaempfer, *Geschichte und Beschreibung von Japan*, edited by Christian Wilhelm von Dohm, 2 vols, Lemgo, 1777-79, reprint Brockhaus, Stuttgart, 1964.
IOR	India Office Library and Records, London.
NFJ	Algemeen Rijksarchief, The Hague, 01.04.21, Het Archief van de Nederlandse factorij in Japan, 1609-1860.
Or.	British Library, London, Oriental Collections.
Scheuchzer	Engelbert Kaempfer, *The History of Japan*, translated by J. G. Scheuchzer, repr., 3 vols, Glasgow, 1906.
Sl.	British Library, London, Sloane Manuscript
VOC	Vereenigde Oostindische Compagnie (Dutch East India Company).

CHAPTER ONE

Introduction:
The Furthest Goal

B.M. Bodart-Bailey

FEW DESCRIPTIONS of foreign countries have stood the test of time so well as Engelbert Kaempfer's work known in English as *The History of Japan.*[1] The work was an immediate success when it was first published in London in 1727 and a reprint became necessary the following year. During the next ten years *The History* appeared in a total of ten editions of translations and reprints, an unusual record for a work of its kind.[2] Even Voltaire, known for his acid pen, praised the work highly and incorporated some of the material into his own writings.[3] Later visitors to Japan, such as Carl Peter Thunberg (1743-1828), Hendrick Doeff (1777-1835) and Philipp Franz von Siebold (1796-1866) who stayed in the country under much less restricted conditions and for longer periods, found it impossible to improve on Kaempfer's account. When the American Commodore Matthew C. Perry set out in the middle of the nineteenth century to 'open up' Japan he carried Kaempfer's book on board,[4] while in England it was used as a reference work by journalists such as Alexander Knox (1818-91) writing for the influential *Edinburgh Review.*[5] Today, Kaempfer's account is compulsory reading for anyone studying the Tokugawa period and Japanese historians frequently cite Kaempfer's account, for it contains material not covered in Japanese sources. Yet in spite of the acclaim *The History of Japan* has received, relatively little research has been published about the author, his personal encounter with late seventeenth century Japan and the way this experience came to reach the public in the form of the well-known work. In view of the paucity of material on Kaempfer's life, especially in English, a brief biographical sketch as background information for the more detailed studies that follow is in order.

KAEMPFER'S EARLY LIFE (1651-1683)

Engelbert Kaempfer was born in 1651, the second son of the *pastor primarus,* the senior vicar, of the merchant town of Lemgo in Westphalia. The cathedral-sized church and the richly decorated masonry of the houses lining the market and the main thoroughfare still bear witness to the former importance of this now somewhat isolated rural township. Kaempfer's father came from an established family and was an educated man. Like his sons he had been a pupil at the local Latin school. Later, he studied at Rostock University and eventually obtained a master's degree. Aged only thirty-four he was promoted to the important post of senior vicar.[6]

Kaempfer grew up in a relatively privileged environment. Although his position as vicar did not permit the father to accumulate great material wealth, he did possess a well-stocked library containing, amongst other valuable works, Adam Olearius's account of Duke Friedrich von Holstein-Gottorp's mission to the court of the Shah of Persia in 1635-39.[7] When Kaempfer eventually followed in Olearius's footsteps and travelled to the Shah's court at Isfahan, he frequently referred to this account.[8]

Not just Kaempfer's life, but also the careers of his brothers testify to the stimulus provided by their childhood environment. Kaempfer's brothers and stepbrothers were all widely travelled and had distinguished academic or official careers; his eldest brother Joachim taught at Leiden University and was later mayor of

2

Lemgo, while the younger, Andreas, was a noted scholar of Hebrew.[9]

The earliest extant written words in young Engelbert's hand are those on his elder brother's matriculation essay. 'Phoebe will reward you if you continue the way you have begun' wrote the fourteen-year- old boy. The title of the matriculation essay was 'Twenty-four Postulates against Atheism',[10] indicating that – as was to be expected – atheism was condemned in the vicarage, but nevertheless still considered a subject worthy of discussion. In his first work on Asia, *Amoenitatum exoticarum politico-physico-medicarum fasciculi V,* (the title is usually abbreviated to *Amoenitates Exoticae*), published in 1712, Kaempfer was to argue that the Japanese were not atheists, only worshipping the Divine Majesty in a different fashion.[11] The tolerance Kaempfer later displayed towards non-Christian religions might well have received its first stimulus from discussions held at the vicarage.

These discussions would also have focused on the gruesome events taking place in Lemgo at the time. The town holds the dubious distinction of having burnt the greatest number of witches: thirty-eight in three years.[12] In 1665, when the fourteen-year-old Engelbert signed the matriculation essay of his brother, the last and most bloody phase commenced. Kaempfer's uncle by marriage, the junior vicar Andreas Koch, was sentenced to death for being in league with the local witches, the only vicar to meet such a fate. Koch had used the pulpit to condemn the murder of these unfortunate women, who were tortured to confess imaginary sins, and thereby had incurred the wrath of the city elders, especially the mayor, for whom the witch-hunt served as stratagem to consolidate his power. In local history he has gone down as the *Hexenbürgermeister*, the witch-hunt mayor. The power of the local government at the time can be gauged from the fact that the city elders succeeded in having Gießen University pronounce and endorse the sentence.[13]

Kaempfer's own matriculation essay, which he sub-

3

mitted at the age of twenty-one at Danzig after having studied, as was customary, at various schools away from his home town, must be viewed with this incident in mind. At a time when a new generation of scholars was arguing for man's natural right to govern himself, Kaempfer defended the authority of the ruler as god-given and absolute. The exercise of justice and just government was too grave a responsibility to be put in the hands of either the nobility or the common man, Kaempfer argued in his thesis. Justice and government had to be subject solely to the will of the country's highest ruler, 'His Majesty', who of course deserved this title only if he governed without regard to personal gain.[14] In short, Kaempfer argued for a system of government under which the locally instigated witch-hunt of Lemgo could not have taken place. Just over ten years later one of the most famous defenders of the natural rights theory, Samuel Pufendorf (1632-1694), would sign Kaempfer's autograph book as a token of their friendship.[15] But apparently Kaempfer's opinion on the subject did not change, for later in Japan he greatly praised the autocratic government of the fifth Tokugawa shogun, Tsunayoshi. In his eyes, Tsunayoshi was a 'great and excellent ruler', fair and compassionate,[16] a judge-ment at odds with the views of the Japanese military aristocracy, who resented the shogun's attempt to curb their power.[17]

The German editor of *The History of Japan,* Christian Wilhelm Dohm (1751-1820), later argued that Kaempfer had travelled the world in search of his personal utopia. 'Once he had found it, his eyes are not to be trusted', Dohm felt compelled to warn even in a pamphlet advertising the work.[18] With this statement, he at-tempted to explain why the author expressed high praise for a heathen country such as Japan. Dohm, who never left Europe, was not in a position to judge whether Kaempfer's praise was justified or not. But he was right in as much as the centralized government of seventeenth-century Japan was closer to Kaempfer's ideal than the fragmented Holy Roman Empire to which the many

German-speaking states belonged, where generally local interests, rather than the universal law of 'His Majesty' prevailed.

If Kaempfer's personal experience predisposed him towards a favourable view of Japan, then his education gave him the tools for his research. Kaempfer studied briefly at Thorn and completed his first degree at Crakow in 1676. A further four years were spent at Königsberg University.[19] His autograph book, one of the few sources of information for this period, contains the signatures of his professors who praise him as a dedicated student, well known for his hard work.[20] In the introduction to his *History* Kaempfer wrote that he did not rely on a large stipend from his family, but had to provide for his own upkeep.[21] In Königsberg he was tutoring the nephew of the 'Abbesse de Tettau', apparently a lady of some influence, for Kaempfer also sought her good offices in 1694 soon after his return to Europe.[22]

Just before his thirtieth birthday, in the summer of 1681, Kaempfer completed his studies at Königsberg and travelled to Sweden. As was his habit, he used the occasion to call on a number of well-known scholars. In Danzig he visited the theologian Aegidius Strauch (1632-1682), who was famous both amongst Catholics and his own Protestant church for his controversial writings. A few days later he met with the chancellor of Upsala University, Peter Hoffwenig (1631-1682), a pioneer of Swedish medicine. Hoffwenig placed his signature in Kaempfer's autograph book 'as a sign of lasting friendship' and praised him as 'a young man remarkable for his scholarship and knowledge of medicine'.[23]

Upsala was also the home of the naturalist Olof Rudbeck (1630-1702), famous for his work *Atlantica,* in which he attempted to show that Sweden was Plato's lost Atlantis and thus the cradle of civilization. But Rudbeck, whose descendent Alfred Bernhard Nobel was to acquire even greater fame, was also renowned for his medical research, especially for his description of the lymphatic glands. Moreover, in 1654 he had established Sweden's first botanical garden and was the author of a voluminous botanical work.[24] The message he wrote in Kaempfer's autograph book was brief: *Invida nobilitas virtuitis comes,* ('Virtue is accompanied by the envy of the nobility'),[25] words which might have been intended as a warning to his young colleague. Olof Verelius (1618-82), noted especially for his works on ancient Nordic languages, also left his autograph in Kaempfer's book.[26] By his thirties Kaempfer was a confident aspiring scholar, who felt no hesitation in approaching his more famous colleagues and apparently was warmly received by them on these occasions.

A year later, in August 1682, we find Kaempfer in Stockholm. Here both Samuel and his elder brother Esaias Pufendorf signed the autograph book. The younger Pufendorf contributed the rather cryptic message *Extremos pudeat redisse* ('It is shameful to turn back before reaching the furthest goal'),[27] an indication, perhaps, that Kaempfer's future travels were already under discussion. For seven months later, in early March 1683, Kaempfer was on the road to Isfahan, as secretary to the Swedish king's delegation to the Shah of Persia.

THE BEGINNING OF THE LONG JOURNEY

With his departure from Stockholm on 20 March 1683, Kaempfer began a detailed diary.[28] We read of his tribulations crossing the still partially frozen sea and his first impressions as the landscape, the people and their customs slowly begin to change. Once the Finnish mainland was reached, the journey continued on horseback, but this was not much easier for a man more experienced in wielding the pen than guiding the reins. On 17 April he noted: 'Today had three dangerous falls on flat ground off two large horses. My saddle, straps and clothes were torn, but I myself suffered no injury.'[29]

The main contingent of the royal Swedish delegation, with its leader the Dutchman Ludwig Fabritius, had left Stockholm some twelve days prior to Kaempfer's own departure. It had been the duty of the newly appointed secretary to wait until the presents for the Shah were ready, and safely deliver them to Fabritius. Finally on 28 April at Narva, Kaempfer caught up with the rest of the delegation and was able to hand over the precious goods. The diplomatic mission now consisted of a total of twenty-four men and forty horses.[30]

Problems arose when the wording of the royal Swedish request to enter Russian territory failed to satisfy the Russian commandant at Novgorod. Kaempfer as secretary wrote letters, took care of the negotiations and ran the necessary errands. Proudly he noted in his diary that during a night journey of some eight miles he had to change his horse only once, while his companion changed three times.[31] Kaempfer, the scholar, was quickly becoming used to life on the road.

In spite of Kaempfer's efforts, a delay of several weeks was incurred. Kaempfer did not sit idly. He discovered four 'tumulos' (*sic*) in the neighbourhood of their camp and used his spare time to excavate them. Disappointed, he noted that they contained only a variety of bones, a few metal rings, some rusted iron, small grindstones, and a metal clip.[32] As he would explain later in a letter, he was still dreaming of following in the footsteps of Alexander the Great and seeing the marvels of the Orient.[33]

More rewarding was the grand reception the delegation received at the court of the two young czars: the mentally retarded sixteen-year-old Ivan and his eleven-year-old half-brother, later to be known as Peter the Great. At the time of the visit the future ruler was still under the authority of the powerful Vassilij Vassiljewitsch Golizyn (1643-1714) and it was not until the latter's return from his country estates that the audience could take place. Kaempfer described the splendour of the court in detail and commented especially on the beauty and vivid expression of the younger boy, who appeared to him to be some sixteen years old.[34]

Kaempfer's description of Russia, where the pomp of endless church processsions stood in stark contrast to the poverty of the masses, gives some indication as to why Peter the Great later pushed for drastic reforms. 'In Russia there are many churches and few who come to listen, many drunkards and few tankards, many prostitutes and few houses of prostitution. The following three are under coercion: the bells, the horses and the women.'[35]

After his arrival in Japan, Kaempfer complained that during the stormy journey his precious notes had been drenched in salt water and had turned into a messy substance.[36] Some of his notes on Russia still show the effects of this journey, the ink having run so badly that they are impossible to decipher. Nevertheless, in his introduction to his *Amoenitates Exoticae,* Kaempfer announced his intention to publish his Russian diary as part of a longer work on his travels. But he died without realizing this project and to date only a rather free and fragmentary transcription of his observations is available.[37]

On 5 September 1683, after a stay of nearly two months, the delegation left Moscow and continued its journey by boat along the rivers Moskva, Oka and Volga towards the Caspian Sea. This leisurely way of travel permitted Kaempfer to sketch the environment and continue comparing his own observations with those of his famous predecessor Olearius.

In theory, the Muscovite empire extended to the Caspian Sea, but the further an area was located from the capital the less law and order prevailed. Already when the party arrived at Tscheboksary on the Volga, they were warned that only a few days previously merchants had been robbed and murdered, and even the soldiers had been stripped of their possessions. Some areas had been set on fire and were totally deserted; in other parts, the delegation found it impossible to purchase any meat because plundering hordes of Calmucks had taken all livestock.

During the daytime the mission attempted to frighten the enemy by firing shots into the air; at night they sought protection from the cover of darkness, silencing even the oars and refraining from using lights. This method proved successful and on 1 November the delegation and the precious gifts for the Shah arrived at

Astrachan on the Caspian Sea without further incident.[38]

It was Kaempfer's duty to call on the local 'duke', who was in fact the Georgian King Artschil (1647-1712), noted for his patronage of Georgian literature.[39]

If the travellers had been worried about their possessions during the journey to the Caspian, they were in fear of losing their lives when they met with heavy storms crossing the sea to reach Nisabad. But fortunately it was only the three greyhounds intended for the Shah that perished in the waves; after a particularly stormy night they were found dead in the dinghy in which they had been transported.

The horrors of the journey could not prevent Kaempfer from investigating the strange currents of the landlocked sea where sweet water alternated with salty currents. Moreover, he discovered that at a distance from the coast the water at times had an unpalatable, bitter taste, something which had not been described by any previous traveller. He came to the conclusion that the same naphtha – now generally referred to as petroleum or oil – that was found on land in this area was also welling up from the bottom of the sea.[40]

Kaempfer was right. Today there are oil rigs where some three hundred years ago he discovered the bitter taste of the sea. Kaempfer included a scholarly discussion of these phenomena both in his doctoral dissertation and in the *Amoenitates Exoticae,* disputing the theory of Athanasius Kircher (1602-1680) that there existed sub-terranean streams that linked the Caspian with the Black Sea and the Persian Gulf.[41]

While the delegation had to wait at Schamachi for permission to proceed to Isfahan, Kaempfer set out to explore the 'eternal fires' of the Apscheron peninsula. His medical skills had turned him overnight into a local celebrity, and since the crowds did not permit him to leave the city during the day, he stole away under the cover of darkness. With only two local guides and two companions he headed for Baku, the fortified town at the entrance to the peninsula. But having neglected to obtain a travel permit in advance, he and his party were arrested as spies and thrown into the local prison. Freedom was obtained by treating the only guard to local wine. While their goaler recovered from the effects of the night's revelling, the travellers escaped at dawn. Yet Kaempfer did not want to miss out on the chance of inspecting this spectacular city built on the face of a cliff at the edge of the sea. He sent his companions ahead and wearing the clothes of his servant, he boldly surveyed fortifications and palaces as day broke.[42]

Kaempfer was the first European to publish a detailed, illustrated description of the oil fields of the Apscheron peninsula, today one of Russia's major industrial centres and petroleum suppliers.[43] Under the guidance of the local population he spent two days surveying the natural spectacle: strange formations of ever-burning flames, deep wells of seething liquid, smouldering fields of hot mud, trembling stone formations emitting clouds of smoke. He recorded carefully the geological environment and distinguished between the different varieties of this evil-smelling bitumen, of which only small quantities were transported in leather skins on the backs of donkeys and sold as fuel. Where oil rigs dot the landscape today, Kaempfer stood sketching and taking notes, wondering why such a precious gift of nature was not carefully guarded and put to wider use in the service of humanity.

Kaempfer did not pay attention solely to the spectacular. His diary records a wealth of detail ranging from descriptions of the local method of ploughing and the effects of polluted water on the health of the population, to accounts of fountain-decked gardens and the food served at the table of the rich. After a decade of theoretical learning, Kaempfer was now gaining the practical experience from which his work on Japan was to benefit. His maps improved in quality: on occasion he found it necessary to 'correct the geographers'. He became efficient in handling the quadrant; his notes regularly contained readings of latitude. Time permitting, he sought out a high point for observation and sketched the layout of major towns. He gained practice in measuring buildings and streets with even steps and supplementing these measurements with hurried sketches. It was this experience which permitted him later to produce, for instance, one of the best seventeenth-century maps of Ayutthaya, the capital of Siam, and unique drawings of the shogunal palace in Japan.

On 29 March 1684, over a year after the departure from Stockholm, the mission arrived in Isfahan. On the advice of his astrologers, the Shah was unable to receive either the Swedish king's delegates or any of the other foreigners waiting to hand over petitions.[44] Kaempfer used the four months' delay for research. Later, the greater part of his nine-hundred-page *Amoenitates Exoticae* was to deal with Persia. The conditions for conducting research were favourable, for the foreigners were permitted to move freely around Isfahan and the countryside. Kaempfer's drawings of buildings and street scenes are detailed and well executed, indicating that he could sketch at leisure, conditions very different from those he would later encounter in Japan. A view of Isfahan shows him drawing on a hill overlooking the city, attired in hat and wig, shaded by the parasol of a servant.[45] He succeeded in striking up a friendship with perhaps the most influential and best-informed foreigner at Isfahan: the Capuchin friar Raphael Du Mans (1613-1696), who acted as interpreter for the Shah and was himself the author of a work on Persia.[46] Even after Kaempfer had left Isfahan, Du Mans fulfilled his requests for specific information and supplied him with various material, including a grammar of the Turkish language.[47] Some two months after the delegation's arrival at the Persian capital, Kaempfer had already completed the first volume of a botanical work on the *flora* of Persia. His carefully designed and decorated title page still exists, but the work was never published.[48]

Notwithstanding these favourable conditions for research, Kaempfer was discontented with his achievements and decided to quit his post as secretary of the Swedish mission. He felt unfulfilled, for even though the delegation was received eventually with great splendour at court, it failed in its objective: 'What did we achieve with these negotiations while the war against the Turks was continuing at home?', Kaempfer would later write in his *Amoenitates Exoticae.* 'We feasted with Persian pomp and in spite of the delay disappointed the hopes of our lord.'[49] In the introduction to his work on Japan, he stated that the threat of military invasion at home, from the most Christian King Louis XIV on one side, and the most un-Christian Turks on the other, had persuaded him to delay his return.[50] Yet in a letter to Herbert de Jager, an employee of the VOC whom he had met in Persia, he explained that he had joined the Swedish delegation driven by 'an insane craving for knowledge' (*curiositates adactus morbo*). But this craving had not been fulfilled in Persia and he wanted to proceed to India to see what the East had to offer. He offered the VOC his services as physician, but assured de Jager that he would even be content to serve as soldier.[51] Kaempfer pursued his aim of travelling to India relentlessly and just over a year after his plea to de Jager, he was in a position to refuse an offer from Germany and inform his correspondent that he was 'travelling via the most noble courts of India to China'.[52]

Kaempfer had succeeded in obtaining the desired position with the VOC, but he was to be disappointed in his ambitious travel hopes. He never reached China nor visited the Moghul Indian courts. Moreover, he would have to serve nearly three years at Bandar Abbas on the gulf of Hormuz before the company would permit him to board a vessel for India. 'The world's most infertile, dryest, hottest, most poisoned, most unhealthy, most damned place, closely resembling hell'[53] is how the usually matter-of-fact scholar described this harbour, then a major trading point for the Dutch. Polluted water, natural poisoned fumes and high temperatures combined to attack the health of locals and visitors alike. But while a large part of the local population sought relief in the mountains during the hottest months, the VOC carried on with its operations, notwithstanding the toll on its manpower. Kaempfer too fell gravely ill, and attributed his survival to two unauthorized trips into the mountains.[54]

'No other scholar would tolerate this climate,' Kaempfer wrote to his brother and added that for this reason there was plenty of scope for research. To the extent that the heat and his duties permitted, he would daily take delight in the strangest natural phenomena.[55] A good part of his doctoral thesis as well as his noted publication on the date-palm,[56] were based on research undertaken during this period. The journey to Bandar Abbas also permitted a visit to the ruins of Persepolis and several days at the city of poets, roses and wine, Shiraz. Later, one of Kaempfer's patrons, Nicolaas Witsen, to whom he had sent reports of his travels at the request of Ludwig Fabritius, arranged to have two of Kaempfer's sketches of Persepolis published in the *Philosophical Transactions* of the Royal Society in London – without, however, mentioning Kaempfer's name[57] – and both these visits provided material for chapters of his *Amoenitates Exoticae.*[58]

India, the country Kaempfer wanted to visit at any price – if need be, even as a foot soldier – was a disappointment. Everything that caught the attention of the scholar appeared to be based on fraud and deception. He soon found out that the apparently highly poisonous snakes were harmless, as they were regularly drained of their poison. The dancing cobras were not bewitched by the spiritual powers of their keepers, but trained in large quantities in some backyard and sold to itinerant entertainers. Even the feats of the fakirs and the frenzied dancing of the entranced temple maidens Kaempfer dismissed as fraud, in as much as he believed to have proof that they were made possible not by the descent of the gods but the administration of drugs. Even his visit to a Hindu temple turned into a disaster. The temple outside the city of Tutikorin appeared deserted and Kaempfer proceeded into the dimly lit interior to inspect the principal image. Suddenly, three wild-looking yogis emerged from the darkness and chased the intruder away with deafening sounds from their conch shells.[59]

Kaempfer never visited 'the most noble courts of India', of which he had dreamt. The schedule of the vessel *Copelle*, on which Kaempfer travelled, permitted him to see only a small part of the coast surrounding the vast continent. Except for a six-months' stay in Quilon, Kaempfer seems to have spent most of his time on board the vessel. But even during his sojourn in Quilon, Kaempfer had little time to explore the interior. He had been summoned because the household of the Dutch governor of the Malabar Coast, Isaac van Dielen, was suffering from a dangerous illness which had already claimed several lives. Kaempfer succeeded in clearing up the medical problem, but refused the offer of a permanent appointment at Quilon and proceeded to Batavia, the VOC's headquarters in the East Indies. One ambition thwarted, another prospect was about to open up, one that was to establish his place in history.

The thread of Kaempfer's peregrinations in Batavia is taken up in chapter 2, 'Writing *The History*'. This essay explains how he came to accept a posting in Japan and collected material for what would be his *magnus opus* on the island empire.

Some scholars now dispute the appropriateness of the term *sakoku* (closed country) to describe Tokugawa Japan. Yet the fact remains that the Dutch – and those who passed themselves off as Dutch – as the only Westerners permitted in Japan, were closely guarded and watched on their tiny island settlement of Deshima in Nagasaki harbour, and the Japanese who came into contact with them had to swear an oath not to divulge any information about the country to the foreigners. These factors were given as an excuse by earlier foreign residents on Deshima for not collecting detailed information about the country, but Kaempfer succeeded in overcoming these restrictions.[60] In the introduction to *The History* he gives due credit to his Japanese assistant and student who risked his life in obtaining written and oral information for him.[61] Both Kaempfer and the Japanese who were party to this breach of the law, successfully concealed the name of the young man and in spite of considerable efforts by both Japanese and Western scholars his identity remained a mystery for nearly three hundred years. Chapter 3, 'The Interpreter Interpreted', reveals the young man's identity and shows his importance in facilitating contact with Europe.

How correct and how significant was the information Kaempfer obtained in Japan? The next two chapters take up this question. In chapter 4, 'Forgotten Practices of the Past', Kaempfer's statements on ritual taboos surrounding the emperor are investigated and it is shown that they furnish a rare glimpse of now lost oral traditions. Chapter 5, 'The Plants that Carry his Name' deals with Kaempfer's description of the Japanese *flora* and his discovery of a number of plants native to Japan.

Kaempfer remained in Japan for two years and finally returned to Europe in 1693. He obtained his doctorate at Leiden University and settled in the countryside near his native Lemgo with the intention of publishing his research. However, his duties as a gentleman farmer, his medical practice and last but not least his responsibilities as physician to the Duke of Detmold consumed more time than anticipated and it was only in 1712 that he was able to publish his first work on Asia, the *Amoenitates Exoticae*. He described this volume of over nine hundred pages as being no more than a sample of his knowledge, a fact also emphasized by the title which translates roughly as 'Oriental titbits'. The work was well received by the scholarly community of the Republic of Letters, but all the same Kaempfer was unable to publish his work on Japan in the four years that remained of his life.

Chapter 6, 'The History of *The History*', unravels the fascinating story of how Kaempfer's manuscripts were purchased eventually by Sir Hans Sloane and how the work was published in London in an English translation some half a century before a complete German version appeared. *The History* shaped European perceptions of Japan for nearly two centuries. Yet Kaempfer's fame should not be judged solely by the written word, for he also executed a number of drawings during his travels. However, the copperplate prints that have accompanied all editions and translations of *The History* since its first publication in 1727 vary significantly from Kaempfer's original drawings. Chapter 7, 'Changing the Image', analyses why and how these illustrations differ from their originals. The volume concludes with an epilogue which examines the place and significance of Kaempfer's work within the wider framework of the Republic of Letters and the scholarly *Weltanschauung* of his times.

CHAPTER TWO

Writing The History of Japan

B.M. Bodart-Bailey

'I AM NOT IN THE HABIT of dishing up reheated cabbage' Kaempfer wrote with a sense of pride and perhaps even a hint of condescension in the introduction to his *Amoenitates Exoticae*. With this down-to-earth simile he wished to assure his readers that unlike many other authors writing about Asia he had not simply collated reports of various travellers. His work contained his own, first-hand experience.

Yet when discussing the subject of Kaempfer composing the manuscript upon which *The History of Japan* is based,[1] one must first deal with the question of whether the work was indeed written by him. J.W. Spalding, a member of Commodore Perry's mission of 1852, discussing the literature on Japan wrote:

> Then there are the books, whose size might well deter the stoutest, but whose pages would well repay the industrious search of the inquirer – the product of the close observation and assiduous notation of Koempfer* [*sic*], Thunberg, Siebold; and the Dezima Opperhoofds – Titsinghe, Doeff, Meylan, ...

The footnote on Kaempfer reads:

> The work of Koempfer [*sic*], to which reference, as to

17

Japanese history, is frequently made, singular to say, was never written by him. It was written by one Camphay, governor-general of the Dutch East Indies, and at one time the superintendent of the trade in Japan. The manuscript was only given to Koempfer to bring home, and to place it in the archives of the Dutch East India Company at Amsterdam; but instead of complying with the trust, he took the pages with him to Germany, and kept them until he died. After his death, more than a century ago, a friend of his named Scheuchzer, residing in London, went immediately to Germany, procured the manuscript, and it was first published in Great Britain in English, and subsequently translated into other languages.[2]

Obviously, Spalding was one of those who had been deterred by the books' size from consulting them for he relied on hearsay. For not only does he misspell the names of Kaempfer and Camphuis, but he is apparently unaware that the information on Kaempfer he cited was a garbled version of that contained in the work of Hendrick Doeff (1777-1835), one of the books he recommended to his readers.

Doeff had spent a record eighteen years in Japan, fourteen as chief of the Dutch factory at Nagasaki. His unusually long residence in Japan was the result of the Napoleonic wars, during which the Netherlands were seized by France, and France's enemy Britain in turn occupied Java, preventing the Dutch fleet from calling at Nagasaki, leaving the company's personnel there stranded. Doeff became fluent in Japanese and in 1816 completed a Japanese-Dutch dictionary.[3] In the introduction to his own work on Japan of 1833 he admitted without reservation that Kaempfer's description of Japan was 'still the best' i.e. difficult to improve upon. But as a long-time resident of Japan he found it impossible to believe that anyone could have accumulated the amount of information contained in Kaempfer's work in just two years, all the more so as he believed Kaempfer knew no Japanese and first had to teach his 'servant' Dutch. Moreover, Doeff was familiar with Onno Zwier van

Haren's biography of Johannes Camphuis.[4] There he found his doubts confirmed. He did not, like Spalding later, suggest that Kaempfer had appropriated a manuscript entrusted to him by the Company, but rather carefully stated that the work was 'less that of this German . . . . than that of governor general Camphuis'.[5]

At the end of his brief biography of Camphius published in 1772,[6] van Haren, on whom Doeff relied for his information about Kaempfer, had written:

> Moreover, the scholarly world is mainly indebted to Camphuis for the only good description of Japan. For it was he who recognized in the physician Kaempfer a man combining extraordinary learning with superior powers of observation when he passed through Batavia in search of his fortune at the time of his governorship, and sent him to Japan, supplied with the necessary instructions and written material to increase the manifold observations and discoveries which Camphuis had made while he was in that country. And when Kaempfer came back from Japan and left for Europe, Camphuis gave him everything he had collected in twenty years concerning the description of Japan. The above I heard from the lips of the governor of the Indies, Imhof [*sic*].[7]

Van Haren added his own explanations: Camphuis had not been interested in gaining fame as an author and similarly had handed the material concerning the founding of Batavia to François Valentyn, the chronicler of the VOC. But while the latter had gratefully acknowledged this fact, Kaempfer had assured the public in the introduction of his work that he had gathered the information himself with the help of his Japanese servant (*knecht*), a boy of twenty-four, whom he first had to teach Dutch.[8]

Van Haren's informer, Baron Gustaaf Willem van Imhoff (1705-1750), was one of Camphuis's successors in the post of governor general at Batavia, but had not known him personally, having been born nine years after Camphuis had died. Camphuis's association with Kaempfer took place during the years 1689-1693 and some forty odd years had passed by the time Imhoff was resident at

Batavia and likely to have heard about the events. Consequently, his own informant was most probably someone who had no first-hand knowledge either, but repeated what he had heard. Van Imhoff died in 1750 and another twenty-two years passed until van Haren cited his conversation with van Imhoff in print. In all some eighty years had lapsed between Kaempfer's association with Camphuis and the first publication of the account.

As van Haren cites no other source of information, one can dismiss the statements with which he attempts to flesh out the words he heard from van Imhoff as speculation or unsubstantiated hearsay. They are interesting only in as much as they demonstrate the distortion of historical facts by uncritical citation and misinterpretation: van Imhoff's report by itself does not permit the conclusion that Camphuis and not Kaempfer wrote *The History of Japan*. However, if van Imhoff's statement can be substantiated by other evidence, then it would throw light on an important aspect of the composition of the work. To what extent was Kaempfer able to prepare himself for the task before he came to Japan? What role did Camphuis play in this process?

KAEMPFER'S MAECENAS

Towards the end of October 1690, less than a month after his arrival in Japan, Kaempfer composed a number of thank-you letters to be taken back to Batavia by the fleet departing at the end of that month. One of them was addressed to Camphuis. 'Oh, Illustrious and Most Magnificent and Most Noble Lord!' the letter begins.[9] Even making allowances for the conventions of the time, the contents of the letter indicate that the author felt deeply obliged to the addressee. He made much of Camphuis's high position and profusely thanks him for sheltering him under the mantle of his authority, granting him refuge in Batavia. 'Another St Martin' he calls him, in reference perhaps to Camphuis sharing his treasures, his valuable material about Japan, just as St Martin divided his mantle with the beggar.

More revealing is the fact that Kaempfer also addresses

20

Camphuis as his Maecenas, a reference to Gaius (Cilnius) Maecenas (c. 70 BC – 8 BC), councillor and chief minister to the Roman emperor Augustus, a wealthy patron of such poets as Virgil and Horace, whose very name has become synonymous with that of the generous patron.[10] Maecenas did not simply exercise his patronage for literature's sake. His aim was to use the poets' talents to glorify the imperial regime of Augustus. Both Virgil's major works the *Georgics* and the *Aeneid* fulfil this purpose.

Kaempfer's work can hardly be said to glorify the 'reign' of Camphuis as governor-general of the East Indies, although in his letter Kaempfer repeatedly refers to Camphuis in terms of a ruler. Nor does it praise the operations of the VOC. On the contrary, Kaempfer is at times extremely critical of its conduct and its employees. Whether at the time this letter was written Kaempfer intended to have Camphuis and the company feature more widely in his work, but gave up such designs when Camphuis died in 1696, is, of course, impossible to tell. Similarities between Maecenas and Camphuis do exist, however, in as much as Camphuis recognized in Kaempfer a man of talent and charged him with the task of writing a specific work. Both van Imhoff's statement and Kaempfer's letter make it clear that a patron/client relationship existed between Camphuis and Kaempfer. This undermines the assumption of later writers that Kaempfer published a work written largely by Camphuis under his own name. However, the question remains what was the extent and nature of Camphuis's patronage and why, having served three times in Japan and having collected material on the topic, did he not write the work himself? What kind of man was Kaempfer's Maecenas?

Van Haren's brief biography of Camphuis throws little light on his childhood and youth. François Valentyn, who knew Camphuis personally, recorded that Camphuis was employed as a servant to a silversmith in Holland, before he joined the VOC to better his life in Asia.[11] Van Haren is uneasy with this statement and claims that he was born to middle-class parents who gave him more than a middle-class education.[12] Whatever the truth, Camphuis had not had the leisure to enjoy a higher education, but spent his life working his way up the career ladder of the VOC. Nevertheless, Camphuis was not uneducated. Kaempfer wrote to him in Latin, rather than Dutch or German, which he frequently used for correspondence with other company employees at Batavia. Moreover, earlier in his life Camphuis had written a brief history of Java. The short work of seventy pages, published as an appendix to Valentyn's multi-volume work on the East Indies, consists mainly of a number of lengthy citations, and shows a minimum of independent scholarship.[13] The experience of producing the work may have been enough to convince Camphuis that he lacked the time and scholarly training to write a comprehensive work about Japan.

As the VOC's governor-general of the Indies, Camphuis carried a heavy responsibility for the whole of the Asian trade, and some 18,000 employees throughout the region.[14] Kaempfer paid due tribute to Camphuis's exacting duties when in his letter he voiced concern that someone like him, 'not busy with public matters', should disturb a man in such exalted position with his pen.[15] The arduous task of scrutinizing and excerpting relevant passages from old documents, meticulously collecting, cross-checking and sorting facts to write a work on Japan was inappropriate for a man of such importance to the giant trading company. It required a man 'not busy with public matters' and in his privileged position, Camphuis, like Maecenas, had the authority to delegate such a task to the appropriate man.

Camphuis's love of Japan was the result of three postings and was well-known to his contemporaries. Valentyn relates that Camphuis loved everything strange and beautiful, but particularly things Japanese. He was so fond of them that he had a Japanese villa built on the island of Edam in the harbour of Batavia. Every Thursday Japanese food was served at his house. Valentyn, for once, was not impressed. He neither thought much of the food nor of the fact that he had to carry rice corns to his mouth by means of two small wooden sticks.[16]

Kaempfer might have been more appreciative of this introduction to Japanese culture, but no material exists to document that he was entertained at Camphuis's house. Kaempfer did not keep a diary during his stay at Batavia and his movements have to be pieced together from the dates on his descriptions and sketches of plants. Thus we know that on 22 October 1689 Kaempfer studied rare plants in Camphuis's garden on the island of Edam and was still on, or had returned to the island, on the 26th.[17] He was not living in Batavia proper, but had been assigned to another island in the harbour, the Onrust where the shipyard was located and the vessels of the company were repaired with a great deal of hammering and other noise.

Kaempfer was extremely unhappy with his billet. There was not even a table at his disposition for he complained that he had to write his letters and notes on his knees. And at night the light was insufficient to do any work. 'I am sitting amongst working oxen, I mean amongst oxen in whose company I, as a good-for-nothing, spend my life, this life which can in no way be relived', the desperate man wrote to his friend Herbert de Jager. He placed all his hope on de Jager and his old patron Vice-Admiral Wibrand Lykochthon to help him to 'come up' in the world again.[18]

Two medical appointments came up at Batavia, but Kaempfer was offered neither.[19] In these desperate circumstances came the proposal, apparently from the governor general personally, to go to Japan and write a work about the country. Kaempfer had good reason to thank Camphuis for sheltering him under 'the mantle of his authority'.

In Kaempfer's work, Camphuis's name is linked with two negative statements about Japan: Camphuis was the director at Nagasaki in 1672 when the Japanese drastically increased restrictions on Dutch trade turning what for the traders had been a 'golden fleece' into a 'shorn sheepskin'.[20] Moreover, Camphuis blamed his journey through the dampness of the Hakone mountains to Edo for a chronic bodily weakness.[21] Yet, based on Valentyn's evidence one may infer that Camphuis generally held a sympathetic opinion of the country and its inhabitants and that Kaempfer's positive attitude towards the nation that kept him under prison-like conditions originated from this early exposure to Camphuis's conversation.

Van Imhoff's statement that the scholarly world had to thank Camphuis for the creation of *The History* seems to be warranted in as much as without the governor general's personal intervention, Kaempfer might never have gone to Japan. Moreover, the statement that Kaempfer was given an account of his 'manifold observations and discoveries' in that country appears to be sound. But what evidence is there to substantiate van Imhoff's statement that Kaempfer was also supplied 'with the necessary instructions and written material' before his departure?

In his letter to Camphuis, Kaempfer refers to a 'request of one departing' which had been fulfilled and a token gift that he intended placing at Camphuis's feet in return.[22] On his journey to Japan, Kaempfer took along diaries written in Japan, invaluable material for the work he was intending to compose. The likely source for this precious material was Camphuis and the 'the token gift' Kaempfer hoped to offer in return might well have been the manuscript he had been asked to write.

In his account of his stormy voyage to Japan, Kaempfer relates how an entry in a diary was instrumental in permitting his vessel to reach Japan. Kaempfer's ship, the *Waelstroom*, had been delayed by insufficient winds on its departure from the bay of Siam and encountered the season's first typhoons in the China Sea. The vessel was badly damaged, the crew mutinied, and the captain was about to return to Batavia when Kaempfer showed him an account, proving that it was possible to reach Japan at that late time of the year. Kaempfer described this account as a Japanese diary – in fact a diary about Japan – given to him to take on the journey by 'a kind person'.[23]

There are extracts from a number of diaries amongst

Kaempfer's notes. The most significant material relevant to this discussion are notes from the diary of the 'Residente', Daniel Six, of his journey to Edo in 1669 written for him by his assistant Joh. Beekhuysen.[24] These notes are not only important because they contain a wealth of detailed information on which Kaempfer built his own observations, but also because they are dated: the notes were made on board the vessel *Waelstroom* on the journey to Siam on 22 May 1690. Consequently, we can be certain that the information contained in the notes was available to Kaempfer before he arrived in Japan.

This account of Six's journey was a virtual blue-print for Kaempfer's description of the journey to Edo, which was conducted annually without change. The diary of Daniel Six supplied him not only with the names of villages and towns on the way to Edo, their geographical environment and the distances between them, but also the procedures the Dutch were required to observe during the journey. Even before arriving in Japan Kaempfer was, for instance, familiar with details of the customary routine of the delegation's departure from Nagasaki: the accompaniment of friends and acquaintances to the outskirts of the city, the seemingly endless stream of well-wishers and the hospitality extended to them – a farewell meal of 'Sakkje und Saccanen' (*sake* and *sakana* – saké and snacks) – which had to be paid for by a generous distribution of coins.

Later, Kaempfer began his own account of the journey in much the same terms with only minor alterations.[25] He cross-checked and where necessary corrected or refined the information in Six's report with reference to other sources and added detail from his own observations and experience. But the reason why he could focus on such details was that prior to his arrival in Japan Kaempfer had been able to familiarize himself with every aspect of the journey to Edo. He knew, for instance, that there was a *daibutsu* (large Buddha) in Kyoto, 60 *pedes* (feet) high, sitting cross-legged. He had recorded in his notes the size of the temple building down to the shape of the roof and was just as well informed about the nearby temple of

'3333 images', *Sanjūsangendō*, and the archery contests that traditionally took place on the temple's veranda. He was also aware of the fact that Osaka was one of the five cities in Japan that stood under direct shogunal control and had noted down not only particulars about the castle, but also the administration, including the information that the two 'governors' who rotated on an annual basis, were not permitted to meet, but left written reports for their successor before departing for Edo.[26]

With special care Kaempfer copied the details of the delegation's visit to Edo Castle. Again, Kaempfer's description of the formal audience, in which the Dutch chief, just like the daimyo, crawled into the presence of the shogun on his knees with his face to the ground, already appears in much the same words in the notes he took from Six's report.[27] However, at the time of Six's visit in 1669, during the reign of the fourth shogun Ietsuna, the Dutch delegation left the castle after this brief audience. The second, informal audience in which Kaempfer was to gain much applause with his singing and dancing, the highlight of his account, was introduced only in 1682, two years after Tsunayoshi succeeded as the fifth shogun.

After the verbal introduction to Japan Kaempfer had received from Camphuis, he was able to study conditions awaiting him in some detail during the sea voyage. Moreover, he was able to acquire some of the Japanese vocabulary he would frequently encounter, such as *norimono* (palanquin), *daibutsu* (large buddha), *sake* and so on, which served as an early introduction to the Japanese language.

While the date Kaempfer wrote at the end of his excerpts from Six's diary permits us to state with certainty that Kaempfer had studied the material before his arrival in Japan, a good case can be made that some of his undated notes were also made before he came to the country. As a Japanophile who, according to van Imhoff, had collected a large amount of material on Japan, Camphuis would no doubt have owned one of the most comprehensive and most recent descriptions of the country, Arnoldus Montanus's *Gesantschappen aen de Kaisaren van Iapan*.[28] Montanus had never been to Japan, but compiled and edited the reports of other travellers. There is a lot of valuable information, but a number of mistakes as well. Kaempfer referred to these errors several times, indicating that he was familiar with the contents of the work. He also took notes from the book where it dealt with the arrival of the first Portuguese in Japan. The fact that Kaempfer took notes makes it unlikely that the book was in his possession when he studied it. It seems reasonable to assume that Montanus's work was available in Batavia and was part of the 'necessary information' which van Imhoff says was provided by Camphuis to the scholar. The same argument applies to notes Kaempfer took from the work *De Rebvs Iaponicis, Indicis, Et Pervanis Epistolae Recentiores* by John Hay, SJ (Ioannes Hayus).[29] In both cases Kaempfer carefully indicated page numbers.

Kaempfer's notes entitled 'Extracten uijt het Dagh Register van d.E. Heer President Nicolaes Coukebacker' (Excerpts of the diary of the noble Mr president Nicolaes Coukebacker) could also have been made in Batavia.[30] Coukebacker (or Coucekebacker) was the chief of the Dutch factory in Japan from 6 September 1633 to 3 February 1639, the important period when the laws for the 'closure of the country' were promulgated, the Portuguese expelled along with the wives and children of foreigners, and only the Dutch and Chinese permitted to remain as traders. No doubt a detailed record of these important events was included among the archives of the governor-general.

Furthermore, Kaempfer excerpted the yearly financial reports submitted by the head of the Dutch factory at Nagasaki to Batavia. Judging from circumstantial evidence listed below, we may assume that this material was available only in Batavia and that Kaempfer consulted it before his departure for Japan. In some cases Kaempfer noted that these reports were submitted at Batavia. In the remaining cases this information can be deduced, for the head of the factory responsible for the report had in all cases departed from Japan several weeks prior to the submission of the document.[31] These documents can be regarded, therefore, as debriefing reports from the outgoing head at Nagasaki submitted on his return to Batavia, and it seems unlikely that they were relayed back to Japan. Kaempfer consulted the reports covering the years 1670 to 1688.[32] The report of Cornelius van Outhoorn, who had left Japan on 1 November 1689 and which would have been submitted in early December of that year, apparently was not available to the scholar at the time. However, even the fact that Kaempfer as a lowly physician was entrusted with reports of past years was unusual and likely to have been due to Camphuis's intervention.

Of a similarly confidential nature was the material which Kaempfer excerpted under the heading 'Extract von verhandelten Gütern' (Excerpts from Goods Traded).[33] This included trading figures for the earlier period such as the years 1636-38. Since these notes end on the upper half of the page on which the notes on the trading reports begin, Kaempfer is again likely to have studied this material before his departure for Japan.

Less confidential, but no less interesting for Kaempfer's work, was the diary of Hendrich Corneliszen Schaep. Schaep's vessel, the *Breskens*, was wrecked on the coast of the province of Nambu in northeast Japan in July 1643. The crew was brought to Edo and kept there till December of that year when the head of the Dutch factory finally appeared in Edo to vouch for them. In the meantime the crew was thoroughly interrogated. Kaempfer was interested in the nature of the questions, for he noted down at some length the points raised by the Japanese.[34] Again it is likely that this diary was consulted at Batavia, and that further notes about the Dutch trade, which continue on the page on which the notes from the diary end, were made at the same time and location.[35]

Such material confirms Imhoff's statement that Camphuis gave Kaempfer access to a considerable amount of material before he left for Japan. Thanks to Camphuis's patronage Kaempfer was well acquainted with, amongst other things, the events that led to the closure of the country, the details of the Dutch trade and the annual voyage to Edo. Kaempfer was fully justified in calling Camphuis his Maecenas, for it was thanks to his good offices he was able to prepare himself thoroughly for writing a work on Japan.

There is reason to believe that the second part of van Imhoff's statement is also sound, namely that Camphuis presented Kaempfer with the material he had collected about Japan when the latter passed through Batavia on his return to Europe. There are a number of items in Kaempfer's collection which fit this description. They include a document containing instructions on the trade in Asia issued by the VOC at Amsterdam on 26 April 1650.[36] The elaborate letters marking the beginning of paragraphs suggest that the copy was made by a professional scribe for official purposes rather than by a scholar or his assistant for private research. Also the confidential nature of the document leads one to suspect that ordinarily a lowly physician like Kaempfer would not have been able to acquire it. A skillfully made copy of the original Japanese patent received by the VOC from the first Tokugawa shogun Ieyasu in 1609 is another document in Kaempfer's possession likely to have been originally produced for Camphuis or the company archives.[37] Somewhat puzzling is the existence in Kaempfer's collection of an official description of the funeral of Kornelis Speelmann (1628-1684), Camphuis's predecessor in the post of governor-general. The wording of the document is more or less identical with that used by Valentyn in his biography of Speelmann.[38] One explanation might be that the document's list of company staff attending the funeral was of interest to Kaempfer.

It is likely that during his three postings to Japan Camphuis, like Kaempfer, collected books, maps and illustrations. Consequently, there is – in line with van Imhoff's statement – a high probability that the present Kaempfer collection in the British Library incorporates items which originally had been in the possession of Camphuis. This would include material with notes which are not in Kaempfer's hand. Any material where there are no notes at all, either on the item itself or amongst Kaempfer's documents, is likely to be from Camphuis's collection, for it is difficult to imagine that Kaempfer acquired Japanese language material without making notes about its contents.

The material discussed above demonstrates that Camphuis did not write the manuscript of *The History of Japan*. However, it indicates that he did play a greater role in the production of this work than is generally accorded to him. In line with van Imhoff's and Kaempfer's own statement, he acted as Kaempfer's Maecenas, without whose intervention the work might never have been written. Moreover, thanks to Camphuis, Kaempfer had access to a large range of material and was able to inform himself about past and present conditions even before setting foot in the country. Yet Camphuis's patronage would not have resulted in *The History of Japan*, if he had not found in Kaempfer a man 'combining extraordinary learning with superior powers of observation'.[39]

EXTRAORDINARY LEARNING

Roughly speaking, descriptions of Japan before Kaempfer can be divided into those based on the author's own experience (the Jesuits, François Caron) and those composed by scholars who compiled information from a variety of reports, but themselves had never left Europe (Varenius, Montanus). Kaempfer was the first author on Japan to combine both.

Unlike most other visitors to Japan, Kaempfer had devoted the first three decades of his life to acquiring scholarly learning. He was well trained, therefore, in handling written sources and was able to put to good use the wide range of material made available by Camphuis. He was an avid and skilled note-taker. Generally, he carefully recorded which source he was excerpting, noting page numbers as he wrote down relevant facts.

For instance, in scholarly manner Kaempfer condensed Montanus's description of the arrival of the Portuguese in Japan, occupying some seven large double-column pages of printed text in the original Dutch version, into twelve lines of notes. A comparison of Kaempfer's notes and his final manuscript shows that these notes were so much to the point that they could be used with only minor alterations. With many abbreviations and an uneven style of writing, the notes are somewhat difficult to decipher, but could be transcribed as follows:

> Von der Portugiesen ankunfft etc.
> Emanuel Rex Portugalliae schiffte anno 1497 Vascari Gama mit 4 schiffen nach Indien (so per Francisc. Mund unterrichtet) kompt nach Calicut zum Sumariin den Keiser, kompt 1499 wieder nah Lissabon. Worauf sie after (?) schikten und den fursten Hidalkam, so anno 1535 starb, die stat Goa erobert und damit festen fus in Indien gefaset u. aus gebreitet. Montanus p. 13 f 15
> Wer zuerst in Japan von Europaer kommen, incertu. Corn. Hazart Jesuit von Antorf schreibt, das die Portugiesen 1539 durch harten sturm in Japan getrieben aber Er nennet kein schiff. Franciscus Xavier (cujus extant 50 Eptlaes.)setzet die Zeit in einem berichte aus Kokin 5 a 6 J. spater, weil Er an einem Jahre zweifelt. J. Petr. Maffaeus Jesuiten, Jac Tuan Ant Galuanus Dicunt quod Antonius Mota, Franciscus Zeimot et Ant. Pexot in 1542 J. aus Dodra nach Sina segelnde, durch sturm in den Japoschen insulen getrieben. hic Montanus p. 17 f.[40]

A more or less literal translation of this passage is:

> About the arrival of the Portuguese etc.
> Emanuel king of Portugal sent Vascari Gama to India with four ships around 1497 (according to Francisc.) He went to Calicut to the zamorin, the emperor, returns 1499 to Lisbon. Whereupon they sent further ships and took the city of Goa from duke Hidalkam, who died 1535, and therewith secured a firm foothold in India and spread from there. Montanus p. 13, f 15
> It is uncertain which Europeans came to Japan first. Hazart Jesuit from Antorf writes that the Portuguese were driven to Japan in 1539 by a hard storm, but he does not

give the name of a vessel. Francis Xavier (of whom fifty letters exist) in a report from Kokin puts the time five or six years later, because he is not sure whether it was a year earlier or later. J. Petr. Maffaeus, Jesuits Jac Tuan Ant. Galuanus say that Antonius Mota, Franciscus Zeimot and Ant. Pexot sailing from Dodra to China where driven by a storm to the Japanese islands. Thus Monatanus p. 17 f 23.

In the manuscript Kaempfer wrote for publication this passage appears as:

Die Portugiesen haben vor allen Europærn zuerst das hertz gefasset, sich im jahre 1497 in das Indische Meer mit 4 Schiffen zu wagen, alwo sie zu calecut angelandet, und mit dem Samorein, als beherscher selbiger Küsten freündschaft zumachen. Sie gewonnen im Jahre 1510 mit eroberung der Stadt Goa den ersten fästen fuß, setzten immer ihre conqueten unter den wehrlosen Indianern weiter fort, und handelten in dessen durch das gantze Orient bis in das abgelegenste grose Reich Sina. Auf der reise nach diesem letzbenanten lande geschahe es, das im Jahr 1542 sie mit einem Schiffe an das noch unbekante Japan verfielen . . .'[41]

Translation:

The Portuguese were the first among the Europeans to venture into the Indian Ocean with four ships in 1497, landing in Calicut, and to establish friendly ties with the zamorin, the ruler of this coastline. In 1510 they gained their first firm foothold with the capture of the city of Goa; they continued their conquest among the defence-less Indians and in the meantime traded throughout the East right to the furthest great empire of China. It happened on a journey to the latter country that in 1542 one vessel drifted to the still unknown country of Japan . . .

Kaempfer omitted excessive detail, rechecked the facts and added some background information, but otherwise stayed fairly close to his notes.

While the arrival of the Portuguese in Japan in the sixteenth century only required brief mention in a work entitled *Heutiges Japan* (Today's Japan), the more recent history of the Dutch in Japan had to be treated in greater detail. The diary of Nicolaes Coukebacker was a valuable source in this respect, being an eyewitness report of the events that led to the closure of the country. Kaempfer's notes are correspondingly detailed. Some sections of the diary are copied verbatim in Dutch. Less significant information is summarized in German or Latin. Marginal headings, underlining and the letters NB (*note bene*) permit quick reference to the most important facts.[42]

Kaempfer did not just summarize his sources, but analyzed the material and, citing the most salient facts, permitted his readers to draw their own conclusions. For instance, examining the annual financial reports from Nagasaki he noticed that the expenses for the year 1686, when Andreas Cleyer (or Andries Cleijer, *c.* 1634-1698) was in charge of the trading post were considerably higher than those for the year 1688 under Hendrick van Buijtenhem (or Buytenhein, Bütenheim). From the large amount of material available to him, Kaempfer selected these two sets of figures for inclusion in his manuscript and used them to demonstrate pointedly what he had otherwise only dared to hint at, namely that the management of the Japanese trading post presented an opportunity for considerable personal profit.[43]

Kaempfer, however, was not content to rely on Western sources only. In all likelihood he was the first foreigner in Japan to study Japanese material extensively – albeit with Japanese assistance – and make detailed notes of the contents.[44] Thus he learnt about the mainly Christian uprising at Shimabara in 1638 not only from the Dutch report on this subject,[45] but also studied in great detail a Japanese eye-witness report, *Shimabara kassenki*.[46] Again, he described the journey to Edo not merely on the basis of Dutch diaries and his own experience, but in addition took extensive notes from works on this topic written by Japanese for their countrymen.[47]

Access to Japanese written material permitted Kaempfer to study topics on which he found no material in foreign accounts. Consulting mainly the work *Dai Nihon*

33

Ōdaiki he produced some forty pages of notes on the succession of early Chinese and Japanese emperors and attempted to translate their dates into Western reckoning.[48] The Second Book of his work was composed on the basis of this information. Not all of the material Kaempfer excerpted from Japanese works found final expression in his manuscript. For instance, he took detailed notes on the Japanese bureaucracy at Edo from *Edo kagami*, but did not incorporate the material as such into his work. It was, nevertheless, important background information, which permitted him to better understand the events that surrounded the shogunal audience at Edo. Kaempfer did not limit his research to printed Japanese material. According to his own statement he consulted a 'Japanese manuscript of a citizen of Nagasaki' who lived at the time of the events he detailed, namely, the first half of the seventeenth century.[49]

Years of theoretical and practical training enabled Kaempfer to consult expertly a wide range of written documentation in three foreign languages and record the relevant information in notes, which were then used in the preparation of the manuscript. There is evidence that Kaempfer was equally skilled in recording information from oral sources.

SUPERIOR POWERS OF OBSERVATION

Not only the people who knew him personally, such as Camphuis, spoke of Kaempfer as a man with 'superior powers of observation'. Later scholars, for example Voltaire, who knew him only by his written work, also praised him in these terms.

By the time Kaempfer met Camphuis in Batavia he had had plenty of opportunity to develop these powers. From the day he had left Stockholm some seven years previously in 1683, as secretary of the king of Sweden's delegation to the Shah of Persia, he had kept a detailed diary of what he could observe and learn from others about the history and culture of the places he visited. Kaempfer had not only years of experience of observing his environment, but even at an early stage of his career showed both considerable talent and persistence in seeking out the best informants and obtaining a maximum amount of material. At Isfahan he succeeded in developing a deep friendship with the French Capuchin Raphael du Mans (1613-1696), himself the author of a work on Persia. [50]

Kaempfer was well aware that the Christian missionaries, especially the Jesuits, were the best informants and spared no pains in seeking them out. At Tuticorin on the south-east coast of India, for example, he had to brave dark passages and crawl through what he described as 'fox borrows' before he finally arrived at the residence of the two local Jesuits. One was out and the other, to Kaempfer's great frustration, did not understand a word of Latin. 'I would never have imagined that there would be members in this society as ignorant as those whom I met in India.' he wrote with indignation,[51] indicating that usually he was much better served. He was more successful in Thailand, where he visited the imprisoned French missionaries, and just one interview yielded several pages of notes on the fundamentals of Buddhist cosmology.[52]

Long before coming to Japan he developed skills in overcoming obstacles which prevented him from gathering information. Thus in Isfahan the topic of the shah's harem was taboo and the living quarters of his wives closed to outsiders. Kaempfer, however, succeeded in collecting enough information on the subject for a whole chapter of his *Amoenitates Exoticae*. He had himself smuggled into the women's quarters as assistant to a certain Mr Warenius, the gentleman in charge of the fountains, and in this capacity carefully inspected his environment. The women, of course, were not present at the time. Hoping to gain some information on their numbers, he began chatting to officials. To his disappointment he found that, however kindly he was treated in other respects, they became like 'wasps and frenzied vipers' when he dared to inquire after the number of the shah's women.[53]

This episode permits some conclusion about what

Kaempfer had come to expect: namely that even total strangers willingly answered his questions. Kaempfer was not only persistent, but no doubt had a certain amount of personal charisma. Already as a penniless student he had succeeded in cultivating the friendship of high-ranking men and aristocrats. Kaempfer's autograph book contains their signatures, often accompanied by words of praise for his learning and poise. An entry from Persia is more direct, describing his eyes as 'bewitching', one glance being sufficient to gain everyone's trust.[54] Such personal magneticism would explain, for instance, his sudden fame as healer while travelling through North Persia. We do not know what drugs he dispensed, nor, apparently, did their nature determine the healing process. His interpreter was so poor at rendering his instructions that a patient with an eye ailment put the prescribed diuretic into his eye. Kaempfer noted that he was healed all the same.

Finally, there is evidence that even before coming to Japan, Kaempfer was in the habit of augmenting his own powers of observation by using assistants. Again, it is only by default that he volunteers this information. Thus he was unable to furnish an accurate list of gifts presented to the shah of Persia by foreign dignitaries, because his clerk or secretary (*amanuensi meo*), whom he had stationed in the garden, lost count.[55]

The extent of Kaempfer's success in applying his experience, skills and talents to his research by the time he left Batavia in the first days of May 1690 is demonstrated by his notes on Siam. Although he spent exactly one month in that kingdom, he gathered more information than most other writers in several years. His map of Ayutthaya is the finest of the period.[56] Typically, he was not content to question only the resident Dutch traders, but sought out the opinion of the disgraced missionaries as well. Skillfully, he took advantage of each individual's capability: a resident Dutch trader with access to the company's mailing system was charged with posting him a grammar of the Thai language which could not be obtained before his departure.

RESEARCH IN JAPAN

No diary exists to provide a record of Kaempfer's daily activities on Deshima at Nagasaki. But there is evidence that Kaempfer wasted no time in commencing his studies.

The outgoing Dutch fleet left Nagasaki on 22 October 1690, less than a month after Kaempfer's arrival.[57] Kaempfer wrote a number of thank-you letters during this settling-in period to be taken back to Batavia.[58] Presumably he had also performed additional duties as physician while the fleet was in the harbour. But ten days after the vessels had departed, on 1 November 1690, his notes on Japanese flora begin.[59] The notes are dated, and as a result we know that except for the duration of the journey to Edo he carried on with these studies more or less on a daily basis. Later, he studied not only the plants themselves, but also referred to Japanese works, such as the encyclopaedic *Kimmōzui*.[60]

From the first day of these notes he tried his hand at writing *hiragana* and *katakana*. His letters are clumsy.[61] Later, he acquired such skill in writing Japanese characters that occasionally one can only judge from errors unlikely to have been made by a Japanese that the characters are those of a foreigner.[62] He studied the Japanese language and wrote his own *vocabulario*, classifying words both with regard to grammatical function and meaning. A large column is reserved for sample sentences and these permit a glimpse of the occasions on which he would practice his Japanese: *Fana bataki ni tsja mutte iki* (bring the tea into the garden), *kono ki wa itz fanano sakimaska* (when does this tree flower?)[63] He was well aware of the various levels of respect language and noted down the many ways of, for instance, giving the same short command.[64] He considered it important to record that *as-ta* (tomorrow) was a word used only by country folk, and that *sakku hitz* was more polite than the simple *kinō* (yesterday).[65] There are other indications that Kaempfer spoke some Japanese, especially when it came to subjects like medicine. When he was asked to discuss medical practices with the shogun's physicians during an audience, he began speaking Japanese, as the interpreters' knowledge was insufficient. The shogun became aware of the fact and inquired what language the foreigner was speaking. The answer was that he was speaking Japanese, but badly.[66]

Even more important than mastering the language, was the need to devise ways of side-stepping government regulations, according to which all Japanese in contact with foreigners had to swear by a host of divinities and sign with their blood that they would not divulge any information about the country to the visitors. Kaempfer soon discovered that this oath, as solemn as it sounded, was not taken altogether seriously by those who took it. 'The Japanese, brave, clever and imperious people will not be tied by an oath which they are forced to swear to unknown gods and spirits, in which they do not believe ...', he wrote in the introduction to his work. Moreover, he was aware that knowledge about the rest of the world was prized highly. Kaempfer had plenty of this prized commodity to offer, but that alone was insufficient. What he had to overcome and take into account was not only an ingrained suspicion of foreigners, but also differences in social rank. As samurai, Japanese officials expected the Dutch to defer to them, for as merchants the foreigners occupied the lowest rank on the social hierarchy. Consequently, Kaempfer took care to conduct himself so as 'to satisfy their sense of superiority and obsession for gain' and, according to his own testimony, was soon on more intimate terms with interpreters and guards then any previous visitor. They came to his house daily to be instructed in astronomy and mathematics. Dispensing medical advice and European drugs without charge, they became even more indebted to him. Sweet European liqueurs did the rest to loosen his visitors' tongues. Kaempfer maintained that no one ever refused him an answer when questioned person to person.[67]

There is no reason to doubt his statement. Firstly, it is in accord with patterns of Kaempfer's behaviour prior to his arrival in Japan. Secondly, there is other evidence that he was trusted, especially by the interpreters. For

instance, when two Japanese were caught smuggling, two
of the interpreters confided to him afterwards that they
had been prepared to overlook the crime in spite of the
fact that were bound by their oath to report all
misdemeanours of others. They had no fears that he
would report this incriminating information.[68] Elsewhere
he refers to 'a Japanese friend'.[69] Thirdly, there is the
large body of notes from his conversations with Japanese.
The material was so diverse and reached such a volume
that Kaempfer began to sort it alphabetically, attempting
to create an encyclopaedic work for his own reference.[70]
Finally, there is the cooperation of his so-called servant,
Imamura Genemon (Ichibee, Eisei, 1671-1736), which
was in total violation of government laws and could not
have passed unnoticed. The fact that the identity of the
young man, who was sent to Kaempfer for instruction in
medicine, has only recently come to light, bears witness
to the conspiracy of silence with which his treasonable
activities were covered.[71]

Kaempfer himself gave due credit to Imamura in the
introduction to his work, calling him a learned as well as
ambitious young man who permitted him to reap 'a rich
harvest' of information about Japan. Kaempfer's critics,
such as Doeff, have questioned the use of such a young
man, to whom, they believe, Kaempfer first had to teach
Dutch. Due to an omission by J.G. Scheuchzer, the
English translator, the fact has been overlooked that
Kaempfer reported not simply teaching Imamura Dutch,
but 'grammatical Dutch', without which, Kaempfer
stated, he would have been of little use to him.[72] As
the son of an interpreter Imamura went to Deshima to
learn Dutch from the age of ten.[73] However, this method
of studying Dutch without grammatical analysis apparently did not produce competent interpreters as the
episode where Kaempfer spoke Japanese in front of the
shogun shows. Kaempfer required more of his assistant
and brought him to a level where he was able to translate
a wide selection of material for him, ranging from classics
such as *Nihon Ōdaiki* and *Heike monogatari* to medical
literature, travel guides and manuals on the Edo bureau-

cracy. Further, Imamura's later success as interpreter – discussed in the next chapter – testifies to the thoroughness of Kaempfer's method.

Kaempfer admits his debt to Imamura, but in turn should be credited with making the best possible use of his assistant. An astute observer, Kaempfer soon learnt how to work the complex Japanese system of obligation, gratitude and honour to his advantage. Obliging the *otona*, the official in charge of Deshima, with medical treatment which required the assistance of Imamura, Kaempfer obtained permission not only for the young man to remain with him for the whole length of his stay, but also to accompany him on his two journeys to Edo.[74]

One of Imamura's tasks on these journeys was to gather plants along the way, as the Dutch were not permitted to walk or dismount at will. Imamura's careful collection of specimens permitted Kaempfer to put together a work on the flora of the country and the herbaria still in existence today,[75] and this apparently harmless cooperation between teacher and devoted student also made it possible to carry out other activity much less acceptable to the Japanese. Under the cover of the plants Imamura supplied, Kaempfer hid a compass, and pretending to study and draw the specimen he was handed, he read his compass and drew maps of minute scale.[76] Most probably some of the other small sketches of strategic localities and fortifications, like those at Akashi, Osaka, Kuwana and Miya (Atsuta), originated in this way. Here Kaempfer adopted the ruse of writing the name of the locality in Arabic script,[77] presumably to avoid detection by the interpreters.

WRITING *THE HISTORY OF JAPAN*: HAKONE

Kaempfer's scholarly competence permitted him to collect material about Japan by studying a wide variety of written sources. His practical experience as researcher allowed him to gather a large amount of oral information in spite of existing government prohibitions. Concluding I will attempt to reconstruct the process by which he combined this diverse material into the manuscript of his work.

An examination of Kaempfer's description of his first journey through Hakone on 11 March 1691 reveals the number of sources consulted and the economy employed in turning notes into the final manuscript. In addition to his own experience of travelling through Hakone four times, Kaempfer's knowledge about the locality came from at least five different sources.

1. He mentions that he heard about Hakone from Camphuis, who, as has been mentioned, claimed that the damp climate was responsible for a chronic bodily ailment.[78]

2. Montanus's work, which we know Kaempfer consulted, contains a description of Hakone. A copperplate print, showing the guard post, is misleading, but the description of the post furnishes some interesting detail, which also appears in Kaempfer's description.[79]

3. The diary of Daniel Six, which Kaempfer studied on the journey to Japan, describes Hakone. Kaempfer noted down various pieces of information, including details about the examination conducted at the guard post and the difficulty of the road. In his account he elaborated on this information and added his own experience.[80]

4. Kaempfer also took notes on Hakone when he studied the Dutch reports of the journey for the years 1684-86. He incorporated these notes into his manuscript, copying some sentences more or less verbatim. Thus in the description of the guard post, the comparison of the station at Hakone with that at Arai and the statement that it was 'a gate for Edo', are both contained in his notes. How close he stayed to his notes in this description of, for instance, the weather may be seen from the following sample. The notes read:

> 'Wetter ist hier ungesundt die lufft kalt schwer u. dampfig so das kein frembder *sed[?] advena* lange dauern kan.'[81]
> (Here the weather is unhealthy, the air cold, heavy and steamy, so that no outsider can last very long).

In his manuscript Kaempfer wrote:

> 'Die lufft ist allhier kalt u. schweer, dünstig u. ungesundt, u. kan ein frembder hier ohne verlust seiner gesundtheit

nicht lange aushalten.'[82] (Here the air is cold and heavy, sultry and unhealthy, so that no outsider can last very long without loss to his health.)

5. A large part of the material used in the description of Hakone is contained in Kaempfer's notes compiled under the heading *Dodzutski Reisebuch* (travel diary). We must assume that these were written on the basis of Imamura's translation of *Edo dōchūki*, of which there are two copies in the collection of books which Kaempfer brought back to Europe.[83]

These notes are sometimes quoted *verbatim*. For instance, the above-cited passage about the weather continues in the manuscript:

> 'Es giebt hier keine fliegen noch Mücken, u. ist des sommers wohl zu schlaffen des Winters aber unbequem zu wohnen . . .'[84] (There are neither flies nor mosquitos and it is good to sleep here during the summer, but living here in winter is uncomfortable . . .')

In the notes from *Dōchūki* Kaempfer had recorded:

> '. . . fliegen gibts hier nicht. ist theurer kost wie ander orten. Sommer ists wol da zu schlaffen, winters schlecht.'[85] (. . . there are no flies here. Food is more expensive than elsewhere. During the summer it is good to sleep here, bad in winter).

Moreover, Kaempfer's description of the 'treasures' of the shrine of Hakone, then known as Hakone Gongen, relies heavily on the notes from *Dōchūki*. The items displayed are listed in the same order, and those are omitted where the notes are difficult to read. Detailed measurements – 'two horns of horses, each two *sun* and six *bu*' – are identical in both his notes and his manuscript. In the manuscript the name of Soga Tokimune is misspelled as *Takimine*, an error easily committed by someone not familiar with the name, because the word is written badly in the notes.[86]

One might question whether Kaempfer had indeed inspected the treasures, especially as in the manuscript he lays no claim to having seen them but simply states:

'there is the little temple Fackone Gongin, which is famous for a number of rare items, which are kept and shown in this temple.'[87] However, if Kaempfer had simply intended to inflate the text of his manuscript with material from *Dōchūki*, one would have expected that other interesting items would have been included. Thus, for instance, he had recorded the story surrounding the founding of Ishiyama-dera as well as the fact that Murasaki Shikibu (Murasaki Skibbu) wrote the novel *Genji monogatari* there,[88] but none of this information appears in his manuscript. Further, when he does include information beyond his own experience he indicates the source. For example, describing the road between Mishima and Hakone, he explained that his Japanese *Dōchūki*, or travellers' guide ('mein Japonischer Dodfutski oder reisebuch'), warned people to take special care on this lonely stretch.[89]

CONCLUSION

The History of Japan is not simply a travel account, but a carefully crafted work reflecting the total sum of Kaempfer's early school and university training in Europe and the decade of travel in the Near and Far East. The work was not written by Camphuis, but its creation owed a large debt to him. Camphuis acted not only as catalyst, but also supplied Kaempfer with important research material and information on Japan. As befits a scholar, Kaempfer used all available means and material to create as erudite a work as was possible under the circumstances. The fact that he did not rely solely on his own observations, but incorporated a wide range of other sources, does not detract from the merit of his work. On the contrary, it makes him the first author on Japan using, in essence, the methods of the modern scholar. Kaempfer lived in an age referred to as Baroque, but his work shows none of the characteristics of that age.

The Interpreter Interpreted: Kaempfer's Japanese Collaborator Imamura Genemon Eisei

Paul van der Velde

> However, fortune presented me with another opportunity and tool in the shape of a learned young man, thanks to whom I could achieve my aims and gather a rich harvest of knowledge ...[H]e had to look for significant information on the state of the country, the government, the court, religion and the history of past ages, family affairs as well as daily events. There was not a book I endeavoured to see, which he did not obtain for me and explain and translate the passages indicated.[1]

WITH THESE WORDS Engelbert Kaempfer acknowledged his great debt to his Japanese assistant, but in spite of efforts by Japanese and Western historians the identity of the young man long remained a mystery and has only recently been established as Imamura Genemon Eisei (1671-1736), or 'Father Ginnemon' as the Dutch called him. However, Imamura's historical contribution was not only Kaempfer's 'rich harvest of knowledge' of Japan. For just as Kaempfer played a crucial role in shaping the image of Japan in the West, Imamura made an important contribution to the transfer of knowledge from the West to Japan. Indeed, his descendant, Imamura Akistune has called him 'the founder of Dutch Learning' (*rangaku no sō*), or the founder of Dutch or Western learning in Japan.[2]

According to the *daghregister*, or diaries kept by the VOC's servants on Deshima, Genemon was descended from a family of interpreters.[3] His grandfather, Imamura Shirobei, had already been in the service of the Dutch when the VOC factory was still situated at Hirado, just off the north-west coast of Kyushu. His father, Imamura Ichizaemon, moved to Nagasaki in 1641, the year the Dutch were forced to settle there and his son Genemon was born in 1671. However, Japanese records do not list the Imamura family amongst the interpreters who followed the Dutch to Nagasaki and the Imamura genealogy lists only Genemon's father as being employed by the Dutch, occupying the post of *naitsū ji kogashira* from 1681 (Tenna 1) to 1694 (Genroku 7) when he retired.[4] According to Kaempfer the *naitsū ji* were 'chamber interpreters'. He writes: 'They may only visit our island at the time of the annual sales . . . they are allotted two to six to every Dutchman to act as interpreters in his room. The truth is, however, that they are spies, for amongst ten there is hardly one who understands a word of Dutch [teütsch]. . .'[5] The Imamura genealogy confirms that the family did move from Hirado in 1641, but apparently they were not considered official interpreters.[6]

From the age of ten Genemon had access to the Dutch settlement and began learning Dutch.[7] As little else is known about Genemon's youth, a description of the environment in which he spent his formative years will be helpful.

DESHIMA

From 1641 to 1853 nearly all news about the Western world and most information about Japan to the West was channelled through the small, fan-shaped, artificial island called Deshima in Nagasaki harbour, originally built in

1634 to accommodate the Portuguese who were expelled from Japan in 1639. The island was connected to the city by a well-guarded bridge. Situated along Deshima's single street were the living quarters of the VOC servants. Deshima was regarded as a regular quarter of Nagasaki and was under the control of an *otona* (mayor). Nagasaki was like Edo, Kyoto, Osaka and Sakai one of the five cities under direct control of the central government (*gokasho*). These cities were governed by two *bugyō*, or magistrates, who took it in turns to reside alternately in Edo and the city under their supervision. However, on account of its unique position, Nagasaki was given a third *bugyō* in 1688 '...to permit closer attention to the arrival of foreigners and to ensure the safety of this world-renowned harbour'.[8]

There was a similarity in the arrangement with the Dutch chiefs (*opperhoofden*) of Deshima. They, too, were allowed to stay only one year on Deshima, returning to Batavia where they often served on the Council of Justice before returning to Japan.

The Dutch chief always held the rank of merchant within the VOC hierarchy and had jurisdiction only over the ten to fifteen Dutchmen and twenty to thirty Malay- and Portuguese- speaking slaves who lived on the island. For their official contact with the authorities at Nagasaki the Dutch were wholly dependent on Japanese interpreters (*tolken*) who formed a guild numbering some 150 members. Membership of this guild was hereditary. The interpreters had their own house on Deshima, adjacent to the watergate, which was paid for by the Dutch. The guild was subdivided into eight ranks among which the Dutch distinguished three main categories: assistant interpreters (*ondertolken*), interpreters (*tolken*) and chief interpreters (*oppertolken*). From the Deshima diaries, we learn that an inner circle of chief interpreters was in control of the information exchanged between the Dutch and Japanese authorities. Apart from these official contacts, the Dutch also had informal contacts with a host of retainers such as cooks, servants, gatekeepers and the like, who were all on the VOC's pay-roll. Furthermore, the Dutch were in close contact with their female Japanese 'housekeepers', or comfort women, who for obvious reasons are never mentioned in the diaries. Only in private correspondence do we catch a glimpse of these ladies. It is no exaggeration to say that many people in Nagasaki were dependent on the Company for their livelihood.

The yearly routine at the factory was determined by the arrival of the ships from Batavia in the middle of August. During the subsequent trading season the Dutch sold their imports which consisted of, amongst other goods, linen cloth from India, silk piece-goods from China and spices, while they bought mainly copper, camphor and minor quantities of lacquerware and porcelain from the Japanese. The ships left for Batavia by the end of October, catching the northern monsoon. From November till February preparations were made on Deshima for the journey to Edo to visit the shogun's court. The participants were the chief, the physician and two other Dutch merchants. During this journey, the status-conscious Japanese ascribed to the Dutch chief a rank equal to that of a minor daimyo and he was treated accordingly. Both on their way to Edo and on the way back to Nagasaki the Dutch stayed for a couple of days in Osaka, where they ordered lacquerware and porcelain. They also stayed in Kyoto and on the outward journey received a safe conduct pass for travel on the *Tōkaidō*, the famous 'Eastern Sea Route'. On their return they where given a tour of the famed temples of Kyoto.[5] While in Edo they stayed at the 'Nagasaki Inn' where court physicians and students were permitted to visit them, but only under strict supervision. After the audience with the shogun in Edo castle the procession returned to Nagasaki.

During the absence of the chief, his deputy supervised the repair of the Company's buildings. Buildings rented from Japanese landlords were repaired by their owners. Upon the return of the chief at the end of May the factory was put in readiness for the arrival of the ships in August. The four VOC sampans, which were used to ship the goods to and from the ships, were repaired and moored at the watergate. During the trading season neighbouring daimyos and the magistrates of Nagasaki would visit the ships. Such was the environment in which Genemon grew up and would spend the rest of his life.[10]

GENEMON ENTERS THE PICTURE

On 22 September 1695 Genemon, with two other Japanese servants, underwent an examination in the Dutch and Portuguese languages in the presence of the Dutch chief, Hendrik Dijkman, and the physician, Matthijs Raquet, whose servant Genemon was at that time.[11] These examinations by the Dutch of future interpreters were held at the request of the magistrates of Nagasaki, but their outcome did not influence the magistrate's decision to make an appointment, although he could use a poor examination result as a pretext to disqualify someone whom he would not have appointed in the first place. However, Genemon, whose family apparently had connections in high places, was appointed without any problem. Four days after the examination, Genemon, wearing ceremonial attire, paid a visit to the chief Dijkman announcing that he had been made assistant interpreter. Dijkman described him as being more proficient in the Dutch language than any of the other interpreters because he had been a servant of the physicians on Deshima since his boyhood.[12] It was this entry in the Deshima diaries that provided the essential clue towards establishing Genemon's identity as Kaempfer's assistant. It had been overlooked by earlier scholars such as Numata Jirō, and even Imamura Akistune, who had studied all the entries in the diaries concerning his ancestor, failed to establish Genemon as Kaempfer's famous student.[13]

The *otona*, Yoshikawa Gibueimon, from whose library Genemon sold many books to Kaempfer, regarded the young and promising Genemon as a suitable partner for his niece and according to the Dutch sources, the marriage compact was sealed in March 1697.[14] On 24 July 1696, only a year after

Genemon had become assistant interpreter, he was appointed full interpreter due to the favourable intercession of Gibueimon, who had pleaded the cause of his future nephew-in-law with the resident magistrate of Nagasaki.[15] While most of the assistant interpreters were never promoted to the well paid position of interpreter, remaining low paid assistant interpreters all their lives, Genemon succeeded in attaining the coveted position in less than a year, an unprecedented achievement. His new position offered him plenty of opportunity to supplement his income.

The Dutch assessed Genemon differently. Cornelius van Outhoorn, the brother of Governor-General Johan van Outhoorn, who was chief at the time of Genemon's appointment, was less impressed by the young man. He considered him to be reasonably fluent in Dutch and not of bad character, but very inexperienced when it came to trade matters.[16] This was an unfair judgement for Genemon would have been able to pick the brains of Yoshikawa Gibueimon, who was regarded as something of an authority on Japan's internal and external trade.

On 8 January 1697, Genemon received a further promotion to the post of assistant reporter interpreter, while Namura Hachizaemon, called Fatsizemon by the Dutch, was appointed chief reporter interpreter (*nenban tsūji*).[17] The reporter interpreters played a key role in the lines of communication between the Dutch and the Japanese officials at Nagasaki. They reported directly to the mayor (*otona*) and the magistrate, and took turns to serve as escorts during the court journey. Dijkman was satisfied with the appointment of the two interpreters, whom he described as good-natured and pleasant company, and considered their command of Dutch unparalleled.[18]

On 25 December 1697, Genemon was given his first opportunity to travel to Edo as the official escort of the Dutch chief during the court journey. He had, of course, travelled to Edo previously with Kaempfer on both of his journeys.[19] But upon his return from Edo in May 1698 the Dutch chief, Pieter de Vos, claimed that Genemon had cheated him in every possible way. De Vos described Genemon as very rude but praised his ability as interpreter.[20] Begrudgingly, De Vos admitted that Genemon had no choice but to act in this manner, otherwise he would lose his credibility in the eyes of the Japanese. 'The more they can squeeze out of us, the higher they are regarded by their countrymen', de Vos remarked.[21]

This was a shrewd assessment. The interpreters were caught between a rock and a hard place and their actions were judged by two quite different sets of values which were difficult to reconcile. They had to explain the demands and behaviour of the Nagasaki magistrates to the uncomprehending Dutch. Accused by the Dutch chief, J. Aouwer, in 1720 of being a liar Genemon replied: 'It seems as if every magistrate directs everything arbitrarily and could not care less what happens after his departure. We interpreters have to bear the brunt and are considered liars although we are not in the least to blame.'[22] The interpreters were suspect not only in the eyes of the Dutch, but the Japanese, too, distrusted them. Every few years an incident occurred whereby an interpreter was punished for some misdemeanour and banished to a remote island. This suspicion waned somewhat when Arai Hakuseki, the Confucian adviser of the sixth Tokugawa shogun, Ienobu, took an interest in Dutch learning. Genemon especially would profit from this interest.

PIONEERING RANGAKU 1710-1720

Japan's interest in and knowledge of the West during the formative years of *rangaku*, was stimulated by the interplay of two Japanese and two Europeans. The Europeans were Giovanni Batista Sidotti (1668-1714), a priest who arrived in Japan in 1708 charged by the pope to convert the Japanese, and the Dutchman, Cornelis Lardijn, who was the chief at Deshima during the years 1711-2 and 1713-4. The Japanese actors were Arai Hakuseki (1657-1725), who wrote several books about the West based on information supplied by Sidotti and

Lardijn, and the individual who translated the source material into Japanese, Genemon. According to Professor Grant K. Goodman '...the interpreting had to be extremely scholarly and detailed [and] it is obvious that were it not for Imamura Eisei, the writings of Arai Hakuseki and the important effects they produced might never have occurred'.[23]

The Deshima Diaries shed more light on the interplay of these actors. Genemon, who had been appointed chief interpreter on 2 September 1707, was the first to interrogate Sidotti upon his arrival in Nagasaki on 18 December 1708. Genemon soon realized that Sidotti was a priest because of the many Christian artefacts he had unwisely carried to Japan. The authorities at Nagasaki were alarmed by the sudden appearance of this man and the display of the Christian symbols outlawed on pain of death more than seventy years earlier. The magistrate of Nagasaki took the precaution of having the interpreters swear a special blood oath that they would not let the priest lead them astray.[24]

However, the only interpreter who could have been led astray was Genemon, because he was the one chosen to interrogate Sidotti, with the occasional assistance of the Dutch. Genemon was ordered to write a report on Sidotti's answers to his questions, which was then dispatched to Edo. The shogunal government decided that Sidotti should be taken to Edo. It was a curious decision in view of the strict laws concerning Roman Catholicism. Sidotti could have been executed forthwith as most probably would have happened a few years before. However, his arrival coincided with the illness and eventual death of the fifth Shogun Tsunayoshi and the subsequent rise to importance of Arai Hakuseki. It is not unlikely that Hakuseki had read Genemon's early reports from Nagasaki and, eager to meet the priest himself, was decisive in having Sidotti sent to Edo. Genemon was ordered to accompany Sidotti to Edo. Before his departure, the Dutch chief, H. Menssingh, advised Genemon to be careful when answering questions relating to religion for fear that unconsidered replies would endanger Dutch-Japanese relations.[25] Genemon promised to take the utmost care not only in his remarks about the religion of the Dutch, but also in guarding himself against suspicion of being a crypto-Catholic.

Once again Genemon had become involved in a delicate and dangerous mission and the party set out during the night of 25 October 1709 to avoid attracting the attention of the local population.[26] They arrived in Edo on 1 December, and Sidotti was put into the Christian Jaskij (*yashiki*) or Christian jail, which had been standing idle for some time. It was probably there that Hakuseki interrogated Sidotti with Genemon as interpreter. Genemon stayed in Edo for two months. During this time Hakuseki must have obtained the greater part of the information contained in his *Seiyō kibun*, a manuscript which included a critical examination of Christianity and which was completed by 1715. On the return journey Genemon met the Dutch chief Hermanus Menssingh at Osaka on 3 March 1710 and was able to give him a progress report.[27]

Genemon returned to Edo in 1712 as interpreter to the Dutch chief Cornelis Lardijn and the interrogation of Sidotti most probably continued at that time. At the request of Hakuseki, Genemon transcribed a list of 300 Dutch words into *katakana* indicating that there was interest in the Dutch language beyond the narrow circle of interpreters.[28] Japanese interest in Dutch books dealing with subjects such as medicine, botany and military science was most probably larger at the time than has hitherto been supposed. The archives of the Dutch factory in Japan contain copies of three Dutch works with Japanese page numbers, permitting them to be bound by someone who did not know Dutch. In my opinion, these form only a fraction of a larger number of copies of Dutch books which were studied by Japanese scholars who had some knowledge of the language. Often these scholars were the descendants of interpreters such as a man known to the Dutch as Inomatta Sosietje. Upon his arrival in Nagasaki in 1722 the Dutch chief remarked that Inomatta could speak Dutch fairly well.[29]

Former servants of the Dutch, such as one the Dutch nicknamed Platje, who lived in Osaka, apparently were also quite proficient in Dutch.[30]

Arai Hakuseki legitimized the study of the West with the authority of his office and this must have encouraged less prominent scholars to continue their endeavours. That his interest was not limited to religion is apparent from his meetings with Lardijn. In November 1710 the Dutch bookkeeper J. Nentwig, at the request of the Nagasaki magistrate, completed a Japanese reproduction of a map of the world by supplying the names of countries and cities.[31] Not long afterwards, the Nagasaki magistrate together with a student cartographer paid a visit to the Dutch chief N.J. van Hoorn, and according to the latter asked 'silly questions' about a fifth continent, as if four were not enough![32] The map was dispatched to Edo as a present for the shogun. His appetite whetted by the map, Hakuseki quizzed Lardijn in Edo in 1712, asking all kinds of questions about cartography, geography and Dutch painting.[33] The information Hakuseki obtained was later included in his manuscript *Sairan Igen*, the first comprehensive and scientifically researched book on world geography in Japanese. Hakuseki also used some of the material in his manuscripts entitled *Oranda kiji* (On things Dutch) and *Oranda fudoki* (Description of the natural features of Holland).

When Hakuseki paid another visit to Lardijn, Genemon was absent. Apparently, the assistant interpreter Namura Hachizaemon (also known as Goheiei and whom the Dutch called Gofe), was bemused when he announced the arrival of Hakuseki to Lardijn because Genemon's presence was essential for a successful conversation. Lardijn wrote: 'He [Hakuseki] asked all kinds of questions about animals but our simpleton Gofe was not able to translate the questions. Annaij Suckingo [Hakuseki] seemed to have taken note of this and after he had drunk a glass of wine took his leave.'[34] Hakuseki's curiosity about the world beyond Japan extended also to medicine. For example, he ensured that his son's stiff knee was examined by the Dutch physician Willem

Wagemans whom he asked if he would be able to cure it. Wagemans diagnosed the problem and gave medicine to Hakuseki.[35] Again in 1716, Hakuseki demonstrated that he believed in the healing powers of Dutch medicine when he used a prescription of the Dutch physician to cure a disease from which he himself was suffering.[36]

Two years later, when Lardijn was in Edo for the second time, Hakuseki again asked questions about customs in Europe. Hakuseki also checked the information he had obtained from Sidotti, demonstrating his thoroughness. Sidotti had told him that the body of Francis Xavier had not decayed and was enshrined in Goa. When Hakuseki, this time accompanied by the interpreter Nakayama Kizaemon, asked Lardijn if this was true, Lardijn dismissed it as Popish nonsense.[37] The day before Hakuseki's visit, Kizaemon informed Sidotti that he had been sentenced to death because he had not refrained from proselytizing. Until that time, Sidotti had lived under fairly comfortable circumstances. Kizaemon made an extensive report about this to Lardijn, who concluded that it should be regarded as a warning to the Dutch to obey Japanese laws. Lardijn added sarcastically that the mission of the Vicar Apostolic had come to an end.[38]

With regard to trade policy, Hakuseki was less open to the world. He favoured restricting the outflow of precious metals, a policy which had already begun under the previous shogun. In an analogy with the human body, Hakuseki called precious metals the bones of the country, without which it could not exist. The Dutch were soon to face the consequences of Hakuseki's economic thought because in 1715 further restrictions were imposed limiting the export of copper to 10,000 piculs and setting price ceilings for Dutch goods.[39] These measures provoked a severe crisis in Dutch-Japanese relations. Both at Batavia and Edo factions advocated discontinuing the trade. In Batavia those in favour of continuing trade with Japan won on the grounds that competitors might step in damaging the Company's prestige.[40] However, the real motives behind the decision to continue trade with Japan were most probably the large profits which individuals could make from private sales in Japan.

Genemon saw the restrictions as a personal defeat and wanted to resign.[41] Instead, he was entrusted with the delicate mission of escorting the Dutch chief Gideon Boudaen to Edo in 1716. Boudaen had been ordered by the VOC to find out what the consequences would be if the Company stopped trading with Japan.[42] On his return from Edo, Boudaen noted in his diary: 'The Japanese do not care whether we leave or stay since they say that they do not profit from our presence.' [43] In Edo the battle was still going on between those in favour and those against foreign trade. The Dutch were mainly in the dark but had heard that the faction of Tokugawa Tsusutomo, which opposed Yoshimune, the eighth shogun, was against continuing the trade with the VOC.[44]

Although Hakuseki favoured restrictive trade regulations, he was by no means unfriendly towards the Dutch presence in Japan. When Boudaen informed him of the wreck of the vessel *Arion* and the drowning of Lardijn during the disaster, Hakuseki replied that he was sorry to hear about the death of his friend Lardijn from whom he had learned so much about the West.[45] He promised to put in a good word for the survivors of the wreck, who were being kept prisoners in China.[46]

Japanese interest in Western learning survived Hakuseki's demise, for the eighth shogun Yoshimune was interested in such knowledge for utilitarian reasons. The personal audience he granted the Dutch chief Joan Aouwer in 1717 lasted an unprecedented six hours. It was a clear indication to Japanese officials that the shogun was not willing to sever relations with the Dutch. Aouwer was invited to the innermost rooms of the shogunal palace where only Yoshimune's next-of-kin were admitted. Moreover, Aouwer was allowed to sit six paces away from the shogun which was as close as one could get to the ruler of Japan.[47]

The news of the exceptional audience spread like wildfire and in Nagasaki there was great relief, for the population was economically dependent on foreign trade. Although fears were revived for a while when the Dutch ships failed to arrive in 1719 and Aouwer was excused from the yearly court journey, the transfer of Western learning was greatly accelerated when in 1720 Yoshimune partially lifted the ban on the import of foreign books. By so doing Yoshimune encouraged the flourishing of *rangaku* the beginnings of which had been greatly facilitated by Hakuseki and Genemon who, in turn, had relied for their information on Sidotti and Lardijn. Due to their controversial nature, the works written by Hakuseki were printed only after the fall of the Tokugawa shogunate in 1868, but many handwritten copies circulated in Japan.

IMAMURA GENEMON AS INTERMEDIARY AND *RANGAKUSHA*

In 1719 the Dutch chief Joan Aouwer described Genemon as the *beschikker en bezorger van alles* (the manager and agent for everything).[48] From then on Genemon was regarded by both the Dutch and the Japanese as an important intermediary between the two countries. His status was further enhanced by Yoshimune's interest in *rangaku*. The shogun sent a number of scholars to Nagasaki to study various aspects of Western learning. Dutch sources mention especially a certain Inomata Sosietje, most probably a descendant of the interpreter Inomata Denbei, as well as Mukai Gensei (1656-1727) and Fukami Kyūdayū (Arichika, 1691-1773). The latter remained in Nagasaki from 1722 to 1727 and during this time questioned the Dutch chiefs on a broad range of subjects on behalf of Yoshimune. His questions ranged from such practical subjects as agriculture, animals, building construction, fire-fighting, food, forestry and navigation, to more theoretical subjects such as astronomy, the calendar, geography, geometry, legislation, mathematics, religion and the structure of the state. The scholar's activities must have greatly burdened Genemon who had to satisfy the curiosity of this 'intelligent person' as the Dutch chief De Hartog described him.[49] After his return to Edo, Kyūdayū became shogunal librarian (*goshomostu bugyō*) and until the end of his life would quiz the Dutch whenever they came to Edo.[50]

Although *rangaku* greatly accelerated under Yoshimune's government, the first Japanese works on more theoretical subjects such as linguistics or mathematics appeared only in the second half of the eighteenth century when a greater number of Japanese scholars had learnt Dutch. By then, the role of the interpreters in the transfer of knowledge had diminished. However, on the less theoretical subject of horsemanship, in which the eighth shogun Yoshimune had a keen personal interest, a successful transfer of knowledge did take place in the earlier period. Here Genemon played an important part.

On 19 May 1725 Genemon was appointed shogunal messenger (*goyō kata*), for which he was paid 500 taels on top of his regular income.[51] His appointment as shogunal messenger coincided with the arrival of the first shipment of Persian horses to Japan on 23 July 1725, which was accompanied by the riding master J.G. Keijser (also Keyserling, 1696-1736).[52] Yoshimune was much impressed by the horses and two years later sent the shogunal horse master Tomita Matazaemon to Nagasaki. Matazaemon stayed for two years in Nagasaki and was taught to ride in Western style by Keijser. Genemon translated his questions about riding and at the end of Matazaemon's apprenticeship Keijser was ordered to return with him to Edo. By then Genemon had been imprisoned on charges of embezzlement.

The Dutch chief Pieter Boockesteijn wrote that if Genemon had not been a shogunal messenger he would have been banished like his accomplice.[53] Boockesteijn signed a petition addressed to the Nagasaki magistrate asking that Genemon be set free. It is impossible to know whether this had any influence, but a couple of days later Genemon was released from prison. The fact that he was a highly able, proven interpreter and therefore difficult to dispense with was almost certainly the main reason for being let off lightly. Genemon was ordered to accompany Keijser and Matazaemon to Edo and he told Boockestein that he feared that he would not return from his journey alive.[54] Genemon, however, did survive his second prolonged stay in Edo, which lasted from October 1729 to April 1730. During this time he was ordered to write a report on what he had learnt about equestrian techniques and medicine. His work incorporated translations from a Dutch book on horsemanship by Pieter Almanus van Coer, *Toevlugt of Heylsame Remedien voor alderhande Siektens en Accidenten die de Paerden Soude kunnen overkoomen* (Resort or wholesome remedies against all kinds of diseases and accidents that can occur to horses, The Hague, 1688), which Keijser must have brought with him to Japan.[55] A number of handwritten copies of Genemon's report are known to have circulated in Japan. The report represents one of the first successful attempts to transfer Western knowledge of riding techniques and horse breeding methods improved considerably thereafter.[56]

When Imamura Genemon died on 22 September 1736 the Dutch chief Bernardus Coop à Groen made only a brief comment: 'Today the shogunal messenger has died...'.[57] One would have expected that the chief would have devoted more attention to the death of Genemon. However, no explanation was necessary, for no doubt every Dutchman who had served at Deshima was aware that over some forty years Genemon had played a crucial role in Dutch-Japanese relations. With regard to trade many a Dutch chief described him as the pivot on which everything hinged, but a similar case might be made with regard to the role he played in the transfer of Western learning. Kaempfer's original assessment and faith in his young informant had not been misplaced.

Forgotten Practices of the Past: Kaempfer's Strange Description of the Japanese Emperor

Carmen Blacker

IN BOOK II, chapter 2 of *The History of Japan*, Kaempfer gives an extraordinary account of the daily life of the Japanese emperor, and in particular of the various taboos applied to his person. So holy was he that he might not touch the ground with his feet; wherever he wished to go he must be carried on the shoulders of men. Nor might he expose himself to the open air, or allow the sun to shine on his head. Nor could he cut his hair, beard or nails, as these parts of his body were considered especially holy. He might be 'cleaned' by night, however, provided that this was done while he was asleep, '...because they say that what is taken from his body at that time hath been stolen from him, and that such a theft does not prejudice his holiness or Dignity'.

Nor was this all. 'In ancient times he was oblig'd to sit on the Throne for some hours every morning, with the Imperial Crown on his head, but to sit altogether like a Statue, without stirring either Hands or Feet, Head or

Eyes, nor indeed any part of his Body, because by this means it was thought that he could preserve peace and tranquillity in his Empire.' For if he turned to one side or the other, or looked steadily in any particular direction, '...it was apprehended that War, Famine, Fire or some other great Misfortune was near at hand to desolate the country'.

Since those ancient times, however, it had been discovered that it was not the immobile, statue-like sitting of the emperor which preserved the land from disaster. Protective power lay rather in the immobility of the crown or cap. The crown or cap acted in fact as Palladium for the country; provided that it was suspended motionless over the throne every day, the emperor could be released from the burdensome daily duty of sitting with it on his head. Further, every time the emperor ate, his food had to be cooked in new pots and served at table in new dishes. These were clean and neat, but extremely plain, 'made only of common clay', so that they could be broken and destroyed immediately after use. Their destruction was necessary, for should they fall into the hands of ordinary men, or worse still, should such a man try to eat from them, the food would at once swell inside him and cause inflammation to his mouth and throat. Similar dire consequences could be expected by any lay person presuming to wear a garment of the emperor without his express permission: the holy clothes would cause 'swellings and pains in all parts of the body'.[1]

Such is the strange list of taboos which Kaempfer tells us were imposed on the sacred *dairi*, the Japanese emperor. All, save for the new pots and dishes, are apparently unknown to court practice in historical times; no shred of direct evidence exists to suggest that the Japanese emperor was ever subjected to such bizarre constraints, or that he ever presented so macabre a figure, with long hair, beard and nails, as is suggested by these statements.

This account of the emperor, together with his remarks on Shinto, was singled out by the English scholar W. G.

Aston, the translator of the *Nihongi*, 1896, and the author of *A Grammar of the Japanese Written Language*, 1877, *Japanese Literature*, 1899 and *Shinto, the Way of the Gods*, 1905, for an intemperate outburst of abuse.

'The old writer Kaempfer, whose ignorance of the subject is stupendous,' he wrote, had given an account of Shinto which was 'grossly erroneous or rather imaginary'.[2] His stay in Japan had lasted two years and two months only. He had lived in semi- captivity in the Dutch settlement, where the Japanese authorities took every possible means of preventing communication between Dutch residents and the inhabitants of Nagasaki. He was '...wholly ignorant of the Japanese language, depending for his information on native interpreters, but chiefly on a young man who was appointed to wait on him as his servant, and at the same time be instructed in physic and surgery'. His 'colossal ignorance' of Shinto was proved by his defining it as idol worship, by his speaking of Tenshō Daijin as male, by his calling Ebisu 'the Japanese Neptune', and Inari the great god of foxes. His statements about the emperor '...seem to consist of a good deal of ignorant gossip mixed with perhaps a few grains of truth', but '...his woeful blundering in Shinto matters deprives him of all claim to our credence, and what knowledge of the domestic arrangements of Windsor Castle would we expect from a Japanese who had lived two years in semi-captivity in Galway, prevented from intercourse with the inhabitants and entirely ignorant of the English language?'[3]

Abuse so vituperative, so lacking in understanding of Kaempfer's circumstances, and so disproportionate in relation to his alleged errors – Ebisu is after all a divinity of fishermen, Inari has foxes at his beck and call, and in Kaempfer's day Shinto was so fused with Buddhism that Buddhist 'idols' were doubtless to be seen in a good many shrines – comes strangely from a scholar such as Aston, and leads us to suspect some further unacknowledged cause of provocation.

Fortunately, however, there were equally respected scholars in England who took a more favourable view of

61

Kaempfer and his statements about the emperor. J. G. Frazer, the celebrated author of *The Golden Bough*, was convinced that he had found in Kaempfer's account a model description of the archetypal taboos which all over the world tend to be imposed on a sacral king. On the correct preservation of the person of the sacral king, on the correct performance of his ritual actions, the safety and prosperity of the country depended. Kaempfer's description of the Mikado accorded so well with what Frazer had read of sacral kings in other parts of the world, that he chose to quote it in full at the beginning of his volume *Taboo and the Perils of the Soul*. The aspersions of Aston he dismissed in a footnote:

> 'Mr W. G. Aston tells us that Kaempfer's statements regarding the sacred character of the Mikado's person cannot be depended on...To me it seems that Kaempfer's description is very strongly confirmed by its close correspondence in detail with similar customs and superstitions which have prevailed in regard to sacred personages in many other parts of the world, and with which it is most unlikely that Kaempfer was acquainted.'[4]

He proceeded to recount examples of other sacred rulers who were subjected to appallingly minute and complex restrictions in the interests of the realm, many of which were similar if not identical to those which figured in Kaempfer's account.

Among the Zapotecs in Mexico, or example, the high priest was forbidden to touch the ground with his feet, or to allow the sun to shine on his head. In Fiji it was believed that to eat from the chief's dishes would cause the throat and body to swell. In Tonga a man who fed himself with his own hands after touching the body of the chief would swell up and die unless he performed a complicated ritual to disinfect himself. In New Zealand the Maoris believed that a man who unwittingly ate food left by the chief would quickly die; similarly a man who wore any of the chief's clothes or blankets.

Likewise to be found in many parts of the world were instances of sacral kings forbidden to cut their hair because it was dangerously holy. The Frankish kings in

France let their hair grow long; so did the king of Ponape in the Caroline Islands, and high priests in Togoland, Borneo and among the Aztec. A Fiji chief might not cut his hair until he had protected himself by a ritual feast. Frazer even found parallel examples for the odd detail that the emperor's hair and nails could only be cut while he was asleep; less danger attended the operation when the soul was absent from the body.[5]

Why should Kaempfer have recorded stories about the emperor which had no apparent foundation in fact, but which did have their counterparts in countries of which Kaempfer could have known nothing? I suggest that first what Kaempfer recorded was neither ignorant gossip nor grotesque fantasy, but genuine oral folklore about the emperor current in Japan in the seventeenth century, and second that this folklore may be an oral and somewhat distorted transmission of extremely old and otherwise forgotten practices.

First, we should not forget that certain items in Kaempfer's account were mentioned by other Europeans in Japan during the sixteenth and seventeenth centuries. More than a century before Kaempfer arrived in Japan the Jesuits in their *Letters* to India and Europe time and again repeated the stories that the emperor never set foot on the ground and always ate out of earthenware vessels.[6] François Caron, in his *True Description of the Mightie Kingdoms of Japan and Siam*, written in the mid seventeenth century, asserts that the Dairi were esteemed so holy '...that they never trod upon the ground, neither was the Sun or Moon ever suffered to shine upon them; nothing of their Body was diminished or paired off, their hair, beard and nails being suffered to grow at length; when they did eat, their meat was (still) dressed in new pots, and served up in new dishes'.[7]

Furthermore, the Dutchman Conrad Cramer noted in his journal of 1626 that the Dairi '...wears long hair which has never been cut in his whole life; in the same way his beard and the nails of his hands and feet have never been trimmed'. Cramer received his intelligence from an old and trustworthy person in the city of Miyako.[8] The Jesuits, it is alleged, first heard the stories from the fugitive Japanese Anjirō, who dictated a description of Japan to the missionaries in Goa in 1548, and who returned to Japan as interpreter to St Francis Xavier.[9]

Second, it should be noted that Japanese sources are not entirely silent on the subject. It is true that there is no direct eyewitness account of any such taboos by a member of the aristocratic (*kuge*) families permitted direct access to the emperor. But a few accounts, indirect and fragmentary, do exist in volumes of *zuihitsu* which give a similar picture of the emperor as a sacral figure, subject to strange, non-human taboos to safeguard his sacrality.

An exceptionally interesting work of this kind is *Tankai*, a collection of stories and anecdotes compiled by Tsumura Sōan between 1776 and 1795. Tsumura collected his material from a wide range of topics, among which, in *maki* 3, the inconvenient restrictions which hampered the daily life of the emperor figure prominently.

First, he writes, no moxa treatment may be applied to the imperial person. However great his need, this form of medical treatment was forbidden to the reigning emperor. Hence, he continues, the very night that the emperor Sakuramachi (1735-1747) abdicated and retired to the newly-built Sentō-gosho Palace, he ordered forthwith an application of the moxa treatment. Second, no metal knife may be used on any part of the imperial person (*gyokutai*). When the emperor's beard and nails grew long, a lady-in-waiting must bite them off to the required length with her teeth. Third, the emperor's food was always strictly prescribed. Every day the menu was fixed, and he was allowed nothing outside these prescribed dishes. Here again the abdicated emperor Sakuramachi, on his retirement to the Sentō-gosho, lost no time not only in ordering a moxa treatment, but also in requesting a dish of soba for his supper.[10] Fourth, Tsumura describes the restrictions and consequent sufferings imposed on the ladies who attended on the emperor. Before and after touching his clothes or his food, they must wash their hands in water. The result was that their hands were always chapped and chilblained. Nor were they allowed to wear anything on their feet while serving the emperor. Only those ladies over sixty were allowed to wear *tabi*. The floors were not covered with *tatami*, so that their feet as well as their hands, were chapped and rough.

What was more, these ladies-in-waiting, whose names Tsumura incidentally notes all ended in -*sa*, were forbidden to serve the emperor while their monthly periods were upon them. They must retire from service for the duration and their places be taken by older ladies.[11]

Lastly, Tsumura tells us that on the night of *Setsubun*, the celebration of the end of winter according to the old calendar, the citizens of Kyoto were allowed access to a restricted area of the palace grounds, where for a few coins they could buy the beans used in the palace *tsuitō*, a ceremony for driving out evil spirits. Steps were nevertheless taken to ensure that no one should look on the emperor's face. As he crossed from the corridor to the Shishinden, the Hall for State Ceremonies, ladies-in-waiting must walk before and behind him, shading his face from view with open fans. Even the temples on the hillside with a distant view of the palace, far away though they might be and in no sense overlooking the precinct, must put out all lights and cover their windows with matting.[12]

Tsumura's account thus differs from Kaempfer's to the extent that no item on his list of taboos actually coincides with anything that Kaempfer wrote. It resembles Kaempfer's account nevertheless in so far as it, too, describes precautions to safeguard a sacral condition. Frazer would have been the first to confirm that iron, in the shape of a knife or razor, is taboo to sacred persons in many parts of the world. It was on account of the taboo against the use of iron on royal persons indeed, that the Frankish kings were forbidden to cut their hair.[13]

Tsumura's extraordinary detail that ladies-in-waiting must bite off any excess growth of the emperor's beard and nails, is not parallelled, however, in any of Frazer's examples. Miyata Noboru in his interesting treatment of the emperor as a sacral figure comments that several of the taboos described in *Tankai* treat the person of the emperor as a *goshintai*, a vessel for a *kami* or sacred spirit. The *kami* were offended by *akafujō* or menstrual blood. Hence the ladies-in-waiting whose monthly period was upon them must yield their place to older ladies. Hands are scrupulously washed before a visit to a shrine. Hence the ladies-in-waiting, too, must wash their hands every time they touch the emperor's food or clothes. Kaempfer's reference to the malignant swellings which any lay person might expect who unwittingly touched the emperor's clothes or ate his left-over food, refers to the same taboo. The emperor in short is treated as a *hitogami*, a *kami* dwelling in a living human body and therefore requiring that body to sacrifice ordinary human comfort and convenience in order to conform with the rules of sacral life.[14]

Tsumura does not reveal the source of his stories, so that it is impossible to judge whether they were factually true in the late eighteenth century. It seems unlikely however, that they were leaked from a source inside the palace, and far more likely that they were drawn from the same source that probably supplied Kaempfer and the other European visitors with their information. I suggest that this was a body of 'folklore', current in the seventeenth and eighteenth centuries, which sought to satisfy curiosity about the mysterious secluded figure of the emperor in the Kyoto palace.

We know that in collecting information for his *History* Kaempfer relied much on the testimony of his students in physic and surgery. Not even Aston accuses these young men of deliberately feeding Kaempfer with falsehoods or wonders. Nor was Kaempfer one to indulge in the kind of marvels so dear to travellers such as Sir John Mandeville and Marco Polo. Consider for a moment the fantastic account given by Marco Polo of the emperor's palace, roofed and floored with thick slabs of fine gold and studded with enormous rose-coloured pearls and of the capital of Japan captured by 30,000 shipwrecked Tartars, who slaughtered all the garrison except eight men who had inserted magic stones under their skin and were hence invulnerable to steel.[15] Kaempfer's information will readily be seen to lie in a different category of sobriety.

Moreover, it should not be forgotten that not once during the seventeenth and eighteenth centuries did the emperor leave the confines of the Kyoto palace. Not once did he leave its precincts to visit a shrine or temple, to take part in any religious ritual or procession, much less to wave to crowds from the palace window or balcony. He lived behind walls, in a palace sealed off from the outside world, visible only to the members of a few ancient noble families. No ordinary citizens ever reported as much as a glimpse even of his dim outline inside a palanquin.

A first principle of folklore is that, like nature, it abhors a vacuum. Where historical fact is lacking, folklore readily rushes in to fill the gap. An empty mansion, an abandoned monastery, a murdered stranger, a vanished girl, are challenges to which folklore quickly responds with stories conforming with well-known fixed motifs and stereotypes. A king secluded behind walls, whom no one has seen, about whose daily life nothing is known, but on whom the welfare of the country mysteriously depends, presents a similar challenge.

But should we not expect the response to have been a picture of glittering treasure and wealth, on the lines of the hidden palaces and *mondes à part* which figure so richly in Japanese folklore? Behind the walls of the Kyoto palace should surely have been a wondrous place resembling *Ryū gū*, the dazzling underwater palace of the dragon king, or the strange paradises, similarly luxurious, upon which travellers stumble in deep mountains or at the bottom of wells. Brocade, silk, orchid and musk, ivory, sandalwood, exquisite music, a continuous round of delicious banquets – these are the images which we should expect to be evoked by the mysterious sealed palace. Furthermore, the emperor at the centre is a stately, priestly figure in embroidered silk robes.

Why then should we find a weird figure with long black hair and beard and claw-like nails, forbidden to set foot on the ground or allow the sun to shine on his head? And why should this figure, though apparently unknown to historical fact in Japan, yet be so similar to sacral kings in other parts af the world? Is it possible that these statements are folk memories of customs which were once widespread in Japan with regard to the treatment of sacral persons?

Let us consider the matter of the emperor's hair, nails and beard, which Kaempfer says must not be cut. The custom of allowing the hair, beard and nails to grow unchecked is still found in certain parts of Japan as an integral part of the prescribed regime of *gyō*, the ascetic disciplines which conduce to a state of greater holiness. In the Nichiren temple of Hokekyōji, in Chiba-ken, a specially severe regime of *aragyō* is undergone for the space of a hundred days. The exercitants must submit to a greatly reduced diet, a ferocious programme of cold water austerities seven times a day, a continuous chanting of the Lotus Sutra and the *daimoku*, the invocation of the Nichiren sect. But in addition they are forbidden to cut their hair or shave during the three month period. They emerge at the end of the hundred days with long straggling hair and beard.[16]

The same penance is exacted of the two *matsuhijiri*, the two specially chosen ascetics of the Hagurosan branch of the Shugendō who for a hundred days before the winter festival *Shōreisai* undergo a similarly rigorous programme of *gyō*.[17] Again, alongside the chanting, the cold water, the reduced diet and the seclusion, is the rule forbidding the cutting of hair and beard. The practice is recorded also among the ascetics known as *nembutsu gyōja* during the Edo period and earlier. Tansei Gyōja, a *mokujiki hijiri* or 'tree eating ascetic' of the late sixteenth and early seventeenth century, who achieved a degree of holiness in which he believed himself to be fused into a single entity with Amida, allowed his hair and beard to grow so long that those who caught sight of him thought he was a demon.

The same disciplines were practised by Chōzen Gyōja (1652-1721), who was believed to be a reincarnation of Tansei, and by Tokuhon Gyō ja (1758-1818) who likewise during a period of special *gyō* allowed his hair to grow down to his knees and his beard to cover his chest.[18]

Lastly, there survive cases among the *tōya*, the laymen who supervise on behalf of the village the arrangements for the *matsuri* or religious festival and its preliminary *kessai* or purification. The *tōya*, chosen to represent the village in this matter, and on whose shoulders the responsibility for correct communication with the divinity therefore falls, is sometimes required during a period before the *matsuri* to refrain from cutting his hair or beard.[19]

In all these examples, the object of the practice is the attainment of greater holiness, greater ritual purity, greater nearness to the *kami* or the Buddha. It seems arguable, therefore, that at some period before history the forebears of the Japanese emperor, whose sacral nature was then more pronounced than in later times, were required to undergo similar penances and restrictions; that such practices disappeared from court ritual as it became more stately, institutionalized and Chinese; that it survived only in remote districts and sects; but that the memory of such practices once observed by the king or chieftain was passed down orally through the centuries, to be committed to writing only when such tales reached the ears of European visitors or of a few curious Japanese with no direct access to the court. Kaempfer, perhaps, collected such tales more carefully than did his predecessors, so that his account is fuller than any previous description by a European. In short, it seems arguable that in Kaempfer's strange description of the emperor we may discern a genuine piece of folklore current in the seventeenth century about the mysterious royal recluse; folklore which uniquely preserves the memory of ancient practices forgotten elsewhere but once observed by the sacral forebears of the Japanese emperor.[20]

The Plants that Carry His Name: Engelbert Kaempfer's Study of the Japanese Flora

Wolfgang Muntschick[1]

IN ORDER to evaluate Engelbert Kaempfer's contribution to the study of the Japanese flora it is necessary to consider the wider scientific context of his time. The following questions require investigation: At what level were botanical studies conducted in Europe in the late seventeenth and early eighteenth centuries? To what extent had the flora of Asia, and Japan in particular, been explored before Kaempfer? How developed were botanical studies in Japan at the time? Further, Kaempfer's methods and achievements need to be examined. How widely was his work known and how was it judged by the acknowledged experts in the field?

THE DEVELOPMENT OF BOTANY IN EUROPE

Otto Brunfels (1488-1534), Hieronymus Bock (1498-1554) and Leonhart Fuchs (1501-1566) are generally regarded as the 'fathers' of European botany.[2] They wrote voluminous herbals which were generously illustrated with woodblock prints. These works were not published for scientific purposes but to offer practical advice on how plants could be put to use, especially in the field of medicine. A description of the plant and its most common habitat was followed by a section labelled 'usus', describing, as the word implies, the use of the plant. It was this latter part which was of real interest to the reader. The description of the plant and its habitat were added merely to permit correct identification and collection of the plant.

In academic terms, botany was part of the discipline of medicine and only those plants which had some medical value were studied. Herbals were written in the vernacular in order to supply the general public with basic medical knowledge.[3] The layout of the herb garden of Padua, established in 1546, indicates how plants were studied at university level. Plants were arranged according to their pharmaceutical elementary qualities, i.e. warmth/coldness and moisture/dryness, attributed to them in different grades.[4]

The scientific study of botany took a step forward when so-called 'useless' plants began to be studied. Here the Dutchman Carolus Clusius (1526-1609) and the Italian Andrea Cesalpino (1519-1603) were prominent. Cesalpino was the first person who did not merely list plants in some arbitrary order, but grouped them according to similarities, especially with regard to their fruits.

However, these two writers did not make reference to other works. By including a survey of all available literature on the subject Caspar Bauhin (1560-1624) established a new model with his *Pinax theatri botanici* of 1623. Moreover, he arranged plants in groups according to their assumed relationship. Bauhin was what the eighteenth century botanist Linné called a 'nomenclator', and was the originator of the so-called natural classification of plants. Bauhin's *Pinax*, which included approximately 6,000 species and was reprinted in 1671, served as a standard reference work until the beginning of the eighteenth century. It was also used as a bibliographical source and was regarded as a model for the description of new species.

Further progress was made with the appearance of John Ray's *Historia plantarum* (vols 1-2, 1686, vol 3,

1704). Ray (1628-1705) used a new method of classification which he had introduced in his *Methodus plantarum nova* (1682), differentiating, amongst other things, between mono- and dicotyledons. His descriptions of plants were extremely detailed and well supplemented with citations from other works. The *Historia* was, in fact, a much advanced synthesis of earlier herbals and Bauhin's *Pinax*.

Around 1700 several new systems of classification appeared, such as those of August Quirin Bachmann (1652-1723) and Joseph Pitton de Tournefort (1656-1708), which enjoyed sporadic popularity. However, Kaempfer appears to have ignored these works, and they will not be discussed here.

The most famous system of classification created in the eighteenth century was that of Carl von Linné (Linnaeus, 1707-1778). In his work *Systema naturae* (1735) he made extensive use of a method of sexual classification which he himself had developed, and in his *Species plantarum* (1753) he consistently employed binary nomenclature specifying both genus and species.[5] As a result of Linné's fame, all previous botanists were judged largely in terms of his personal evaluation of their work.

EUROPEAN BOTANISTS IN ASIA

The publication of the first volume of *Hortus Malabaricus* by the Dutchman Hendrik Adriaan van Rheede tot Drakenstein (1636-1691) and his assistants in 1678 marks the beginning of European botanical studies in Asia.[6] Kaempfer witnessed the creation of this work at close quarters while serving with the VOC.[7] He was so impressed by it that in 1689 he dedicated his *History of the Date Palm* to van Rheede and humbly asked him for guidance in his own botanical studies.[8] Alas, because of van Rheede's early death this guidance did not materialize.

While van Rheede studied the flora of South India, another member of the VOC, George Rumphius (1628-1702) carried out research at Ambon in the Moluccas. His *Herbarium Amboinese* (*Het Amboinsche Kruidboek*) is in no way inferior to van Rheede's work, but was published only posthumously in 1741-51 by Johannes Burmann.[9] In the introduction to his *Amoenitates Exoticae*, Kaempfer stated modestly and deferentially that he intended to publish a manuscript entitled *Herbarium Trans-Gangeticum* which would deal mainly with the flora of Java and Thailand, but would do so only after Rumphius's work had appeared.

Less significant was the work of the Jesuit Georg Joseph Kamel (1661-1706) who had arrived in Manila in 1688. Kaempfer does not appear to have been aware of his studies. The greater part of Kamel's work appeared in the third volume of Ray's *Historia Plantarum*.[10]

A common feature of these studies was that they recorded the local name of the plant and, if applicable, noted any variants. Kaempfer employed this method as well, and considered this feature important enough to include it in the formal title of his *Plantae Japonicae*, which will be discussed below.

The Englishmen James Petiver (*c.* 1658-1718) and Leonard Plukenet (1642-1706) edited and published botanical research done in China, especially work by James Cunningham (between 1698 and 1709). In addition, East Asian plants were occasionally imported into Europe and studied by botanists there. For instance Jacob Breyne (1637-1697) discussed in some detail exotic plants cultivated in Dutch gardens.

EUROPEAN BOTANICAL STUDIES IN JAPAN

Rightly, Engelbert Kaempfer has been called the first European to study the flora of Japan; prior studies are insignificant. Basically, there was little incentive to study the flora of Japan, for plants which functioned as trading commodities, such as tea and camphor, were already known from other Asian countries. The level of knowledge about Japanese flora can be gauged by the fact that the Guernsey lily, the first plant to be given the name 'japonicus' by European botanists (*Narcissus japonicus*, today: *Nerine sarniensis* [L.] Herb.), was native to Africa and was unlikely to have reached Japan at the time.[11]

The Germans Andreas Cleyer (1634-1698) and Georg Meister (1653-1713), a gardener who had been employed by the VOC as Cleyer's assistant and servant, were the first Europeans who wrote in some detail about Japanese plants. Cleyer's notes were published in the journal *Miscellanea Curiosa* between the years 1686-1696, while Meister's observations entitled 'Japponische Baumschule' (Japanese Nursery) made up the tenth chapter of his *Orientalisch-Indianischen Kunst- und Lustgärtner* (Oriental-Indian art and pleasure gardener).[12] Cleyer described a total of fifty-five plants, Meister eighty-eight. (Forty-six descriptions are common to both works.) The method of description was far below the accepted level of the time. No reference is made to standard works such as *Pinax*. The various parts of the plant, for instance flowers and leaves, are insufficiently described, with Cleyer providing somewhat more detail than Meister. Most of the descriptions consist of details about the medical and economic value of the plants. Meister sometimes adds anecdotal material, and while Cleyer's descriptions are badly illustrated, Meister's are not illustrated at all.

The German political economist Johann Beckmann (1739-1811) wrote about Meister: 'He knew nothing of botany, a science which was well developed at his time.'[13] This judgement, which in some ways applies to Cleyer as well, appears somewhat harsh but the fact remains that future botanists, except those interested in the history of botany, took little notice of Cleyer and Meister. Later Thunberg named one genus 'Cleyera', but it would not be surprising if Kaempfer had been unfamiliar with their publications. Linné did not refer to their work, although he owned a copy of Meister's book and would have been acquainted with *Miscellanea Curiosa*, in which Cleyer's work was published. In short, Kaempfer far outranked his predecessors and consequently was given much greater credit for his work on Japan.[14]

Nearly a century after Kaempfer's visit to Japan, Carl Peter Thunberg (1743-1828) spent the years 1775-76 in

Nagasaki and made a major contribution to Western studies of Japanese plants.[15] Botanists have differed greatly in their judgement of Thunberg's work. While some regarded him as the best naturalist of the generation that followed Linné,[16] the botanist Gerhard Zuccarini (1797-1848) wrote: 'Thunberg was one of the most hardworking but least gifted students of Linné. He received the word, but not the spirit of the great man.'[17] Indeed, most of Thunberg's classification of plants – of which his *Flora Japonica* contains some eight hundred – were revised by other botanists soon after they appeared. Nevertheless, he should be given credit for bringing a large sample of Japanese plants to Europe, enabling his colleagues at home to conduct their research.

Finally Philipp Franz von Siebold (1796-1866), who first visited Japan in 1823-1830, deserves a mention among the early students of Japanese botany. On his return to Europe he cooperated with Zuccarini in the analyses of plants which he had brought back from Japan.[18]

JAPANESE BOTANICAL STUDIES AT THE TIME OF KAEMPFER

In 1829 Siebold wrote: 'At the time of Kaempfer's visit to Japan, the empirical study of plants in that country had reached a higher level than in Europe, a level somewhat comparable to that reached in Europe only at the time of Thunberg's departure.' Siebold went on to say that there existed in Japan a commonly accepted classification of plants into genus, species and varieties, which was indicated by the Chinese character. Siebold maintained that it was only due to the advanced stage of botanical studies in Japan that Kaempfer and Thunberg achieved what they did under the conditions they had to conduct their studies. 'It was unnecessary at that time to search distant forests and mountains for new genera or a series of species. These were cultivated in gardens and virtually begged for Thunberg's attention,' Siebold wrote.[19]

Siebold is correct as far as nomenclature is concerned. Names of plants underwent relatively little change since

918, when Fukane-no-Sukehito wrote his *Honzō-wamyō*, a Japanese version of a Chinese medical work. Moreover, some botanical knowledge was part of the standard education of the upper classes. The texts used were mainly works of lexicographical nature, which does not mean that they were of no interest to Kaempfer.

In his *Flora Japonica*, Kaempfer claimed that he had provided '*nomina & characteres Sinicos*' for all plants described.[20] Plants of which he could not ascertain the name either by questioning informants or consulting Japanese (Chinese?) herbals, were excluded.[21] Kaempfer does not cite these herbals in his text, but in the case of two drawings he supplied the name of his source. A drawing of the Japanese lacquer tree is labelled '*Icon arboris ex Herbario Japonico Kinmodsjui*' (p. 792)[22] and an illustration of the orchid *Dendrobium moniliforme* bears the indication '*Icon ex Herbario Japon. Kinmodsjui*' (p. 865). These references refer to *Kimmōzui*, the only identifiable Japanese source for Kaempfer's *Plantae Japonica*.

Kimmōzui, written by the Confucian scholar Nakamura Tekisai (1629-1702) consists of twenty Japanese volumes plus index and is an encyclopaedia rather than a herbal in as much as it deals with the whole environment, both animate and inanimate, natural as well as man-made objects. Only volumes sixteen to twenty describe plants. The work was first published in 1666. Kaempfer's copy in the British Library is a reprint of the 1668 edition. There are several entries in his hand, mainly transcriptions of plant names.[23] *Kimmōzui* was Japan's first, and at the time of Kaempfer's visit, only illustrated encyclopaedia. It was of enormous value to a foreigner with little knowledge of the language.[24]

It is doubtful whether the exploration of Japanese gardens would have furnished Kaempfer with additional scientific knowledge, as Siebold suggests. Kaempfer described in some detail the little gardens in the backyards of inns, which he saw during his journey to Edo, but his descriptions cover aesthetic aspects only.[25] One garden in Osaka, Hiranomachi, he considered worthy of special mention on account of its 'marvellous flowering Fudsi trees', but he does not indicate that he made any botanical discoveries in those gardens.[26] Kaempfer mentioned a garden in Nagasaki, set up for the acclimatization of imported Chinese plants, which existed only between 1680-88,[27] but he does not seem to have been aware of the medicinal gardens in Edo and Kyoto.[28]

In Kaempfer's time, Japanese gardens were divided into ornamental gardens and those in which non-ornamental, useful plants were cultivated. The latter contained mainly plants valued for pharmaceutical purposes. These gardens had advanced greatly under the patronage of the third Tokugawa shogun Iemitsu (1604-1651), who in turn encouraged the study of pharmacology. A major work on this subject had become available earlier when Hayashi Razan (1583-1657) translated Li Shih-chen's (1518-1593) *Pen-ts'ao kang-mu*, published in 1612 under the title *Tashikihen*.

Literature on ornamental gardens appeared somewhat later. The first work during the Edo period was Mizuno Motokatsu's *Kadan kōmoku* (1664). A much more detailed work, Itō Ihei's *Kadan chikinshō* was only published in 1695. The Genroku period, during which Kaempfer visited Japan, is well known for its cultural attainments, and it was at that time that new strains of ornamental plants appeared. Some of them were described in monographs. Kaempfer listed a number of these new strains, but his record is poor and provides only an incomplete picture of the variety of plants existing at the time.

Besides *Kimmōzui*, other books dealing with botany were available in Japan at the time of Kaempfer's visit, but works which could have qualified as 'flora' were missing. There was no system permitting comprehensive classification of plants. However, on account of the language barrier and his own fairly basic knowledge of botany, Kaempfer might not have been aware of the lack of scientific literature. Hence, *Kimmōzui* appeared to him a most welcome aid in his studies of the Japanese flora.

KAEMPFER'S STUDY OF BOTANY

Kaempfer studied medicine in Crakow and Königsberg from 1674 to 1681 and in the course of these studies acquired some botanical knowledge. But there is no indication that his enthusiasm for botany dates from these early years. Only with his travels in Asia does he begin to display any botanical knowledge. While there is no specific information about his botanical training, there is plenty of evidence of his superior skills of observation and description – both visual and literary – a pre-requisite for all descriptive scientific work. These skills permitted Kaempfer to excel also in other fields to which he turned his attention.

The method Kaempfer adopted was that of the sixteenth-century herbals, works still greatly respected while he was a student of medicine. A description of the plant was followed by information on its pharmaceutical properties, economic value, cultural and historical aspects. He also used this method when he wrote the manuscript for his history of the date palm, completed in 1689. This work, which was later included in the *Amoenitates Exoticae*, established his reputation as a botanist among his contemporaries. His description of the Japanese flora, however, was to secure him an important place in the history of botany among future generations.

DID KAEMPFER WRITE A *FLORA JAPONICA*?

Kaempfer's contribution to European knowledge of Japanese botany is his *Plantae Japonicae*, which he published as the fifth 'book' of his *Amoenitates Exoticae*. Linné described this work succinctly as follows: '*Nomina vernacula, propria, descriptiones plurimae. Flora japonica est*' (native names, many descriptions. A Flora Japonica).[29]

Even in the nineteenth century it was apparent that Linné's judgement had been too generous. While Kaempfer listed 526 species,[30] the Japanese scholar Ōi has concluded that according to today's system of

79

classification the plants Kaempfer described amount to only 324 species.[31] This is a fraction of the more than 6,000 different species found in Japan. Kaempfer gives no indication in the *Plantae Japonicae* that when collecting plants he had been greatly limited in his movements due to the restrictions imposed upon the Dutch in Japan, although he does mention the prison-like existence of the Westerners in Japan in his discussion of the closing of the country contained in the same volume (*Amoenitates Exoticae*, p. 479). Linné ignored this essay and appears to have believed that Kaempfer had travelled throughout Japan or at least had received samples from all over the country. For this reason he credited Kaempfer with having produced a *Flora Japonica*.

Nevertheless, the work rightly lays claim to being a 'flora'. One condition for a work of this kind is that the author has personally inspected all plants described either *in vivo*, fresh, or *in sicco*, dried. Kaempfer's many sketches of plants and the herbarium he brought back testify to the fact that this condition was met and his text shows that he made full use of his informants.[32] For example, he describes the white sandalwood tree and mentions that according to his sources this tree is native to Japan (a mistake) but that he had not seen the tree personally (*non vidi hic eam*, p. 905). Describing *Lithospermum officinale* he noted: '*vidi siccam (herbam) ex Japonia septentrionali oblatam*' (seen by me, dried [as a herb], brought from northern Japan, p. 784); describing *Chaenomeles japonica* he wrote: '*perfectum non vidi*' (not seen by me in a perfect state, p. 808) and in the case of *Nymphoides peltata* he added: '*florigeram non vidi*' (not seen by me flowering, p. 900). These comments indicate that these were exceptions; in other words, he had personally inspected all other plants. There is only one case where we can be sure that this was not so: that of a plant entitled '*Arundo bifurca*' (p. 898), an imaginary plant, which he could only have seen in the illustrated encyclopaedia of Nakamura Tekisai.[33]

Linné's brief description of Kaempfer's *Plantae*

Japonicae implies that one aspect of Kaempfer's work is inadequate: it neither refers to *secundum systema* or *systematice* – expressions with which Linné described other works of this genre. In this sense, Kaempfer's work did not conform to the botanical method current at the time. Therefore, the wording *nomina vernacula, propria* must be viewed as a negative comment, for it implies that Kaempfer had failed to create Latin names for newly-described species. For Linné this was an important aspect of botanical research.

KAEMPFER'S METHOD

After briefly describing the characteristic habitat of the plant, Kaempfer placed the various parts of the plant 'under the botanist's knife', as he once put it. He described the plant in the following order: root, stem and branches or stalk, leaves, flowers, fruits and seeds. Nearly all illustrations contain larger-than-life drawings of the flower and fruit or parts thereof. Sometimes cross-sections are added. In the introduction to the work, Kaempfer explained that he had classified his material rather more roughly than intended (*proposito crassior*, p. 767) into five categories:

1. Plants bearing berries or stone-fruits
2. Plants bearing malaceous fruits or nuts
3. Various vegetables, types of grain and leguminosae
4. Plants valued for their flowers
5. Various

In the first two categories, and to some extent in the remaining three, Kaempfer uses the form of the fruit for classification. This method as well as that used in the determination of species is based on Bauhin's *Pinax*, to which Kaempfer referred explicitly thirty times – implicitly more frequently – within the 144 pages of his work. Kaempfer was not up-to-date with recent advances in botany, a fact which he admitted in his introduction, explaining that he composed the 'catalogue' of plants during his first trip to Edo (February-May 1691), 'before the present method of botanosophy was current'. He is referring to the first two volumes of John Ray's *Historia plantarum*, which he only acquired and studied after his return to Europe.

To my knowledge, neither Kaempfer's contemporaries nor later generations of botanists have accused him of using outdated methods. Rather, judgement of his work has been based on the quality of the descriptions of the plants. As to nomenclature, Kaempfer frequently used European terms in cases where he discovered strong similarities with European plants. Often he committed the error of believing that in Japan he had come across species existing in Europe, a mistake common at a time when botanists had no knowledge of the evolution of plants or of their geographical distribution. When a species did not appear to be related to a European one, Kaempfer pointed out those parts which were similar to known plants. Even then he did not create new names for the genera or species, but was content to give the Japanese name.

An examination of the descriptions contained in Kaempfer's five categories shows that sub-categories are implied. Kaempfer's first category are plants bearing berries, most of which are woody plants. In the sub-category '*Laurus*' (*Amoenitates Exoticae*, pp. 769-773, 905) he included *Podocarpus nagi* on account of its berry-like fruit, in addition to members of the family of *Lauraceae*, which today are still classified as having berries. It did not worry him that the 'blossoms' were totally different from those of the *Lauraceae*. In the descriptions that follow he occasionally avoided the term *bacca* (berry) in favour of the wider term *fructus* (fruit). Only in the case of plants belonging to the *Vitaceae* family as well as *Rohdea japonica* (p.786) did he use the term '*acinus*', which literally means 'vine berry' with the extended meaning of 'berry with several pips'.

The plants *Fragaria* and *Rubus* (p. 787), as well as the mulberry tree are listed in this first category, because at the time the clusters of fruit were thought to be berries and Kaempfer erroneously considered the stone fruits of *Prunus tomentosa* and *Elaeagnus* species (p. 789) to be berries. It should be remembered, however, that these berries with one stone do look like stone fruits and that at the time they were not systematically distinguished from stone fruits. Kaempfer concludes his first category with *Prunus* species, *Myrica rubra* and *Aphananthe aspera*, and lists them as belonging to the family of stone fruits (p. 798).

Kaempfer began his second category with malaceous plants ('*Malus*', '*Pyrus*', etc.) belonging to the family *Rosaceae*, as well as the pomegranate-tree ('*Malus punica*') and citrus fruits ('*Malus aurantia*,' etc.), the fruits of which resemble malaceous fruits, although anatomically speaking they are quite different. He also included the fig amongst the malaceous fruits (p. 803) and added persimmons, which are actually berries, as a variety of the fig '*Ficus hortensis*' (p. 805ff.). With all these species, where at least the genus was known in Europe, Kaempfer followed Bauhin's system. Further 'genera' of malaceous plants such as '*Mespilus*', '*Pyrus*', and '*Mala*' are listed from p. 809. After this there follows a discussion of species of *Cucurbitaceae* (p. 810ff.), which on account of their multi-seeded berries were considered to be a malaceous plant. The ginkgo tree introduces the nut-bearing plants (p. 811ff.), followed by *Torreya* (p. 814), *Fagaceae* (oak) family plants, etc. However, Kaempfer was mistaken regarding *Distylium racemosum* (p. 816ff.), believing the gall-nuts, which often cover the whole tree, to be its fruits.

The title of Kaempfer's third category indicates that there are three sub-groups: vegetables (pp. 818-33), types of grain (pp. 834ff.) and legumes (pp. 835-43). The first sub-group contains mainly root vegetables, species whose roots are officinal, such as ginseng or more accurately the Japanese variety of ginseng (pp. 818ff.). They are followed by the common onion (pp. 827, 830), mushrooms, lichen, algae and swallow's nests, even though the latter is not a plant (pp. 832ff.). Related species are usually, but not consistently, grouped together (for instance *Apiaceae, Brassicaceae, Zingiberaceae*).

The grains sub-group, as might have been expected, contains, in addition to *Gramineae* (grasses), buckwheat

(p. 835). Kaempfer's '*Siliquosae*' (p. 818) include notably the legumes (pp. 835-43). Besides herbaceous species with edible seeds, he includes some woody species in this family and also the Indian bean Catalpa, which is not a legume, but bears similar fruits. Since the flower of the Indian bean differs greatly from the legumes, this shows again that Kaempfer – in accordance with Bauhin – considered the fruit the most important criterion for classification.

The fourth category of plants 'valued for their flowers' is roughly subdivided into shrubs (pp. 844-55), climbers and creepers (pp. 856-58), herbaceous perennials (pp. 862-870), lilies and other monocotyledons (pp. 870-73) as well as asters (pp. 875-77). However, many species do not fit into any of the above sub-groups, which is not surprising in view of the label Kaempfer attached to this category.

The fifth category deals with conifers (pp. 883ff.), species of bamboo and other *Gramineae* (pp. 898-900). Frequently two or three related species are grouped together, but on the whole the material has not been systematized.

In his introduction, Kaempfer calls his *Flora Japonica* a 'catalogue' amplified by descriptions and drawings of some species (p. 767). There are descriptions of 29 species which are illustrated by 28 drawings. In addition, three species not native to Japan are described and illustrated with two drawings each: two south-east Asian orchids (*Dendrobium crumenatum*, p. 867, and *Arachnanthe moschifera*, p. 868) and *Kaempferia galanga* (p. 901). Kaempfer included monographs and illustrations of four additional Japanese plants in other chapters of his *Amoenitates Exoticae*: the paper mulberry tree *Broussonetia papyrifera*, musk seed *Abelmoschus manihot* and the creeper *Kadsura japonica* in the thirteenth chapter of the second book bearing the title *Chartopoeia Japonica* (p. 466ff.) and the tea plant *Camellia sinensis* in the thirteenth chapter of the second book under the heading *Theae Japonensis Historia*. (p. 605 ff.) These four plants are also briefly mentioned in the fifth book (pp. 895, 858, 785, 817).

All in all, Kaempfer described thirty Japanese plants in detail. Some were already known in Europe but Kaempfer considered the available knowledge insufficient and thought it worthwhile to add his own findings about such matters as botanical detail, the history of cultivation and economic significance. One reason why he might have done this is that he believed experts in Europe would be more interested in corrections of the known facts than descriptions of plants which were totally unknown and unobtainable. An example is the wide currency given to Kaempfer's description of the date palm. When his work on the date palm was published, nobody could have forseen that one day Kaempfer would earn greater fame for 'discovering' the ginkgo tree than for any other part of his botanical studies.

KAEMPFER'S *DESCRIPTIONES*

What was the impact of Kaempfer's *descriptiones* on European botanists? The starting point is Linné's *Species plantarum* (henceforth Sp.pl.) of 1753, the origin of modern taxonomy.[34] Linné had already cited Kaempfer in earlier works, praising his botanical research. Kaempfer was in his eyes one of the finest botanical explorers and in recognition of this fact he named the genus *Kaempferia* after him.

Another seminal work is the *Vollständige Pflanzensystem* (Complete Plant System) of Gottlieb Friedrich Christmann (1752-1836) and Georg Wolfgang Franz Panzer (1755-1829) (henceforth: Christmann). This was a revision of the *Natuurlijke Historie* (Natural History) of Maarten Houttuyn (1720-1798), the Amsterdam physician who had employed the system of the twelfth edition of Linné's *Systema Naturae*. Houttuyn cited other sources, often adding his own critical commentary. These included Kaempfer's *Flora Japonica*, which he frequently translated or discussed in long passages. When Linné relies on Kaempfer, as he usually does, the fact is not immediately obvious from the brief text which also draws on other sources. Christmann's work, on the other hand, usually indicates clearly that the descriptions are based on Kaempfer.

By 1730 Linné had developed the so-called sexual system of classification according to which plants were classified with regard to the number and arrangement of gender-distinctive parts of the flower, i.e. the male stamens and the female carpels. As a consequence, only those plants could be incorporated into his system where a complete description of these parts was available or where Linné could examine the species personally. Mistakes made by Kaempfer in the description of these parts caused Linné to misattribute or leave out some specimens from his system.

In the following listing the conventions of taxonomy are followed. These require a brief explanation for the layman. A change in the species name (epithet – the second element in the scientific name) indicates – according to the Priority Rule – mistakes or errors in the epithet first applied. However, changes in the assignation to genus (i.e. the first name element) take place for higher-order taxonomic reasons, usually on account of general changes in methodology and classification. In this case the author of the initial genus name is always indicated in brackets: e.g. (L.).

In the first edition of his *Species plantarum*, Linné referred to Kaempfer as his sole source of information in the case of five plants, and as a source used in conjunction with other material in the case of 10 plants. All of the latter were already fairly well known in Europe at the time. They are:

1. *CINNAMOMUM CAMPHORA* (L.) J.S. PRESL (pp. 770-3)
The camphor tree had already been mentioned in *Pinax*. Jacob Breyne described what he called *Arbor camphorifera japonica*, a specimen of which Willem ten Rhijne (1647-1700) had sent to Holland in 1674.[35] Another tree was grown in the garden of H. v. Beverningh (1614-1690) and reached a considerable size but Breyne had not seen it in flower.[36] In 1715 Johann Friedrich Gronovius (1686-1762) wrote a more detailed treatise about the camphor tree in which he cited the 'Doctissimus Kempferus' or

'Clarissimus Kempferus'.[37] While Gronovius was of the opinion that the camphor tree should be classified as a genus on its own, Linné described it as *Laurus camphorifera* (Sp.pl. 369). The name used today, *Cinnamomum camphora*, was devised by Theodor Nees von Esenbeck (1787-1837) and Carl Heinrich Ebermaier (1802-1870). Christmann's work of 1777 contains a corrected translation of Kaempfer's description. (I:518-520)

2. *SMILAX CHINA* L. (pp. 781-784)
The China-root ('*Radix chinae*') was the first vegetable product imported from China into Europe in large quantities by the Portuguese. Generally speaking, it was the only Chinese root known. Surprisingly, no proper botanical description of the plant existed until Kaempfer. From 1769 the China-root was cultivated at Kew. Christmann translated Kaempfer's description in a shortened version (IV:601) (Sp.pl. 1029).

3. *RHUS VERNICIFLUA* STOKES, SYN. *TOXICODENDRON VERNICIFLUA* (STOKES) BARKL. (pp. 791-794)
Linné (Sp.pl. 265) did not distinguish between the lacquer tree of East Asia and the poison-ivy (*Rhus toxicodendron*, syn. *Toxicodendron quercifolium*) of North America, which had already been cultivated for some time in the botanical gardens of Holland and England, and called both '*Rhus vernix*'. In 1757 John Ellis explained in some detail that this was an error. Christmann translated Kaempfer's description (I:395-7)

4. *FICUS PUMILA* L. (pp. 803-5)
Already in 1744 Linné had published on the fig tree. The tree had also been described by Rumphius (Sp. pl. 1060).

5. *DIOSPYRUS KAKI* L.F. (pp. 805-7)
Linné considered the persimmon to be a variety of the species *Diospyrus lotus* (Sp.pl. 1057). In 1781 Linné's son defined the tree as a genus on its own, most probably due to the influence of Thunberg. For a brief period after 1880 the plant was known as *Diospyrus kaempferi* Naud.

6. *GLYCINE MAX* (L.) MERR. (pp. 837-40)
This is the cultivated soya bean, which had already been described in volume III of John Ray's *Historia plantarum* (1704, pl. 438). Linné called the plant 'Dolichos soja' (Sp.pl. 727). In 1794 Conrad Moench (1744-1805), citing Linné and Kaempfer created the generic term *Soia*. In 1845 Siebold and Zuccarini classified the plant as *Glycine*.

7. *CATALPA OVATA* G.DON (pp. 841-3)
Linné made the mistake of not distinguishing this species from the north American *Catalpa bignonioides* which had been introduced into England in 1726 and called both *Bignonia catalpa* (Sp.pl. 622). In 1838 George Don recognized the plant as an independent species and gave it the name in use today. For a brief period the name *Catalpa kaempferi*, created by Siebold and Zuccarini, was common.

8. *RHODODENDRON INDICUM* (L.) SWEET (pp. 845-8)
In 1680 and 1687 Jacob Breyne and Paul Hermann respectively described East Asian azaleas cultivated in Dutch gardens as ornamental plants. Linné, whose knowledge of geography was limited, called this species *Azalea indica*, although he knew that it originated in East Asia (Sp.pl. 150). The genus *Azalea* was later synony-mized under that of *Rhododendron*. In 1853 J.E. Planchon (1823-1888) created the name *Rhododendron kaempferi*, but this was not commonly accepted.

9. *BROUSSONETIA PAPYRIFERA* (L.) VENT. (p. 471 ff.)
The paper mulberry was already fairly well known in Europe on account of its wide distribution throughout India, China and Polynesia. The Amsterdam collector Albertus Seba, basing himself on Kaempfer, described the plant before Linné (*Morus papyrifera*, Sp.pl. 986). E.P. Ventenat (1757-1808) distinguished between *Broussone-tia* and *Morus*.

10. *CAMELLIA SINENSIS* (L.) O. KUNTZE (S. 605 ff.)
The first European to describe the tea plant was Bontius (1631), who admitted to not having examined the plant in person. In 1658 Piso completed Bontius's description

and added an illustration. Other descriptions include that of Breyne, who noted that the plant was cultivated in Amsterdam. Linné created the name *Thea sinensis* (Sp.pl. 515). In 1818 Robert Sweet combined the genera of *Thea* and *Camellia* and the name *Thea* was dropped.

In his descriptions of the following plants Linné used Kaempfer as his sole source:

11. *TORREYA NUCIFERA* (L.) S. & Z (pp. 814-6)
Here Linné adopted Kaempfer's term '*Taxus nucifera*' (Sp.pl. 1040), but Siebold and Zuccarini created a new species for *Torreya*. Kaempfer's description was translated by Christmann (II:480 ff.).

12. *SIUM SISARUM* L. (in part) AND *PANAX GINSENG* C.A. MEY., SYN. *PANAX PSEUDO-GINSENG* WALL (in part) (pp. 818-23)
Kaempfer had mixed up two species, namely the sugar root and ginseng. His first three illustrations show the former, while the last is an accurate depiction of the root of the latter, but it shows no other parts of the plant. Linné relied on Kaempfer and created a species entitled *Sium ninsi* (Sp.pl. 251), which he believed was closely related to the sugar root. While the sugar root was cultivated all over Eurasia, so much so that it was impossible to define its origin, the wild and rare species of ginseng native only to northern Korea and Manchuria was discovered much later by Europeans. The first authentic description of the whole plant was made in 1711 by the French Jesuit Pierre Jartoux in Manchuria. The Russian botanist C.A. Meyer is credited with the first scholarly description (1842). Long before these descriptions existed, ginseng was known in Europe as a drug and from the end of the seventeenth century was used for medicinal purposes. Kaempfer stated that he had sent ginseng seeds from Japan to Holland. This is impossible since the plant reached Japan only at the beginning of the eighteenth century. Similarly Kaempfer must have mistaken the sugar root for ginseng when he attempted to bring back plants to Europe on his return by boat.

13. *CAMELLIA JAPONICA* L. (pp. 850-2)
Linné ignored the detailed description of a Chinese camellia by James Petiver. No matter that the plant was also found on the Chinese continent, he designated the species as *Japonica* (Sp.pl. 698). From 1841 the name *Camellia kaempferi* Reboul was used for a brief period.

14. *DENDROBIUM MONILIFORME* (L.) SW. (pp. 864-6)
Linné called this epiphytal orchid *Epidendrum moniliforme* (Sp.pl. 954). In 1799 O.P. Swartz (1760-1818) changed the name of the species.

15. *KADSURA JAPONICA* (L.) DUN. (p. 476)
Surprisingly, Linné accepted Kaempfer's description of the plant, even though the latter gave no information about the flower of this liana. Linné considered the plant to be closely related to a South-East Asian species, which had been described in detail and created the name *Uvaria japonica* (Sp.pl. 536). In 1810 A.L. de Jussieu relying on Kaempfer created the new species *Kadsura*, one of the few scientific names borrowed from the Japanese language.

During the last two decades of his life Linné continued to consult Kaempfer's material. In the tenth edition of his *Systema naturae*, 1759 (henceforth Syst.nat.) he added the following two plants, basing himself on Kaempfer's material:

16. *ILLICIUM ANISATUM* L. (pp. 880-3)
Although Kaempfer did not state that the fruits were used as spice, Linné mistakenly concluded that this tree produced the star-anise. The misleading scientific name is still in use today. Kaempfer's description was translated by Christmann (II:65-7) (Syst.nat., p. 1050).

17. *ZANTHOXYLUM PIPERITUM* (L.) DC. (pp. 892-4)
Linné called the tree *Fagara piperita* (Syst.nat., p. 897). De Candolle classified it as *Zanthoxylum*. Christmann translated an abbreviated version of Kaempfer's text. (III:122 ff.).

Linné added the following plants from Kaempfer's

work to the second edition of his *Species plantarum* (1763, henceforth Sp.pl. II):

18. *PONCIRUS TRIFOLIATA* (L.) RAF. (pp. 801-3)
Linné called the bitter orange *Citrus trifoliata* (Sp.pl. II:1101). Rafinesque-Schmaltz included the plant in the new genus *Poncirus*.

19. *PHYTOLACCA ACINOSA* ROXB., SYN. *PHYTOLACCA ESCULENTA* HOUTTE (pp. 828-30)
Linné called the plant *Phytolacca octandra* (Sp.pl. II:631), but believed it to be native to Mexico. Only Roxburgh (1751-1815) distinguished between the Asiatic and American variety and named the former. Asa Gray (1810-1888) attempted in vain to introduce the name *Phytolacca kaempferi*.

20. *CHIMONANTHUS PRAECOX* (L.) LINK (pp. 878-80)
Linné described this variety under the name *Calycanthus praecox* (Sp.pl. II:718). In 1819 Lindley introduced the new genus *Chimonanthus*. Christmann translated a condensed version of Kaempfer's description (III:683).

21. *COMMELINA COMMUNIS* L. (pp. 888-90)
Linné had already included this species in 1753 (Sp.pl. 40), but stated at the time, as he did again in 1763, that its origin was America. The plant is in fact native to East Asia and was imported into America, where it spread rapidly. Since Kaempfer's description of the flower is extremely accurate, it is surprising that it took Linné a number of years to discover that the so-called American variety was identical with the Asian variety (Sp.pl. II:60).

In his *Mantissa plantarum altera* of 1771, Linné again referred to two additional species described by Kaempfer:

22. *RHUS SUCCEDANEA* L. (pp. 794-6)
Kaempfer noted that except for the shape of the leaves being somewhat narrower, this plant was identical with the lacquer tree (see 3 above). Consequently, Kaempfer had only produced one drawing of the flower and fruit, but different illustrations for the leaves. It was probably

for this reason that Linné decided only in 1771 (Mant.pl.alt. 221) to define *Rhus succedanea* as an independent species, pointing out differences in the size and colour of the fruits.

23. *GINKGO BILOBA* L. (pp. 811-3)
The ginkgo tree is the most famous among the plants which Kaempfer brought to the notice of European botanists. The tree apparently first reached England in 1758 and a sample was sent to Linné in Upsala by the gardener James Gordon. Departing from his habit, Linné adopted the native name, perpetuating the mistaken spelling which Kaempfer had transmitted. (Generally Linné had such an aversion against 'uncivilized' names, that he even considered changing the word 'Thea', borrowed from the dialect of the Chinese province Fujian, to 'Dea', the Latin for goddess). Neither Linné nor Thunberg (1784:358 ff.) were aware of the special place this tree occupies in the classification of plants as a 'living fossil'.

Moving from Linné's to others' use of Kaempfer's material, the Frenchman Michel Adanson (1727-1806), who developed his own system of classification in his work *Familles des Plantes*, preferred names of native origin and, with reference to Kaempfer, included the taxa *Tsutsusi* (p. 164; see 8 above), *Tsubaki* (p. 399; 13 above), *Tsia* (p. 450; 10 above), *Mondo* (p. 496; 27 below) and *Mokof* (*sic*; p. 501; 29 below). He also referred to *Gingko* (*sic*) and *Nagi* (*Podocarpus nagi*, both: p. 510; nrs. 24, 23).
But the botanist who explored Kaempfer's work most thoroughly was Linné's student Thunberg. In 1788, after his return from Japan, he studied Kaempfer's material at the British Museum in London and published his *Kaempferus illustratus*. While in Japan, Thunberg had examined plants previously described by Kaempfer. Thunberg classified the remaining species of Kaempfer's *descriptiones*, but his examination was far from thorough and in most cases the nomenclature was revised soon afterwards.

24. *PODOCARPUS NAGI* (THUNB.) ZOLL. ET MORITZI EX MAK. (pp. 773-5)
Thunberg mistook the Japanese *Podocarpus* for *Myrica rubra* Sieb. & Zucc. (1784, p. 76: *Myrica nagi*) although the latter does not have opposite leaves with parallel venation. Joseph Gaertner (1732-1791) had created the name *Nageia japonica*. But it was only with Siebold that an adequate sample was brought to Europe enabling Zollinger and Moritzi to produce a satisfactory description.

25. *PITTOSPORUM TOBIRA* (THUNB.) AIT. (pp. 796-8)
Thunberg had named this shrub *Evonymus tobira* (1784, p. 99). In 1797 Willdenow classified it as *Pittosporum*.

26. *HOVENIA DULCIS* THUNB. (pp. 808-10)
The name created by Thunberg (1780, pp. 7-9) has remained in use.

27. *OPHIOPOGON JAPONICUS* (L.F.) KER-GAWL. (pp. 823-5)
Thunberg (1784, p. 139) had named this plant *Convallaria japonica* var. *minor*, to distinguish it from var. *major*, known today as *Ophiopogon jaburan* (Sieb.) Lodd. In 1807 J.G. Ker-Gawler (1764-1842) created the new genus *Ophiopogon* for both plants.

28. *PAULOWNIA TOMENTOSA* (THUNB.) STEUD. (pp. 859-861)
Thunberg (1784, p. 252) had named the paulownia *Bignonia tomentosa*. In 1835 Siebold and Zuccarini described the plant as *Paulownia imperialis*. In accordance with taxonomic convention, the epithet was changed to the present one.

29. *TERNSTROEMIA GYMNANTHERA* (WIGHT ET ARN.) SPRAGUE, SYN. *TERNSTROEMIA JAPONICA* THUNB. (pp. 783-5)
Thunberg gave a detailed description of this plant, but its identity has been disputed till the present day.

30. *ABELMOSCHUS MANIHOT* (L.) MEDIC. (p. 474)
Thunberg (1784, p. 224) identified the plant correctly as Linné's *Hibiscus manihot* (Sp.pl. 696; Kaempfer is not

mentioned). In 1787 Medicus revised the name to the present one.

THE SIGNIFICANCE OF KAEMPFER'S RESEARCH FOR TODAY'S NOMENCLATURE

Kaempfer's *descriptiones* were used by European botanists only after some delay. One explanation may be that Thunberg was the first to study Kaempfer's herbarium. Linné had classified the plants only on the basis of Kaempfer's descriptions and drawings as lectotypes. Consequently, he reached a number of wrong conclusions. For example, in three instances (*Rhus, Catalpa, Phytolacca*) he assumed that the American species, which was well known to him, and the unknown East Asian species were identical. This was not Kaempfer's fault. All in all Linné found much more material in Kaempfer's *Flora Japonica* than in comparable *exotici*.

Kaempfer's work remained of interest even after Thunberg published his *Flora Japonica*. In 1791 Joseph Banks (1743-1820) published a number of Kaempfer's drawings of Japanese plants.[38] It is noteworthy that Banks's selection of drawings included both unknown plants and those which had been classified by or before Thunberg. Was Banks trying to make the point that the flora of Japan had not been adequately investigated and that botanists could still learn from Kaempfer? Siebold and Zuccarini used Kaempfer's work and praised it highly.

In order to record for posterity their appreciation of Kaempfer's achievements, a number of botanists have used the term *kaempferi* in naming species. In addition to those mentioned above, these are: Seringe (*Morus kaempferi*), Willdenow (*Aristolochia kaempferi*), de Candolle (*Viscum kaempferi*), Siebold (*Iris kaempferi, Clerodendron kaempferi*), K. Koch (*Vitis kaempferi*) and Lambert (*Pinus kaempferi*).

Finally, mention must be made of a dispute which lasted well over a century and is generally known as the 'Pseudolarix saga'. In 1853 Fortune had discovered the golden larch in China. In 1858 Gordon called this tree *Pseudolarix kaempferi*, for he believed the plant to be identical with the Japanese larch described by Kaempfer. (p. 883; formerly *Pinus kaempferi Lamb.*, latterly *Larix kaempferi* [Lamb.] Carr.) It was soon discovered that this was a misidentification and the name *Pseudolarix kaempferi* Gord. was disputed until 1987 when it was finally agreed to officially drop this name.[39] Thus, even a plant which Kaempfer never saw, native to a country which he never set foot in, carried his name for a long time. This alone is sufficient compliment to his standing in the botanical world.

The History of The History: The Purchase and Publication of Engelbert Kaempfer's The History of Japan

Derek Massarella

IN HIS INTRODUCTION to *The History of Japan*, Johann Gaspar Scheuchzer, the translator and editor of the English edition, provides some information about the provenance of the manuscript on which his translation was based. He states that he was a substitute translator, appointed by Sir Hans Sloane because 'a Gentleman of better abilities, who intended to do it [the translation]' had been 'called abroad, and employ'd in affairs of a different nature'. He notes that Sloane, president of the Royal Society, first became interested in Engelbert Kaempfer's East Indian curiosities after reading the latter's inaugural thesis and the *Amoenitates Exoticae*, and that he instructed Dr Johann Georg Steigerthal, physician to George I, to visit Lemgo (he was accompanying his royal master on a visit to Hanover) to find out about the fate of the collection. According to Scheuchzer, the good doctor obliged, made the detour to Lemgo and, finding out that the collection, in the possession of

Kaempfer's nephew, Johann Hermann, was on the point of dispersal, notified Sloane, who authorized Steigerthal to purchase it. This he did, procuring not only the curiosities but Kaempfer's drawings and manuscripts, including what became *The History of Japan*, all 'for a considerable sum of money'.

Thus the Kaempfer collection was transfered from Germany to England, and eventually, through the Sloane connection, to the British Museum and later the British Library.[1] However, there is a great deal more to the story of the publication of the English edition than Scheuchzer lets on, and, as we shall see, about the appearance of the German edition some fifty years later in 1777-79.

* * *

The purchase of Kaempfer's collection of curiosities and manuscripts owed much to Sir Hans Sloane's passion for natural history, his compulsiveness and competitiveness as a collector and his extensive network of colleagues and clients who were on the look-out for materials that would interest him and who were prepared either to do his bidding and buy in his name, or else send him specimens that they believed would enrich his invaluable collection.[2] In the case of the Kaempfer material, the purchase was facilitated by the fact that the elector of Hanover had acceded to the British throne in 1714 and made frequent trips to his native domains.

It was on the occasion of the king's third such visit to Germany in 1723, when George I hoped to conclude a marriage contract between Wilhelmina, daughter of Frederick William of Prussia, and Frederick, eldest son of the Prince of Wales, that Steigerthal first made contact with Johann Hermann Kaempfer. On 12 July 1723 Steigerthal wrote to Sloane that the royal party was at Bad Pyrmont which, he noted, was near Lemgo where the book 'by the late Mr Kaempfer' (the *Amoenitates Exoticae*) had been published. This had reminded him of Sloane's request that he should find out what he could about Engelbert Kaempfer's manuscripts and other curiosities.[3] Steigerthal complied with Sloane's request

97

and discovered that the collection had been bequeathed to the nephew. Later in the month, with the king newly returned from Bad Pyrmont to Hanover and in excellent health, Steigerthal was given permission to make the short trip to Lemgo to visit Johann Hermann. There he was able to inspect the collection and ask that a catalogue of its contents be drawn up.

His preliminary observations of what he judged to be the highlights are of interest. Steigerthal wrote that the dried plants, although very rare, were few in number and in great confusion with some already decayed. Engelbert Kaempfer had been unable to sort them out, leaving only a piece of paper affixed to each specimen. The drawings of animals and fish were similarly few and in black and white. In Steigerthal's opinion they were not especially rare. The manuscript about Japan he described as 'very interesting', but it was written in German, while the maps of the world, of Japan and of its immediate surroundings were precisely drafted, with the roads joining the principal Japanese cities clearly visible. The plan of the capital, Edo, was also 'interesting', with the streets and bridges marked. In addition, there were drawings of 'idols', illustrations of Japanese and Chinese clothing and Japanese houses, and some gold and silver specimens of acupuncture needles which, Steigerthal noted, Sloane was already familiar with from the *Amoenitates Exoticae*.[4]

It is at this juncture that Philip Henry Zollman, who was employed as a secretary to Lord Townsend, secretary of state for the northern department and a member of the royal party visiting Germany, enters the picture. Zollman came from a solid service nobility background (his father was Johann Ludwig Zollmann, *Geheimer Rat*, councillor, to the Duke of Saxony, Moritz Wilhelm, in Jena). He arrived in England in 1714 as tutor to the family of Hans Caspar von Bothmar, ambassador and then minister for Hanoverian affairs in London, and played a small but not insignificant and certainly not uninteresting part in Leibniz's on-going controversy with the Newtonians. Besides German and English, Zollman was fluent in Latin, French, Dutch, Italian and Spanish.[5] He enjoyed the patronage of a number of well-connected individuals in English government and intellectual circles. His principle patron was the diplomat Stephen Poyntz while amongst the fellows of the Royal Society he was on intimate terms with John Jurin, William Sherard and, of course, Sir Hans Sloane to whom Zollman felt especially obliged for his advancement in the Royal Society.[6] Over the years Zollman became one of Sloane's most punctilious informants and correspondents.

In the same package as Steigerthal's letter, Zollman sent Sloane a letter. He enclosed a copy of a new map of the Caspian Sea and the eastern edges of Asia which had been published recently by the Nuremberg cartographer, Johan-Baptista Homann, and was said to be based on the information available from the latest discoveries in that part of the world. The map, not part of the Kaempfer collection, outlined 'Oku Jedso' (present-day Kamchatka) and showed it adjacent to Japanese territory. Zollman's curiosity had not been sparked by Japan but by his deep interest in Russian history. He planned a history of the country and was busy gathering material. A cautious man by nature, Zollman informed Sloane that as a means of fulfilling his recently acquired duties as 'Assistant to the Secretaries in managing foreign correspondence', a post to which he was appointed on 11 April 1723, the first holder of the office, he intended to inquire of Homann the exact provenance of the map.[7]

This he did, and we can clear up one of the questions surrounding the maps incorporated into *The History of Japan* for Zollman was informed by Homann in September that the cartographer had received a draught of the map from Muscovy in October 1721 from a friend, a great minister at the Russian court, and that he judged it authentic.[8]

Zollman also translated the catalogue of the Kaempfer curiosities which had been sent to Hanover and this was despatched along with a copy of the German list to London for Sloane to study.[9] At this juncture, Steigerthal estimated the price for everything in the catalogue at between £300 and 300 guineas, but doubted the collection, which he judged unremarkable, was worth that much. He suggested that he might be able to persuade Kaempfer to sell the herbarium and shells, which he judged of greatest interest to Sloane, separately, and quite cheaply because of their poor and disorganized condition.[10]

As with the map of Kamchatka, it was not a fascination with Japan that attracted Zollman to Kaempfer's writings and in particular the manuscript of *The History*. It was the opportunity he discerned in a possible translation to advance his standing in the Royal Society and help him attain the fellowship he coveted so much. He intended to inspect the manuscript himself at Lemgo.[11]

At this time, of course, the manuscript did not bear the title it would be known by. Kaempfer himself had entitled it 'Heutiges Japan' (Today's Japan). Zollman usually referred to it as 'Kaempfer's manuscript of Japan', but for the sake of convenience I shall refer to it as *The History*. Unfortunately, Zollman's heavy workload for Townsend ruled out a visit to Lemgo, but Steigerthal, who noted that the manuscript had already been prepared for the printers by its author, informed Sloane that because Johann Hermann Kaempfer refused to sell the manuscript itself Zollman intended to reach an agreement to obtain a copy with a view to publishing an English translation. The doctor believed such a course would be most appropriate in order to ensure that the work received the circulation in the Republic of Letters that it deserved.[12] No correspondence between Zollman and Kaempfer survives for these months but it is clear that Zollman faced a tough job in trying to woo the nephew.

Johann Hermann's stubborn resolve not to part with the manuscript stemmed from his fear that it was being snapped up by a collector who would let it languish unpublished. He wanted to be sure that he had found a purchaser with a firm commitment to publish thereby realizing his uncle's ambition. From Johann Hermann's perspective, the language in which *The History* first appeared was not important. The main consideration was that it finally appeared in print. The fact that it made its debut in English was purely circumstantial. Firstly, Zollman was based in England where he was establishing a career. A successful translation of a major work would give him much credit among the Fellows of the Royal Society and win him plaudits in the Republic of Letters. Secondly, there was a precedent for the publication of such a major work in English, Sir Hans Sloane's *A Voyage to the Islands of Madeira, Barbadoes, Nieves, St Christopher, and Jamaica.* In the introduction to the second volume, Sloane recorded, with obvious satisfaction, that the favourable reception of the first volume had been beyond his expectation considering that it had been published in English.[13] Finally, it was an age of translations. Foreign language editions of major works usually followed hard on the heels of the original language version.

In the meantime, Johann Hermann had sent a specimen of the manuscript to Hanover along with a breakdown of the chapters and Steigerthal recommended Zollman to send it to Sloane for an opinion as to whether an English translation should be undertaken. The work comprised forty-seven chapters divided into five books, the manner in which Engelbert Kaempfer had conceived the work.[14] Zollman's rough translation of 'The Heads of M. Kaempfer's Manuscript relating to Japan' has survived.[15] The most notable difference between these heads and the printed version of *The History of Japan* is the fact that the latter comprises forty-nine chapters. The two additional ones are the first chapter of the first book, 'Journal of the author's voyage from Batavia to Siam with an account of what happen'd during his Stay there', and chapter 8 of the fourth book, 'Some more Particulars concerning the Dutch Trade in Japan'. The additions can be accounted for. The first one was added by Scheuchzer from material separate from the manuscript version of *The History* while the second is a subdivision of the long chapter 7 in the manuscript.[16]

After viewing the outline of Kaempfer's manuscript,

Sloane gave his support to the plan to acquire *The History* and for the preparation of an English edition. At this stage neither Zollman nor Steigerthal conceived of buying the manuscript. What they expected to obtain was a copy. But Johann Hermann's resolve not to part with the manuscript itself soon weakened for monetary reasons. His dire financial plight became more serious and he needed every penny he could get. (He would soon be forced to sell the family house to pay his creditors).[17]

The question of money appears to have been brought up by Johann Hermann himself, who mentioned a sum of £40 for a copy. This was unacceptable to Zollman and Steigerthal. As the preparation of a copy would have been time-consuming, subject to unforeseeable delays and would have involved the additional expense of employing a copyist, Zollman, by now determined to take up the challenge of translation, and Steigerthal, looking for value for money, changed tack. Zollman would attempt to convince Kaempfer that priority should be given to an English edition of *The History* and offer to buy the manuscript itself. Kaempfer's reservations melted at the prospect of cash in hand, and he was won over to this plan. It should be emphasized that Zollman enjoyed a completely free hand in negotiating with Johann Hermann, and it was because of his determination to secure the manuscript that Kaempfer relented. Zollman had acted in consultation with Sloane, but not as his agent as was the case with Steigerthal. The price finally agreed upon for the manuscript was 200 thalers (£36.40p), exactly one half of what Steigerthal paid for the curiosities.[18]

Johann Hermann made two contracts, one with Steigerthal the other with Zollman. Sloane had chosen to disregard Steigerthal's opinion about the merit of the collection and returned the catalogue with a number of items marked for purchase which Steigerthal then bought on Sloane's behalf for 400 thalers, plus Kaempfer's costs for transporting them from Lemgo to Hanover, an additional 50 thalers. Sloane had been prepared to pay up to £100 (approximately 549 thalers) but Steigerthal, good agent that he was, had managed to knock down the price. Payment was arranged to be made by letters of credit drawn on a Hanover merchant.[19]

In response to pressure from Kaempfer, who was disappointed that Sloane was interested only in a part of the collection, Steigerthal had agreed to help Johann Hermann secure a post as a provincial doctor (*Landphysicat*). Even if Steigerthal felt a measure of compassion, possibly a twinge of guilt, about having driven a hard bargain with the unfortunate Johann Hermann, his philanthropy was calculated to make the nephew more amenable to Sloane's bid. The offer of assistance was entirely Steigerthal's responsibility. Sloane, a man who did not gladly entertain claims on his patronage, had made it clear that no extra conditions were to be attached to his bid. Steigerthal regretted making the offer. He found it more difficult than anticipated to help further Johann Hermann's career and hoped that the latter would not insist after he had the money in his hands. Steigerthal discovered that no post was available for Kaempfer and that for any post that was likely to crop up there were already many able and better-connected suitors. Nevertheless, Steigerthal did what he could and approached no less a person than the king's confident and chief minister, Andreas Gottlieb Bernstoff, with a request that the latter intercede with the Princess Royal, under whose patronage these posts were lodged, to have Johann Hermann's name added to the list of applicants. Thanks to Bernstoff's intercesion, it was.[20]

No copy of Zollman's contract with Johann Hermann survives but its provisions can be pieced together from the writings of the two men.[21] According to Johann Hermann, there were at least six clauses. First, Zollman paid 200 thalers in silver coins for the manuscript and all materials belonging to it (the draughts of the illustrations that Engelbert Kaempfer had selected for publication). Second, he undertook not to leave out any of the sixty-odd illustrations that Kaempfer had marked for inclusion at specific points in the text and which the author considered essential to his work.[22] Third, a German edition, which Zollman was to arrange, was to be prepared immediately after publication of the English translation to prevent anyone from producing a German retranslation from the English. Fourth, the German edition was to appear under Johann Hermann's name, as editor, prefaced with a dedication of his choice. (Ultimately, he settled upon George II because he was a fellow-countryman of Engelbert Kaempfer.)[23] Fifth, Johann Hermann was to receive fifty copies of the German edition 'halb druck papier, halb schreib' (half printing paper quality, half writing paper) free of all costs, but he was obliged not to sell any of these, only to dispose of them among friends or patrons.[24] Sixth, Zollman would endeavour to oblige the German bookseller who would handle the publication and distribution of the German edition not to print a second edition of *The History* without paying a royalty to both Zollman and Johann Hermann.

Of especial significance for the subsequent history of *The History*, and for explaining why Johann Hermann was won over by Zollman's arguments to sell the manuscript itself, is the fact, until now unknown, that Johann Hermann kept a copy of the manuscript in Lemgo. Aware of the danger that the precious manuscript could easily perish in transit, Zollman was happy with this arrangement, although he was commercially-minded enough to insist that Johann Hermann was not to allow this copy to be used in the preparation of any other edition of *The History*.[25] As Zollman met Johann Hermann for the first and only time in Hanover in December 1723, he had no idea about the nature and condition of the copy left in Lemgo. As we shall see, neither had Johann Hermann.

Johann Hermann delivered the manuscript and other materials relevant to *The History* to Zollman in Hanover on 3 December (NS) and the contract was signed. (He had brought the manuscripts and the curiosities from Lemgo at the end of November, handing over the curiosities separately to Steigerthal.) Zollman immediately informed Sloane of the successful conclusion of the deal. He was confident that the money had been well spent and that the projected translation would quickly win recognition in the Republic of Letters. Convinced that his credit with Sloane had risen sharply, he requested that he be looked upon favourably at the next election of fellows to the Royal Society.[26] For his part, Johann Hermann had received badly needed cash to ease his financial problems and, with a bit of luck, he would soon have a new job with a secure income. He could also take heart from the fact that he had successfully embarked upon the first steps towards having his uncle's work published. Everyone appeared happy.

Zollman returned to London with the English ministers and, with Sloane's encouragement, immediately began work on the translation. Sloane had been enthusiastic about the project from the start. When news of Zollman's interest in purchasing the manuscript first reached him in the autumn of 1723, he wrote to Steigerthal expressing his hope that Zollman would procure the manuscript and his confidence that the young man would see it 'translated extreamly well'. He believed that publication of Zollman's translation could be financed by a subscription 'without Booksellers intermedling'. This would make it more financially rewarding to the translator.[27] Over the following weeks, Sloane hatched grander but ultimately impracticable ambitions for presenting the Kaempfer material to the Republic of Letters: a double edition, comprising an English translation of the *Amoenitates Exoticae*, and Zollman's translation of *The History*.

Zollman worked hard on the project, always in close contact with Sloane. On 7 February 1724, he wrote to Johann Hermann, keeping him abreast of the latest developments. He mentioned that he was hard at work on translating the manuscript. He had encountered only three minor problems. First, a part of the manuscript had been written in a hand other than those of Engelbert and Johann Hermann and this third hand was out of sequence with the other two. Second, many proper names had been badly spelt and, third, several blanks for place names had been left in the manuscript. Zollman said he would draw up a list and send the queries to Johann Hermann so that he could check his copy.

The letter is especially interesting, however, because Zollman reveals that Sloane intended to buy more of Engelbert Kaempfer's collection. According to Zollman, Sloane would not limit his selection to the master list that Steigerthal had sent over in the autumn. Not only did Sloane have his eye on the remaining curiosities, but he wanted the original manuscripts of the *Amoenitates Exoticae*, to help Zollman with his planned translation, and he was greatly interested in acquiring any remaining manuscripts belonging to Engelbert Kaempfer. For his part, Zollman informed Johann Hermann that in order to see the project through, it was 'absolutely necessary' for him to have 'the 50 Japanese paintings' (*meisho-e*), the maps of the principal Japanese cities, and the map of the world that remained among the curiosities in Lemgo. He requested Johann Hermann to send him exact information about what remained in Lemgo. Finally, he noted that there would be additional work involved in preparing new copper plates for the press as the ones used to illustrate Japanese flora in the *Amoenitates Exoticae* had been poorly engraved when judged against Engelbert Kaempfer's original drawings.[28]

Sloane's renewed interest in the collection can be explained easily. Like Zollman, Steigerthal had kept in touch with Johann Hermann after returning to England. No letters between the two survive from this time but we know of the correspondence from Zollman's letter and from a later one from Kaempfer to Zollman. Johann Hermann had written to the doctor around the turn of the year mentioning that another person had been making enquiries about purchasing the remaining Kaempfer curiosities, a certain councillor Rott in Bielefeld. The latter had made both direct and indirect approaches to Kaempfer and had his eye on various Buddhist artifacts (the *kannon*, the small statues, and a rosary) and books and maps relating to Japan. Rott was promising a good price for them.[29] News of these approaches had already reached London and had prompted an immediate response from Sloane. Through Dr Steigertahl, Sloane let Johann Hermann know that he was ready to do business again, but only on the right terms. Jealous collector that he was, Sloane was determined that the curiosities would not fall into another's hands.[30]

In his reply to Steigerthal in early February 1724, Johann Hermann confirmed that Rott had been in touch but he informed his new-found patrons that Rott had been told bluntly that Sloane had first option on his uncle's collection. He assured his 'dear patron' that everything he had requested for Sloane was in a good condition, just like the first batch, which he was glad to learn had arrived safely in London. He emphasized that he would rather sell the rest of the curiosities to Sloane than to anyone else, especially the books and maps which he said his deceased uncle considered the cream of his collection because they contained 'all the knowledge of the Japanese from the rudiments to the sublimities of Astrology'. Johann Hermann's enthusiasm for another Sloane-purchase had been hightened by Sir Hans's additional payment of two guineas for a Japanese statue, which Johann Hermann interpreted as 'a new manifestation of your [Steigerthal's and by extension Sloane's] benevolence and a sign of its continuation'. These were fine-sounding words, but in the rest of the letter he made it obvious that his obligation to Sloane was solely a consequence of the efforts that Steigerthal had already made to obtain a post for him and that he expected to reap the fruits of patronage in the future (he mentioned that he would be going to Hammeln or the Harz in the spring to seek a job).[31]

Sloane made an offer of 300 thalers for the second batch of Kaempfer curiosities but Johann Hermann asked for, and received, 600 thalers. He mentioned his price in letters to Steigerthal and Zollman. An agreement was concluded by March and the goods were despatched for London via an agent in Hamburg.[32]

What did this second, larger and more costly batch from the Kaempfer collection comprise? Among the Sloane manuscripts in the British Library is a list of

Japanese items, each one ticked. It includes examples of Japanese flowers made of silk, portraits of Japanese men and women on Japanese paper, a rosary, mirrors, the box of idols, the fifty paintings, a kettle, accounts in Japanese, maps of Japan, its principal cities, one of the world and fifty-four manuscript volumes in Japanese covering Japanese history, chronology, geography etc. The list appears to be in Scheuchzer's hand and one suspects that it is the check-list of the items Sloane wanted to purchase.[33] Towards the end of his letter to Steigerthal, Kaempfer mentions that he would personally take the items Sloane wanted to Hamburg, expenses paid, of course, but that he would not bring the portraits of the Japanese men and women, the box of idols, the glass, and the fragment of the bird of paradise all of which, he suggested 'on aura marque [*sic*] par quelque meprise'. But as the portraits made their way into the Sloane collection they were certainly included in the purchase.[34] The items were shipped to Hamburg along with the manuscripts of the *Amoenitates Exoticae* and other manuscripts relating to Engelbert Kaempfer's travels, including the diaries of his voyage from Batavia to Siam and of his return to Amsterdam.

Meanwhile, Zollman had been thinking long and hard about how to proceed with the Kaempfer project. He knew – from Sloane – that several booksellers were keen to publish a translation of the *Amoenitates Exoticae*, and he was in agreement with Sloane's plan for a double edition. But he realized that there was no chance of completing such a huge, time-consuming job quickly, even if Sloane's purchase of Engelbert Kaempfer's original papers for the *Amoenitates* would, as was hoped, shed light on several obscure passages and subjects in the *Amoenitates*. It turned out that the original papers for the *Amoenitates* were imperfect in several places with a number of sections in the second and third fascicules wanting entirely.[35] A double edition was a major publishing enterprise in itself and Zollman suspected that the public would prefer to see a translation of *The History* in print as soon as possible rather than wait for a double edition to appear. Besides, the painstaking work involved in preparing the illustrations had to be taken into consideration and if, as was intended, publication should be paid for largely by subscription, there was a serious risk that subscribers would be unhappy and even withdraw their financial support if there was a long delay.

Zollman judged it better to gain experience by translating *The History* while dissuading the booksellers from proceeding with a separate translation of the *Amoenitates* until he was better equipped to perform this work. This, he believed, would not prove difficult once the booksellers were made aware of the fact that Sloane had acquired a whole range of curiosities unmentioned in the Latin edition and illustrations of a far higher quality than those in the earlier publication. Zollman could not hazard a guess at costs until he had made some headway with the translation and had a clearer idea about how many copper plates would be required for the illustrations and whether they should be cut in England, either by 'Mr Virtue', who would be expensive, or the engraver who did the job for the *Philosophical Transactions*, or in Holland where it was cheaper. Zollman judged that at present his energies would best be focused on the translation of *The History* alone to get some idea of the length and likely cost, and that he should seek advice from people who were familiar with the procedures for raising subscriptions.[36]

Yet, his resolve to press ahead was undermined by one nagging imponderable, the question of 'how soon I may be able to finish the Translation of Kampfer's Manuscript relating to Japan'.[37] The uncertainty did not stem from any lack of self-confidence about his qualifications and ability to produce the translation, but from a new call upon his talents by the British government. The distractions of these duties eventually forced him to relinquish a project to which, for a few months, he had devoted much time, thought and effort.

In the spring of 1724, Zollman was overseas once again, in Paris, in the service of the British government,

Kaempfer's manuscript of *The History* in his possession. This time he was secretary to the British plenipotentiary, Horace Walpole, in the latter's delicate negotiations with the French court. In mid-May, Sloane informed Zollman of the purchase of the second batch of Kaempfer material and assured him that there would be 'something more for yor history of Japan'. He suggested that Zollman investigate the possibility of having the plates engraved in Paris where they would be done better and cheaper than in London and that Zollman should consider the possibility of including more illustrations than Engelbert Kaempfer had intended for publication in proportion to the sheets of paper used to print the text. Yet, sensing the probable negative impact of Zollman's new employment on progress on the translation, Sloane begged Zollman to 'lett me know what you do in it, for people expect it with great impatience'.[38]

Sloane's premonitions of delay were realized for in his replies Zollman conceded that the pressure of work was indeed preventing him from making any headway with the translation of *The History*. He saw no let-up in the foreseeable future but assured Sloane that the manuscript of *The History* was in safekeeping. He appreciated Sloane's encouragement and his generous offer to ensure that the translation would appear in a high quality edition. As for getting a subscription underway, Zollman was reluctant to bother Walpole with such a relatively trivial matter in the midst of delicate diplomatic negotiations.[39]

While Sloane understood Zollman's situation and indeed sympathized with his predicament, he realized that a Zollman translation of Engelbert Kaempfer's *History* would take too long to reach print. Practical as ever, he suggested that Zollman give up the job and offered to buy the manuscript from him. Zollman hesitated. He thanked Sloane for his offer and said that he would make up his mind after he had reviewed his obligations to Johann Hermannn.[40] His procrastination is understandable. By giving up the translation he would be saying farewell to an undertaking that would give his name wider recognition in the Republic of Letters.

His strong sense of obligation to Johann Hermann is evident from his papers which contain notes that he penned as conditions for parting with the manuscript and draughts. He stipulated that because of the 'Engagement with the Gentleman I bought it of' the manuscript should be copied and the copy retained until the English translation was ready for the press as '...a precaution against the work's being entirely lost to the World by unforseen accidents' (the bearer of this expense was left undeclared). The copy was then to be returned to Zollman '...to be printed in the original Language which is High Dutch [German]; This I am engaged to do in order to prevent any edition done after the English Translation'. Finally, the plates to be used in the English translation were to be fashioned in such a manner that they could also be used in the planned German edition and a sufficient number of cuts were to be made and delivered to Zollman 'upon my paying for the expence of the printing of the paper'.[41]

During the summer of 1724 Zollman returned briefly to London prior to taking up a new appointment overseas in the autumn as secretary to the British ambassador to the Swedish court in Stockholm, Stephen Poyntz, his English patron and one of the subscribers to *The History of Japan*. Thus, the manuscript of *The History* was brought to England for the second time. But because Zollman had decided against proceeding with the translation it was only then that Kaempfer's work came into Sloane's possession. No formal contract was drawn up let alone signed; rather Sloane and Zollman reached a gentleman's agreement incorporating the assumptions in Zollman's earlier notes. But Sloane reimbursed Zollman for his outlay in purchasing the manuscript and draughts.[42]

Commenting on the purchase of the manuscript, Steigerthal told Sloane that he doubted there would be any profits to be made from publication, perhaps even a loss would be incurred, but he noted that as Sloane was not motivated by financial gain anyway but by the superior vocation of promoting the public good '...the world at large will esteem your generosity; at the very least it will be eternally grateful', a view with which subsequent generations can concur wholeheartedly.[43] From Steigerthal's letter it is also clear that Johann Hermann's importuning manner had further alienated Sloane and Steigerthal. Over the summer of that year Johann Hermann had requested payment for two small manuscript volumes and some cardboard figures with straw hats which he had given to Steigerthal in Hanover. Steigerthal had taken them to be a gift, possibly a gesture of goodwill, and had presented them to Sloane. He urged Sloane, whom he said had paid more than enough already for the material from the Kaempfer collection, to disregard Johann Hermann's demand, dismissing him as this 'poor indebted man' who would not have got the half of what he had received had he tried to sell the collection in Germany.[44] Johann Hermann had burdened himself with a reputation as a pushy and ungrateful client, grabbing indecorously at what he considered to be the just rewards of patronage instead of showing the appropriate degree of deference and gratitude for any rewards that came his way.

Finally in possession of the manuscript, and eager to press on with the project, Sloane quickly designated a new translator, Johann Gaspar Scheuchzer, who started work immediately. Until now only the broad outlines of Scheuchzer's brief career have been known, even if he was thought sufficiently important to be included in the *Dictionary of National Biography*. His father, Johann Jakob Scheuchzer, was the distinguished Swiss virtuoso and author of the *Iter Alpina*. Johann Jakob had longstanding links with the English *virtuosi* of the Royal Society, including Sloane and the irascible Dr John Woodward whose *Essay towards a natural history of the earth* (1695), he translated into Latin for wider circulation in the Republic of Letters and he put those contacts to good use to help find employment for his son in England.

Encouraged by Woodward's promise of assistance to help him find his feet in England, the young Scheuchzer arrived in London at the end of 1722 only to become imbroiled in the bitter rivalry between Woodward and his adversary, Sloane. A stranger in a foreign land, uncertain of his future, frustrated in his present employment and resentful of his treatment by Woodward, who did not have much to offer him beyond work of a routine clerical nature, Johann Gaspar gave vent to his feelings. The prickly Woodward, short-tempered as ever, washed his hands of the young man, informing Johann Jakob that his son had received his 'Civilities...very coldly' and '...had been so insolent to me that I will never more personaly have any Thing to do with Him', although he assured his correspondent that Johann Gaspar's 'misdemeanour' would not alter '...my sentiments of you, or letting my Friendship to you cool'.[45]

Fortunately, Sloane stepped in, showing compassion for the miserable youth who had been 'disappointed by his friends'. He took the young man under his wing and employed him in his library, indexing and putting the books into order. In January 1725, Sloane wrote to Johann Jakob that he found Johann Gaspar 'very sober, modest, & diligent' and that in order to '...keep him from being chargeable to you...advised him to betake himselfe to the study of the practice of physical which here or in all places will make a man qualified, able to live handsomely & have the good will of his neighbours'. He had taken the necessary steps to have Johann Gaspar examined for a licence from the Royal College of Physicians, which would cost a good deal of money. He added that '...in matters relating to yor son [he had] gone much beyond any thing I ever did in the like condition'. He noted that he had formerly encouraged similar 'young gentlemen in his circumstances' only to 'have mett in some of them returns of ingratitude', but he had no doubt that Johann Gaspar '...will by his behaviour deserve all I have done, or may hereafter do for him'.[46]

Sloane's confidence was not misplaced, and Johann Gaspar responded with diligence, enthusiasm and energy to the challenge of working for his new-found English patron. At the end of April 1725 Sloane wrote to Zollman, who was still in Sweden, that '...Dr Scheuchzer works hard at Kempfer's Japan & gives you his service'.[47] And hard he did work. On 13 August Sloane wrote to Zollman mentioning that Scheuchzer '...labours very hard in getting thro Kempfer [and] is alrerady gott to ab[ou]t 2/3 of it'.[48] Zollman, who continued to take a keen interest in the project, asked Sloane to convey his respects to Scheuchzer '...and to wish him good success in his work on Kaempfer's Japan'.[49] He continued to look out for curiosities and manuscripts that would be of interest to Sloane and on 23 November 1725 he sent Sloane an extract of a voyage to Japan which he had acquired at an auction. The original had been published in Swedish and had been written by Oloff Erickson Willman, a marine officer in the Dutch East India Company's service who had visited Japan in 1651-1652. He asked Sloane to look it over and give an opinion as to whether it would be worth translating and adding to the forthcoming edition of Kaempfer's *History*. It was not included but Scheuchzer mentions it in the introduction to *The History of Japan*.[50]

Meanwhile, in 1725 Steigerthal met Johann Hermann again at Bad Pyrmont on the occasion of the fourth royal visit to Germany. Steigerthal informed him about progress on the translation of *The History* and Johann Hermann told him that he still possessed some of his uncle's letters which he thought could form a sixth fasicule of the *Amoenitates Exoticae* (there were five in the Latin edition). Steigerthal reported to Sloane that the letters covered illnesses prevalent in Persia and India, and a natural history of some plants and animals. He suggested that Scheuchzer would find it useful when he came round to translating the *Amoenitates* after finishing his work on *The History*. Steigerthal agreed with Johann Hermann that it could be added to make an additional fasicule. Sloane was interested in acquiring the new batch of material and Steigerthal asked Johann Hermann to provide a list of what was available and send it to Hanover. Steigerthal assured Sloane that he would endeavour to keep the sale price low.[51]

On 4 September (NS), after a number of letters from Steigerthal, which went unanswered, Johann Hermann finally sent the list to Steigerthal in Hanover. The manuscripts, both Japanese and Dutch, were arranged according to their size (folio, quarto, octavo, etc.) and included extracts from *Osaka monogatari, Edo kagami,* a chronological succession of the Japanese emperors, *kana* tables, two volumes, described as 'Collectanea Japonica' covering numerous aspects of Japanese medicine, culture, religion, geography etc, extracts from the *Dagh Register* (Diary) of the Dutch factory in Japan and other Dutch source material, and the collection of letters in octavo which was intended to form the basis of the sixth fasicule of the *Amoenitates Exoticae*. There was also a printed volume called the *Sapienta Sinica,* a Jesuit publication, printed in China in 1662. Johann Hermann said that he was reluctant to part with the *Sapienta* and the letters but that he would do so nevertheless. He suggested that some of the new material could be added as an appendix to *The History*. He also mentioned his terms. He requested that a sales contract be drawn up 'much after the same manner with that of Mr Zollmann', which Sloane should sign, seal and send over to Lemgo. He specified the changes that should be made. These were minor. Johann Hermann gave no price but expressed his hope that '...Sr Hans would be pleas'd to make the conditions [the financial ones] still better, which I shall be very glad of'. He also asked for more up-to-date information about work on *The History* '...that I may resolve upon the dedication of the German edition, which I reserv'd to myself'.[52]

Steigerthal dispatched Johann Hermann's proposals to Sloane, noting that as he felt sure that Zollman would have left a copy of his original agreement with Johann Hermann in Sloane's custody, Scheuchzer would be able to inform him of the allusions to the earlier contract.[53] Sloane, realizing that he already had the cream of the collection in England (he wrote as much to Zollman in Stockholm in August) and by now fed up with Johann Hermann's importuning, instructed Steigerthal to purchase the papers but to offer no more than £20, just over half what Zollmann paid for *The History*. Sloane emphasized that no other conditions were to be entertained. Steigerthal forwarded the details to Lemgo on 2 October (NS) and Johann Hermann, who would have preferred to receive 200 thalers (the price of the first purchase), reluctantly accepted Sloane's offer of 100 thalers, plus the expenses of bringing them to Hanover. He added that he wanted to receive twenty-five copies of any publication that resulted from the sale and he emphasized that publication should advance speedily.[54]

It is impossible to reconstruct Johann Hermann's state of mind from the surviving evidence. He was concerned about the delay in publishing *The History*. Two years had passed since the purchase of the manuscript with still no publication in sight and the individual who had undertaken to put *The History* into print, was now divorced from the project, while he himself was being fobbed off with vague reassurances. Perhaps there was the tug of a guilty conscience. Equally plausible is the view that he wanted to see an early publication not just to satisfy his sense of obligation to his late uncle's wishes but to savour the rewards he expected his association with such a prestigious work would bring.

As usual, the conscientious Dr Steigerthal relayed Johann Hermann's comments to London estimating that transportation would add between 20-30 thalers to the overall cost depending on whether Kaempfer came directly to Hanover or stopped on the way. He would await Sloane's instructions regarding payment and whether he should accept Johann Hermann's request for the free copies. Steigerthal hinted that it might be better to pay a small additional amount so that Johann Hermann would have no excuse to demand more money in future. He also asked Sloane to let him have the precise details of what Kaempfer had offered for sale, suggesting that he no longer trusted Johann Hermann. But Johann Hermann was offered no more, and on 6 December (NS) he handed over the manuscripts to Steigerthal in Hanover and received 112 thalers in Hanoverian currency.[55] Thus two years after the first purchase, the third and final batch of Kaempfer material was ready to be transferred to

England. The total amount spent by Sloane to acquire Engelbert Kaempfer's curiosities and manuscripts was 1,162 thalers, plus the 200 thalers reimbursed to Zollman for the original purchase of *The History* and the 2 guineas paid for the Japanese idol in January 1724, a total of approximately £250.[56]

No matter Johann Hermann's fears, work on the translation and publication of *The History* was proceeding smoothly. On 13 December 1726 Sloane wrote to Zollman that half of the book had already been printed and the copper plates for the illustrations engraved. He said that Scheuchzer intended to send him a copy to Stockholm by Lady Day (25 March 1727).[57] Scheuchzer had already submitted proposals for printing the book earlier in 1726. We know this from a reference among the original manuscript catalogues of Sloane's collection.[58] The efforts to raise a subscription had been a success. *The History of Japan* would be published with the Royal Society's *imprimateur*, not with its money; the Society did not have the funds for such ambitious, non-commercial publications. By the time that Sloane wrote to Zollman not only was the printing well under way but steps had already been taken to advertise the publication to the Republic of Letters through the Republic's most widely read literary review, the Paris-based *Journal des Sçavans*.

The first notice appeared in the edition for October 1726 and announced that Johann Gaspar Scheuchzer, son of the Zurich savant, Johann Jakob Scheuchzer, had translated *The History of Japan* into English by the late author of the *Amoenitates Exoticae* and that the work would soon be in the press (it already was). There followed a brief outline of the contents and it was noted that the author had visited Japan in the employ of the VOC and had seen what he described. The *Journal* added, that judging from the synopsis that Scheuchzer had prepared, the work will be 'very curious' and comprises over 100 folios and forty plates, all well engraved. The following February, the *Journal* noted that subscriptions for *The History* were going well, adding

117

that Scheuchzer had also included two journeys to the imperial court, Kaempfer's return voyage to Holland and his journey from Batavia to Siam.[59] The account of the return voyage was dropped, and what has become the first chapter of the first book of *The History*, the journal of the author's voyage from Batavia to Siam, was added by Scheuchzer and the chapter numbers in the manuscript changed accordingly.[60] (Kaempfer's manuscript begins with his description of Siam.) A few of these changes are noted in an entry in Sloane's manuscript catalogue, describing the 1728 edition: 'The Title, The Index, the Author's life, the Introduction, the Preface partly changed, Explanation of ye cutts, severall Annotations intermixed in the text very materiall, The two appendixs, all added by Dr Scheuchzer & not contain'd in ye German MS.'[61] It seems likely that Scheuchzer's additions and amendments were thought to be of little or no consequence to the intended readership and were thus not mentioned in his introduction to the English edition. But, as we shall see, they were to affect the German edition.

Thus, just over three years after Zollman's purchase of the manuscript Engelbert Kaempfer's *The History of Japan* was finally published in Scheuchzer's English translation. The Journal Book of the Royal Society notes that on 27 April 1727 the new president, Sir Hans Sloane, '...gave his imprimateur to Dr Scheuchzer's Translation of Kempfer's History of Japan'. A month later, on 28 May, the Journal Book records that Scheuchzer presented his translation to the Society 'and was ordered Thanks'.[62]

During the months before publication, Scheuchzer had not been alone in applying himself to Kaempfer's *History*. Pierre Des Maizeaux, Huguenot refugee, journalist, literary agent and English translator and biographer of Pierre Bayle, had been putting Scheuchzer's text into French. Des Maizeaux had first learned of *The History* from Zollman in August 1723.[63] Their acquaintenceship goes back to Zollman's early days in London and the Leibniz-Clarke correspondence.[64] Recognizing a hot property, and with unrestricted access to Scheuchzer's work, Des Maizeaux signed himself up for the French translation which he arranged to be published by his customary publishers in The Hague, Pierre Gosse and Jean Neaulme. He did not neglect his own public relations. In September 1727, the *Journal des Sçavans* announced that Des Maizeaux had translated the English edition of *The History of Japan* into French and that it would be published in the Hague in two volumes. Subscriptions were invited at a cost of 20 florins, half payable on subscription, the balance on delivery. Subscriptions would remain open until 15 November (NS) at all reputable booksellers in France, Britain and Germany, and publication would follow eight months later.[65] Such confidence was unwarranted for the publishers had difficulty in raising a full subscription and the two-volume edition did not appear until 1729, dedicated to the Prince of Orange.[66]

Mindful of the undertakings to Johann Hermann, neither Zollman nor Sloane had been negligent about attempting to find a German publisher and to ensure that copies of the translation reached Kaempfer. In his letter to Zollman of 13 December 1726, Sloane mentioned that Scheuchzer had corresponded with Johann Hermann '...and will fulfill all agreements with him as much as he can possibly, but finds a great difficulty to gett it [*The History*] printed in Germany'.[67] It seems that Zollman had secured the services of an agent, one Mattheson, in Hamburg to find a suitable publisher for the German edition.[68] But Mattheson's efforts ran into the sand. Kaempfer began to fret.

On 22 July 1727 (NS), Steigerthal, back in Hanover, after accompanying George I on what turned out to be the king's last journey to his native land (he died on 12 June, terminating Steigerthal's duties in England as royal physician), wrote to Scheuchzer that he hoped Sloane had received the two letters that he had forwarded from Johann Hermann. Unfortunately, they are no longer extant. He was at a loss to understand what Johann Hermann was after. In particular, Steigerthal could not understand what the younger Kaempfer expected the publisher in England (Thomas Woodward) to perform. Possibly, Johann Hermann expected Woodward to use whatever contacts he had to help set up the German edition; more likely, he wanted Woodward to send him the copper plates for the German edition, according to the contract with Zollman. No matter, Steigerthal, who had been entrusted with the task of delivering a set of *The History* to Johann Hermann noted that he had the volumes in safekeeping and had already been in touch with Kaempfer about the best way to send them, either by post or through an acquaintance of Johann Hermann's. Steigerthal had given presentation copies of *The History* to the Prince of Wales and the Duke of York, both of whom had been suitably impressed. The publication of *The History*, authored by a German, reflected glowingly on Sir Hans Sloane and the Royal Society.[69]

The question of a German edition rested there, or so it seemed. During the following two years Pierre Des Maizeaux's French edition and a Dutch edition appeared, Johann Gaspar Scheuchzer died suddenly in April 1729, much to the grief of his many friends in England and on the threshold of what appeared to be a promising career, and Johann Hermann fulminated in Lemgo, feeling frustrated and shamefully treated. In October 1730 (NS) he broke silence. On the 6th (NS) Steigerthal wrote to Sloane that he had received a long letter from the 'unfortunate' Dr Kaempfer four days previously lamenting Scheuchzer's death and Zollman's absence. (From 1728 Zollman was in France as secretary to Stephen Poyntz, British commissioner at the Congress of Soissons, but, unknown to Kaempfer, he had returned to London with Poyntz during the summer of 1730 and resumed his duties at the Royal Society as assistant secretary for foreign correspondence.) Despairing that help would ever be forthcoming from London now that Scheuchzer was dead and Zollman abroad, Johann Hermann had decided to take matters into his own hands. He claimed that at last he had found a publisher prepared to undertake a German edition, H. W. Meier, the Lemgo publisher and bookseller who had published the *Amoenitates Exoticae*. But there had been a few unpleasant surprises when Johann Hermann had started to prepare his uncle's work for publication.

To his horror he discovered that the manuscript that he had retained in 1723 was far from complete. Book two was missing entirely and books three and five were so badly written as to be virtually indecipherable. Moreover, he lacked the plates which Zollman (according to the contract) and, in his absence, Scheuchzer, had promised he would receive. Steigerthal, sympathetic to Johann Hermann's plight, felt sure that out of charity for the poor man's miserable condition, Sloane, no matter the inconvenience involved in searching out the manuscript and plates, could arrange for a copy of the manuscript to be made in London by a member of the Hanoverian mission and for it to be forwarded to Lemgo along with the plates, at Kaempfer's cost. Steigerthal said he would await Sloane's instructions before replying to Johann Hermann.[70]

Sloane did not delay long in responding. On 1 December (NS) Steigerthal thanked Sloane for a letter in which he assured the doctor that a copy of the manuscript and the plates would be prepared. Steigerthal promised to inform Johann Hermann of the good news and was confident that the latter would feel obliged for Sloane's good graces in helping to advance publication of the German edition.[71]

Nothing happened. Isolated in Lemgo, Johann Hermann became increasingly angered by what he read as betrayal and breach of contract by his distinguished contacts in London. On 2 May 1731(NS), he wrote a long despairing letter to Zollman, bitterly complaining about his shabby treatment and, despite Sloane's promises, the lack of any progress towards the preparation of a new copy of the manuscript, or at least of the gaps in his copy. He rehearsed the main points of the contract they had signed in Hanover in December 1723 and said that he could not but feel injured by what had happened. He had stuck faithfully to his side of the bargain, only to witness publication of Dutch and French editions of *The History* before the debut of the promised German one, which, he argued, should have appeared simultaneously with the English one. He feared someone would soon be tempted to produce a pirated German edition.[72]

He informed Zollman about Meier's interest in publishing a German edition and that he had been working day and night to decipher the third and fifth books, even attempting to match them with the English translation, but the horrendous complexity of this task and the complete absence of the second book had frustrated his efforts. He mentioned his request to Steigerthal, apparently submitted through official channels, for a copy to be made of the second book, but nothing had come of this. He felt that he was the victim of an injustice. After all, his request had been both modest and legitimate and he was in no doubt about who was responsible: Sloane and Scheuchzer. He felt that he would be well within his rights to demand that the manuscript itself should be returned.[73]

The anger was ignited by Johann Hermann's despondency and the letter the last recourse for a despairing man. He had already sought to petition the king for redress, to compel Sloane to return the original manuscript or a copy of the missing and illegible parts, but had been rebuffed. The expense of the postage alone was crippling him financially. To cap it all, Meier had lost interest in a German edition because of the gaps in the manuscript. Johann Hermann's back-breaking work had been in vain. In one final, desperate plea, he reminded Zollman of his obligation and appealed to his sense of honour and his Christian conscience, begging him to take steps to ensure that at least he received an accurate copy of the three books so that he could proceed with the German edition.[74]

One cannot but have sympathy for his plight. As his contract with Zollman had only mentioned English and German editions of *The History*, technically the publication of French and Dutch editions was not a breach of the agreement. It was, however, a breach of the spirit. Yet there is no question but that Zollman, Sloane, Scheuchzer (while he was alive), and Steigerthal believed that they were acting honourably. Sloane and Zollman, even while overseas, had taken what steps they could to try to set up a German edition. Scheuchzer's sudden death, Zollman's absences abroad, and Sloane's numerous other activities and concerns had further complicated the situation. (Steigerthal's direct involvement with Johann Hermann had ceased with his purchases in 1725.) They were all busy men who believed they had fulfilled their commitments to the tiresome, German country doctor as best they could.

Zollman received Johann Hermann's letter on 25 May but it was not until March of the following year that Johann Hermann received satisfaction. Why such a delay occured can only be surmised. Johann Hermann had impunged the honour and *amour propre* of Sloane and questioned the integrity of the deceased Johann Gaspar Scheuchzer. The affair threatened to stir up a scandal in the Republic of Letters. But Sloane and Zollman concluded that the most sensible way to settle the matter, and one that did not imply any wrongdoing on their part, was to send Johann Hermann a copy of his uncle's manuscript and to allow him to do what he wished with it. Johann Jakob Scheuchzer was informed about what had happened and gave his approval to the decision to send the copy to Johann Hermann. The preparation of such a manuscript obviously would have taken time, even for an accomplished copyist for Engelbert Kaempfer's handwriting is not easy to follow, but it was finally completed and dispatched to Dr Steigerthal in mid-March 1732, much to the relief of Sloane and Zollman, with the request that he forward it to Lemgo.[75] The question of whether this was a copy of the whole manuscript or only of the parts Johann Hermann had specified will be taken up later.

Zollman enclosed a letter for Johann Hermann which was both polite, conciliatory and sympathetic, stressing that he wanted to remain on good terms with Johann Hermann and would be willing to help him with any difficulties that he encountered in reading the new text.

He wished him well with his work on the German edition of this 'fine book'.[76] Johann Hermann's reply, on 21 April (NS), was equally gracious, emphasising his goodwill towards Zollman and his complete satisfaction that the controversy had been stilled. Johann Hermann felt relieved that he coud now work in peace towards early publication of the German edition as soon as he could find a suitable publisher, implying that Meier had given up on a highly ambitious but commercially dubious project.[77] The decision to send Johann Hermann a copy of the manuscript won approval in the Republic of Letters. On 8 June 1731 Zollman received a letter from Gerhardt Reiche congratulating him on his efforts. Reiche, who later became one of the executors of Zollman's will, said that he was impressed and felt sure that Zollman had managed to outflank and 'shut up' ('Ferme la bouche') Johann Hermann so that he would be unable to cause any further trouble.[78] Scandal in the Republic of Letters had been avoided, natural justice had triumphed and stubborn, but righteous, perseverance had been rewarded.

But a German edition of *The History* was not published for another forty-five years. Johann Hermann Kaempfer died in 1736, frustrated about having failed to fulfil his uncle's ambition for a German edition of *The History*. The remnants of Engelbert Kaempfer's collection and the library were inherited by Johann Hermann's sister, Maria Magdalena Kaempfer, who, like her brother, had chalked up debts. After her death on 29 January 1773(NS), her possessions were sold off to her creditors. It was during the preparation of the sale of the library, which numbered at least 2,111 volumes, that the two manuscripts of *The History of Japan* came to light (the one that Johann Hermann had retained in 1723, and the one sent from London in 1732). Both were acquired by the then owner of the Meier publishing house, Christian Friedrich Helwing. Helwing could not believe his luck, imagining that he was party to a major discovery about an already well-established work. As a publisher he could sense an opportunity. Helwing sought the best available advice.

He consulted Anton Friedrich Büsching, one of the most distinguished German geographers of the eighteenth century then director of the Berliner und Kölner Gymnasium. The Büsching connection introduces another son of Lemgo into the story, his pupil Christian Wilhelm von Dohm, one of the brightest of Büsching's young epigones, the eventual editor of the German edition of *The History*, and future luminary of the German Enlightenment.

Dohm was a young man in a hurry (he was only twenty-two in 1773), determined to make a name for himself among the German savants. With the endorsement of his mentor and patron, Büsching, who had announced the Lemgo find in his *Wöchentliche Nachrichten* in July 1773, Dohm announced his intention to prepare a German edition of *The History*. It would be another step towards securing his reputation which was already being established with the appearance of a number of important publications in this highly productive decade of his life.[79] Dohm's appointment as editor was announced in the *Wöchentliche Nachrichten* on 9 August 1773(NS), and in March 1774, in a short pamphlet that was both an address to fellow scholars and future subscribers as well as a sales pitch, Dohm outlined his plans for editing and publishing *The History*.[80]

Dohm emphasized the originality of Kaempfer's work, provided additional information about the state of the Lemgo manuscripts, blasted the inadequacies of the published translations and invited subscriptions to cover the high costs of publication. Dohm also announced his own long-term ambition to produce a systematic encyclopaedia of Japan, including a critical bibliography. The encyclopaedia would cover the country from the arrival of the Europeans to the present and would, he hoped, be a model for an eventual 'allgemeine Weltgeschichte' (universal history).[81]

Dohm referred to the Lemgo manuscripts as the 'Oheims' and the 'Neffens'. The 'Oheims', or uncle's, he suggested was in Engelbert Kaempfer's own hand and was the author's rough draft. The 'Neffens', or nephew's, he claimed, was a clean copy prepared for publication by Johann Hermann (its title-page bore his name as editor) but abandonned as no publisher could be found. Dohm emphasized that the differences between the manuscripts were minimal, even if the uncle's contained many corrections, deletions and additions, had duplicate pages and pages missing. Dohm also speculated about the manuscript which Scheuchzer had used (by then in the British Museum and only available for consultation in London). He suggested that Steigerthal (*sic*) had bought only a copy, sold to him either through ignorance or else deliberately so that the original would remain in Germany, although he revised this view in his introduction to the *Geschichte* conceding that '...it might be the case that the manuscript in the British Museum is really also in Kaempfer's hand, perhaps written later and more fully'.[82]

Unfortunately, Dohm's initial supposition that, deliberately or otherwise, Steigerthal had only received a copy of Kaempfer's manuscript has coloured subsequent accounts with a patina of nationalism wholly at odds with the facts and the spirit of the original transaction and with the more modest vein of national pride underpinning Dohm's enterprise.[83] Dr Meier-Lemgo argues that Johann Hermann kept the Lemgo manuscripts a secret from the 'English' (*sic*) buyers; Dr Hüls, that Johann Hermann purposely concealed them from Steigerthal and speculates, on the basis of Dohm's statements, that the version in the British Library might be a copy and not the original in Engelbert Kaempfer's hand.[84] This is nonsense, an old canard that can be laid to rest finally.[85] We now know conclusively that the copy in the British Library is largely in Kaempfer's hand.[86]

What then were the Lemgo manuscripts? Unfortunately, and astonishingly considering the manner that their discovery was trumpeted before the world of learning, they have disappeared. But given the new information presented here we can make some confident statements about them. We know that Johann Hermann received a copy of his uncle's manuscript from London in April 1732. But was this a copy of the *entire* manuscript or only of books two, three and five, as he had requested? Zollman's letters are inconclusive on this point. If only a partial copy had been sent, Johann Hermannn would have incorporated the three books into a fresh manuscript for the printer, either as written by the scribe in London, or into an entirely new manuscript which he himself laboriously rewrote. The former hypothesis, simple substitution, can be discarded immediately. The difference between the writing of the unknown *amanuensis* at the Hanoverian legation in London and Johann Hermann's own hand, as well as differences in paper size and quality, would have been obvious and would have been noted by Büsching, Dohm and the others who examined the manuscript in Lemgo.

The second hypothesis, while entirely plausible, can also be rejected. The fact that this laborious task would have taken up too much time, especially for a man already anxious about the long delay in bringing out a German edition is an insufficient basis in itself to reject such a hypothesis. What seems to me to clinch the argument beyond reasonable doubt that the nephew's manuscript is identical with the one sent from London, and that this manuscript was not a partial but a complete and authentic copy of the one in Sloane's possession, is the fact that Dohm's edition of *The History* retains Scheuchzer's additional chapter – chapter 1 of the first book, the journal of the voyage from Batavia to Siam – and his division of the original long chapter 7 of the fourth book into chapters 7 and 8, a division added by Scheuchzer to the Sloane manuscript. These ammendments would only have existed in a copy made from Sloane's manuscript; they were alien to Kaempfer's conception and would not have occured in the version of the manuscript left in Lemgo. Dr Bodart-Bailey's argument that Dohm's translation of chapter 1 has all the hallmarks of being a translation from the German rather than a translation from Scheuchzer's English version supports this argument.[87]

127

Dohm's suggestion[88] that the Sloane manuscript was possibly a later and *longer* copy of *The History* in Engelbert Kaempfer's own hand can be explained simply. Dohm believed that it was lengthier because he assumed that it contained chapter 10 of book 4 ('Some Proclamations, Pasports, Orders, etc. mentioned in the foregoing Chapters'). There is only a chapter heading for this in the Sloane manuscript, no space for documents.[89] Kaempfer had made his selection of documents but these were in a batch separate from the manuscript. Confronted with a gap, Scheuchzer made his own selection from what he could read from among Kaempfer's batch and Dohm translated Scheuchzer's choice into German for his own edition.[90] A further circumstantial reason to believe that what was sent to Lemgo in 1732 was a complete copy of the Sloane manuscript is Zollman's own concern in 1724 that a copy should be made. The uncle's manuscript presents less of a problem; it was the incomplete version retained in Lemgo in 1723, the one that had frustrated Johann Hermann's labours to prepare a German edition, and which he had kept, with Zollman's knowledge and approval lest anything untoward happened to the other manuscript. It is from this version that Dohm, as he states, was able to insert, and perhaps modify, the map of Deshima into his edition. Scheuchzer had not included it in his version although it is sketched in the Sloane manuscript.[91] Oversight somewhere along the line of production or an editorial decision that it was too crude to reproduce are plausible reasons for this omission from Scheuchzer's edition.

Dohm's description of the Lemgo manuscripts, their similarites and differences is contradictory and plainly wrong and we are left with the inescapable conclusion that Dohm, a young man of boundless ambition, was not telling the truth about them. Granted that his ignorance of earlier developments made it reasonable for him to assume from the title page of the nephew's manuscript that it had been written by Johann Hermann, although a cross-check between the handwriting of the German copyist in London and that of Johann Hermann might have raised suspicions. After all, letters or other writing by Johann Hermann must have been extant in Lemgo.[92] But, this does not alter the fact that his description of the Lemgo manuscripts is largely invention. He was not the first, nor the last, to distort or ignore inconvenient evidence or bend it against the dictates of more reasoned judgement to support his own thesis. In his determination to present the German reading public with a sensational new discovery, and to advance his career, Dohm was carried away on a tide of enthusiasm and emotion that drowned his judgement leaving him exposed and vulnerable to the promptings of his imagination and what it wanted him to believe.

Dohm was not alone in this self-deception. His teacher, Büsching, the *eminence grise* behind the project, was determined to ensure that Kaempfer's substantial and already much-acclaimed work appeared in a German edition which, Büsching believed, 'would bring much honour to the Fatherland', and, of course, strike a blow against the continuing French influence in the German world of *belles lettres*. But, even by his own admission, Dohm reveals that he was not presenting 'pure' Kaempfer to his readers. He doctored the Lemgo manuscripts to make the style less grating to the more refined linguistic sensibilities of a late eighteenth-century German readership. This is evident from the few comparative samples of the different Kaempfer texts that he gives in his introduction, and the alterations are not all necessarily of a linguistic nature. Dohm was not presenting to the world an authentic edition of Kaempfer's work even if contemporaries took his claims at face value.[93] This makes his attacks on poor Scheuchzer, the individual who has been most maligned in the history of Kaempfer's *History*, particularly distasteful. It is a matter of historical injustice that Dohm's rubbishing of Scheuchzer's considerable, and still inadequately recognized, achievement has been accepted so uncritically until now.

Péchés de jeunesse have come back to tarnish the reputation of one of the leading luminaries of the German enlightenment. By the time that the German edition of

The History appeared in 1777-79, Zollman, Steigerthal and Sloane, the individuals who could have set the record straight were already dead.

* * *

Finally, one other mystery about Kaempfer's writings remains to be cleared up. In his introduction to the German edition of *The History*, Dohm dropped his grander ambitions for an encyclopaedia of Japan. Instead, he argued that a comprehensive edition of all the material relating to Kaempfer's travels in the British Museum should be published and drew attention to Sloane's plan to do just that.[94] Dohm mentions an advertisement in the *Journal des Sçavans* in November 1731 announcing that the publication would apppear in two volumes with fifty plates the following year and that it had been edited by Cromwell Mortimer, secretary to the Royal Society, who had taken over the job on Scheuchzer's death.[95] Dohm could find no trace of such a publication and surmised that none had actually appeared. On this point, at least he was correct, even if, and not for the first time, he gives a wrong reference to the *Journal des Sçavans*.[96] The manuscript catalogue of Sloane's library notes: 'J. G. Scheuchzer['s] proposals for printing Dr Engelbert Kaempfer's travells thro Muscovy, Persia & ye East Indies, 1728' and Cromwell Mortimer's proposals 'of ye same, 1729'.[97] In June 1734, the *Journal des Sçavans* made a new announcement about Mortimer's intended publication noting that, because of the success of *The History of Japan*, Mortimer was hard at work preparing an edition of the other travels. Ambitions were more modest this time. Only one folio volume was planned, although it would be illustrated and the paper would be of the same quality as that of *The History*. Subscriptions were invited, two guineas for 'le petit papier', four 'pour le grand', half due on subscribing, the remainder on delivery. The *Journal* had been assured that publication would not be delayed.[98] Alas, Mortimer's duties for the Royal Society were time-consuming and the challenge of transcribing, translating and editing Kaempfer's manuscripts proved too great. His colleague, Zollman, had lost interest in Kaempfer. In 1728, he became a Fellow of the Royal Society, his ambition satisfied. The edition never appeared. In June 1737, Mortimer informed the distinguished scholar, Theophilius Bayer in St Petersberg, that he had put this particular task aside.[99]

CHAPTER SEVEN

Changing the Image: The Drawings and Prints of Kaempfer's The History of Japan

Jörg Schmeißer

SO FAR THE DISCUSSION in this volume has focused on Engelbert Kaempfer's written work. However, Kaempfer is also an important source of visual information concerning Asia. This information is to be found among the books, loose leaves and prints which he had purchased, and among his own sketches which he brought back to Europe with him.[1] Until their recent rediscovery, some of these sketches were not known to the public at all, in others the images had undergone considerable change by the time that they were published.[2] The majority were reproduced as copperplate prints to illustrate the *Amoenitates Exoticae* and *The History of Japan* (subsequently referred to as *The History*). What follows is a comparison between the original drawings and their reproduction and an examination of the changes that took place during the transition from sketch to print.

After outlining the technical possibilities of printmaking in the eighteenth century, I will turn to the specific problems encountered in turning Kaempfer's drawings into prints. I shall examine the differences between Kaempfer's originals and the images that reached the public and compare the prints to other illustrations of a similar nature. Photography, and recent developments in printing and laser technology, have made it possible to produce illustrations so closely resembling the original artwork that the ordinary reader is unable to recognize the difference. In Kaempfer's time only two very different and much more cumbersome printing processes were available to turn a drawing into a print. One was the relief print (woodblock printing), the other the intaglio process, more commonly known as etching and engraving.

In relief printing the image is drawn onto a block of wood and then either the artist or a woodcutter cuts away what is not to appear on the print with a knife, gouge or chisel. The remaining areas are covered with printing ink by means of a roller or some similar tool. A sheet of paper is then placed on the inked block and pressure applied through a printing press so that the ink is transferred from the block to the paper. The advantage of such a process is that the printing can be done at the same time as the printing of the text, for the block with the image and the typeface with the text can be aligned at the same height. The disadvantage is that the method does not allow for particularly fine and detailed work. For more detailed work the intaglio process had been in use since the middle of the fifteenth century.

In the intaglio process a copper plate is commonly used. Fine lines and indentations are either scratched, engraved or etched into the metal with a needle or with an engraver. For printing, the whole plate is covered with ink and the excess is wiped off, usually by hand so that the ink remains only in the etched or cut lines and indentations. Then the plate is placed on an etching press. The plate is covered with a slightly moistened piece of paper and the etching blankets. This is then pulled through the etching press at high pressure. The advantage of this technique is that it allows for very fine line work, the representation of texture and volume as well as shades of light through cross-hatching and other methods. The disadvantage – in the eyes of the publisher at least – is that it entails a process which is quite distinct from that used for printing the text. It is more time-consuming, requires a separate press, and the paper needs a different preparation and aftercare, all of which, of course, affects the final price of the work.

The prints in the *Amoenitates Exoticae* and *The History* are done mostly by intaglio with the exception of a few images in the *Amoentitates* and one print in the German edition of *The History*, which are in relief. One example of relief printing is the illustration of the *daruma* in the *Amoenitates Exoticae*, possibly derived from a Japanese woodblock print. Others are the mountainous landscapes where the power and ruggedness of the rocks come across vividly and dramatically in the relief printing technique. The print of Deshima in the German edition of *The History* was cut from a small sketch by Kaempfer and is the only woodblock print in that book.[3]

In order to understand the differences between the original drawings and the published prints, it is necessary to explain briefly the early eighteenth-century mechanics of producing a print from a drawing. The artist supplied the originals in the form of a pen or wash drawing to the printer. This drawing was then copied, either by tracing the lines with a sheet of paper which had been made transparent with Venetian oil, or by copying it freehand. The drawing could also be transferred through a mirror device which reversed the image at the same time. Once the preparatory drawing from the original was complete, it was transferred to the plate, either by needling (by piercing the paper), or by applying ferric oxide powder to the back of the intermediate drawing and then pressing through the image with a blunt needle onto the prepared plate. The brown acid-resistent varnish on the plate would have been covered with whiting so that the lines of the tracing were visible to the engraver who then began the next part of the process by scratching through the varnish with a sharp needle thus exposing the metal of the plate. The acid would bite these exposed areas in the etching process and the plate would then be ready for printing.[4] Artist/printmakers today sometimes do all the work from the preparatory drawing to the printing themselves. However, in book publication several hundred years ago some four or five individuals were often involved in the process, but most probably only the person who did the intermediate drawing had seen the original. This could lead to some changes in the image.

When Kaempfer returned from the Indies to Westphalia he employed the engraver A. W. Brandshagen. Brandshagen lived with Kaempfer and they had plenty of opportunity to discuss or clarify difficult parts of the drawings. No matter the advantage of such close proximity between author and engraver, and despite the fact that the pictures Kaempfer planned to publish were not particularly exotic or difficult to reproduce, Kaempfer was unsatisfied with Brandshagen's work and that of another, unknown, engraver who was employed. In an unusual move, Kaempfer, in the introduction to the *Amoenitates Exoticae*, complained bitterly about the clumsiness and stubborn attitude of his engravers. He blamed them for the shortcomings of the illustrations and stated that he had even considered leaving out the illustrations altogether.[5] He had attempted, unsuccessfully, to find another engraver. Sometime in 1710 or 1711 he visited Holland to investigate the posssibility of having the cuts made there. Nothing came of this and for whatever reason he did not contact the man who would have been able to help him most, Nicholaas Witsen.[6]

By way of comparison, another near-contemporary traveller-author who was unhappy with his engravers was John Gabriel Stedman, an accomplished artist and observer. Stedman's publisher employed 'name' engravers to do the engraving job, including William Blake. But Stedman was furious with the poor quality of a number of the engravings from his original sketches and watercolours, although it is not clear whether this was more on grounds of workmanship than accurate visual transfer from his raw data.[7] There is also the case of William Hogarth. In 1732 he drew and etched himself the series 'A Harlot's Progress' as he was not satisfied with the work of his assistants.[8] In 1760 Luke Sullivan made an etching after a painting by Hogarth ('March of the Guards Towards Scotland') but then in later prints of this etching there is the following addition to the original address: 'Retouched and improved by William Hogarth, republished June 12th 1761'. This remark not only acknowledges the new edition but points to an improvement in the print by the artist who seems to have been dissatisfied with what his engraver had achieved.

Such dissatisfaction is not confined to Western authors. In a letter to his publisher, the Japanese artist Hokusai Katsushika (1760-1849) complained:

> I suggest that the engraver should add no lower eyelids where I did not draw them. As to the noses: these are my noses [he drew two examples] and the noses usually engraved are the noses of Toyokuni, which I do not like at all and which are contrary to the laws of the art of drawing. It is also the fashion to draw the eyes like this [a black point in the centre], but such eyes I like no more than the noses.[9]

It was not until late in life, long after the *Manga* had been launched, that he was able to report to his publisher that at last an engraver had been found who could cut into wood what he, Hokusai, had submitted on paper.

* * *

Why is it so difficult to make exact copies or truthful images of the things that we see? The main problem is that we all see things differently and that we all draw or describe what we see in different ways, forms and terms, depending on what we see, within what framework of reference we pereceive it and according to how we have learned to describe it. The representation of the same object by several different artists can show clearly the highly subjective and limited information that results from such an exercise, even though the draughtsman might attempt to be objective.

William M. Iving, the former curator for prints at the Metropolitan Museum of Art in New York, demonstrates this with a number of prints depicting the head of the Laokoon group [Pl. 1].[10] Each print contains only what each artist saw in that sculpture and in turn is defined by how each of the engravers went about his work. If we were to take these illustrations as reliable source material and were to discuss the representation of arm muscles and beards in antiquity from the evidence of these prints, we would come to a number of different conclusions, depending on which print we took as an authentic representation of the sculpture. Iving also points out that Lessing did not see Laokoon, but only prints and drawings, and that for a long time the discussions and arguments among art historians relied heavily on prints such as these. It was only with the invention of photography in the middle of the nineteenth century that a way was found to represent an object, living being, or landscape with relative authenticity and objectivity. Until then, individual or collective ways of seeing and the skill and work methods of the artist and the engraver defined the form and content of any printed image.

The representation of something completely alien to an audience with no idea of the forms and features with which it is being confronted is extremely difficult. According to Partha Mitter:

> Whenever we attempt to understand something unfamiliar we proceed from the known to the unknown. The human mind is able to record its impressions of the external world only by first classifying the received information under a general category and the initial generalized 'schema' serves as the essential framework for this. In the field of art, when artists choose to represent a new subject, a pre-existing general formula serves as the starting point which may then be modified and adapted in the light of the actual individual subject. But the problem arises when the artist is not able to adapt his schema because either he lacks the relevant schemata or his starting-point is too far removed from his motif.[11]

An example of the use of a European schema to introduce the Indian deity Ganesha to the Italian reader is provided by a woodcut [Pl. 2a, 2b] from Cartaris's 'Le vere e nove imagini' (Padua, 1615). A comparison of this print with Lucas Cranach's painting of Venus and Cubido in Munich reveals striking parallels. There the print artist works within the Renaissance convention of 'deity and consort' and adds to that, without really understanding what he does, the new information 'elephant'. We can find similar combinations of Western conventions and Eastern 'novelties' in many prints or paintings from the seventeenth century onwards, including the illustrations in Kaempfer's books.

* * *

Kaempfer was an unusually accurate observer, but not a gifted draftsman or artist. His drawings range from detailed and carefully executed illustrations to copies of Japanese prints or watercolours and half-finished sketches of scenes and places. It appears that Kaempfer had no artistic ambitions. He produced no truely inspired drawings, none of the exquisite renderings of a Wenzel Hollar, a contemporary of Kaempfer who similarly recorded events and drew places, landscapes and objects. It is to Hollar that we owe the only surviving print of Shakespeare's Globe Theatre. Hollar also worked on the illustrations of Jan Nieuhof's book on China,[12] combining the talents and skills of draftsman, artist and engraver.

Kaempfer had no claims or pretensions to such brilliance. His aim was more modest; to record what he saw and witnessed as faithfully and reliably as possible. The sketches and drawings he made in Japan indicate that time was often limited. Drawings were sometimes done furtively or from memory. Many sketches remained incomplete. For example, when travelling on the Inland Sea on his trip to Edo, his boat may have passed the building he was sketching before he had a chance to draw all the details. The end result is a sketch that shows part of the building from one side and parts from the other [Pl. 3].[13] The drawing of the *daibutsu* or large Buddha in Kyoto shows similar haste. It is a rough sketch with numbers and a legend indicating that Kaempfer intended to complete the drawing later.[14] The political realities of Japan were such that Kaempfer could not ask a Japanese to do his intermediate drawings for him. It would have laid the individual vulnerable to the serious charge of espionage. Kaempfer had to wait until he had left Japan to complete his preliminary sketches or to work them into more detailed drawings. In the case of the *daibutsu*, however, this never happened. The drawing remained incomplete and in such a state posed a problem for the engraver, for the lack of detail left plenty of scope for different interpretations.

From the multitude of his sketches and drawings, Kaempfer selected approximately sixty pieces as illustrations for his *History*.[15] In many cases he had indicated where these should be bound in the text. The exact number of plates was to depend on how many single motives could be accommodated on a single plate. But Kaempfer did not live to see the publication of *The History*.

Once Sloane had acquired the manuscript, the job of preparing the text and the illustrations for publication was assigned to Johann Gaspar Scheuchzer who did not follow Kaempfer's instructions for arranging the visual material.[16] Scheuchzer selected many more images than Kaempfer had indicated.[17] He added a considerable number of maps as well, whereas Kaempfer had only planned to include one map. More than 130 single images are presented on the forty-five plates in the English edition and in the subsequent Dutch, French and German translations. Scheuchzer aimed at providing an elegant and informative addition to the text and by including a substantial number of images from contemporary Japanese books such as *Kimmōzui*, he added an exotic flavour that appealed to the readership, even though it was not strictly in accordance with Kaempfer's original conception.[18] The combination of so many single images onto one plate was also financially advantageous, for it reduced printing and binding costs.

Scheuchzer prepared the majority of the intermediate drawings from Kaempfer's sketches and from the books and objects which Kaempfer had brought back from the Indies. In all likelihood this was done to protect the originals which might have been damaged or even destroyed when treated with oil, ferric oxide or with needles during the process of preparing the plates. Scheuchzer states in the introduction to his English translation:

> As to the cuts, but very few were left finished by the Author: All the rest I have drawn with my own hand, either from his unfinished originals, or from the prints and drawings of the Japanese, in the Collection of Sir Hans Sloane.

Sensitive to possible charges of misrepresentation, he added, that '. . .if they should appear to some to fall short in point of elegance, though even as to that I have taken all possible care, I have the satisfaction at least, that I can vouch for the truth and accuracy of them, and their conformity with the originals.'[19]

How accurate and true to the originals are the prints? The prints in Kaempfer's *History* can be grouped into 1) architecture and landscapes, 2) illustrations based on Japanese water-colours, 3) copies of Japanese woodcuts, 4) Kaempfer's drawings from the journey from Nagasaki to Edo, 5) maps and plants, 6) miscellaneous. After giving a few examples for each group and examining the originals, I shall discuss the relationship between drawing and print, and the informational value of the latter. The numbered sequence of the plates in the 1727 edition are the same in all subsequent editions and translations.

1) ARCHITECTURE AND LANDSCAPES

Plate 5 of *The History* depicts the Berklam's temple at Ayutthaya, Thailand, a building which still exists today [Pl. 4a, 4b].[20] Various images of the temple have been combined in this plate. We know that the plan of the temple was taken from one of Kaempfer's sketches, for the paper has traces of ferric oxide on the reverse side. The inside of the temple is based on a number of Kaempfer's sketches.[21] It appears that the five small figures were drawn first and the larger ones placed above, possibly being an enlargement of the small ones. Similarities in form and body position suggest that the main figure is also an enlargement of the small central figure, but other points, notably the fact that the smaller figures partly obscure the larger form, suggest otherwise. The draftsman made further sketches and developed them into an intermediate drawing and placed the figures in a hall. He continued his arrangement, positioning the hands of the central figure under the breast and in the folds of the loincloth, so that it now resembles a baroque sculpture rather than a Thai figure of Chinese origin. The head decoration has been simplified to a string of beads and the face has become mask-like. The lotus on which the figure sits in Kaempfer's original now resembles a Graeco-Roman altar-piece. The position of the hands, which Kaempfer draws differently on each figure, appear to be joined as if in prayer with no differentiation at all. Components 3 and 4 of this plate also lack some of the detail contained in Kaempfer's sketches. Thus the informational value is limited, except for the precision with which the temple plan has been drawn. The sketches on which the plate was based were lacking in detail, paricularly concerning the figures' position within a room, and many of the forms were either not understood or purposely simplified by Scheuchzer, the draftsman, or the engraver. The resulting print is detailed but lacks accuracy.

Another architectural image is entitled *Kuruma Do* (Plate 33), the only representation of a Japanese multi-storey pagoda in the book [Pl. 5a, 5b].[22] The original sketch accurately depicts the typical features of a Japanese pagoda,[23] but the print shows a building which resembles a massive castle tower rather than a pagoda. The original has a wavey line on the first roof indicating the use of round tiles, but this is not shown in the print. The number of roofs increases from seven to an improbable eight and the steps from four to seven. Neither in general outline nor in detail is the print as informative as the drawing and the engraver appears to have relied on pictures of Chinese palaces rather than

Kaempfer's drawings from Japan.[24] There is an obvious inclination to make things bigger, taller and more impressive, a tendency evident also in other prints.

The first drawing [Pl. 6a, 6b] for plate 4, depicting the Puka'thon Pagoda in Siam, is more freely drawn than the Japanese pagoda.[25] At first sight it seems impossible to comprehend it fully, yet the intermediate drawing and the printed plate convincingly show the typical forms of the stone pagoda.[26] The form of the stone pagoda was most probably known in London by 1720. The first sketch contains all the relevant information in shorthand, the plan from above, the well observed concave and convex forms, as well as enlargements of details. The drawing was made quickly, but as the basic form was known, the engraver could incorporate without too many difficulties all the details that Kaempfer had sketched. A closer look, however, reveals a number of differences. The gable of the small gates where Kaempfer sketched the shapes of flames is diffused and represented as a baroque scroll. A part of the decoration at the corner of the enclosing wall is drawn so vaguely by Kaempfer that various interpretations are possible. One cannot blame the engraver or the draftsman for choosing forms known to them from baroque architecture and, on balance, the print is a convincing rendering of a large architectural form, if inaccurate in some fine detail.

Plate 24 is an atttempt to show one of the most spectacular structures in Kyoto, the temple Kiyomizu with its famous platform high above the valley supported by huge pillars [Pl. 7a, 7b]. However, this print is totally misleading. Kaempfer visited the temple but made no drawings. The relative accuracy of the ground plan and the positioning of the buildings suggests that the draftsman and engraver constructed their image from Kaempfer's text and a map, although not from the one of Kyoto in the Sloane collection which is more accurate and quite different from the Kiyomizu print that appears in *The History*.[27] The most obvious mistakes are the odd shape of the pagoda and entrance gates, the grass on the wooden platform of the temple, and the poor rendering of the unique lines and forms of the roof of the main hall. At least the engraver resisted the temptation to design a baroque palace!

2) ILLUSTRATIONS BASED ON JAPANESE WATER-COLOURS

Amongst the material Kaempfer brought back from Japan are a set of fifty brush paintings (*meisho-e*) showing famous sights and the life that went on around them.[28] They have no great artistic merit but furnish an abundance of folkloristic detail and a range of architectural information. They are colourful, elaborately drawn compositions, although the use of perspective is inconsistent and haphazard.

Plate 35 shows Hōkōji, the temple in which the famous large Buddha (*daibutsu*) of Kyoto was housed [Pl. 8a, 8b, 8c]. Kaempfer had carefully copied the brush painting to give as much information about the building as possible and accurately portray the activities taking place in the vicinity.[29] However, he must have seen the traditional clouds of gold dust typical for this kind of painting as only hiding information and he attempted to reconstruct what was hidden by the clouds. He made several attempts, but without much success. The remaining picture is copied faithfully: details such as the bridge, the tiles, the temple roof, the stone lantern and the figures are accurately depicted, but the drawing remained unfinished. Scheuchzer's drawing for the print has not survived, but we can assume that the engraver followed it closely. There is considerable loss of precision: the tiles become paint-dot patterns, the figures limp and lifeless and European fashion has crept in. The wooden construction has changed into a solid building and the tiles have made way for metal sheeting or roofing paper. The cross on the stone lantern is not in the original.[30] However, even in the etched and printed version of the brush painting there remains a distinctly Japanese quality. This is partly because the parallel perspective has been maintained. The plate also retains the strength and right angular qualities of Japanese architecture which was almost unknown in eighteenth-century Europe. The transformation of the brush painting of the Sanjū-sangendo temple in Kyoto [Pl. 9] into plate 36 is comparable to the previous plate.[31] The rendering of the roof and tiles is unresolved and the figures look stiff and uninspired in the print. There is no accuracy in the depiction of dress and hairdo. The trees are odd and exotic plants because the engraver was unaware that Kaempfer had copied the plants in the manner commonly used in Japan for representing pine trees. Scheuchzer also omits the building above the main hall and introduces a horizon, sky and clouds to suggest depth. Shadows are used to indicate volume even where there is only a flat wall in the original.[32] The print has a hybrid quality. The foreground is Western, the middle-ground is drawn in Eastern parallel perspective, while the background returns to Western conventions.

Plate 17, Matsushima, is likewise hybrid. The view *onto* the landscape has become a view *into* it.[33] The hill is positioned like a theatre prop at the lower part of the print and creates a foreground (*repoussage*). All other parts of the image become middle and background. A horizon has been introduced and the figures have not been copied faithfully. The light and casual mood of the original has become sombre and serious. The prints based on these brush paintings were intended to provide information about architecture and the customs and habits of the common people. They convey a good part of the information contained in the originals, but there are inaccuracies and faults. These result from the attempt to change unfamiliar forms and ways of representation into shapes and modes known to Europeans. The purpose was to make the information more accessible, but the price was distortion. Kaempfer copied several more brush paintings from this set, but they are even more sketchy and were not reproduced as prints.

³) COPIES OF JAPANESE WOODCUTS

These constitute reproductions in the form of etchings (Plates 9-14) of Japanese woodblock prints from Nakamura Tekisai's pictorial encyclopaedia *Kimmōzui*.[34] Kaempfer had brought a copy back to Europe and chose a few of the prints as illustrations for his *History*.[35] Anyone who has tried to copy the seemingly simple lines of a Japanese brush drawing or woodcut knows how difficult it is to retain the strength and tension of even a blade of grass depicted in a fine work. The simpler the design and the easier the lines flow over the paper, the more difficult it is to reproduce that quality in a copy or print. Most of the prints from *Kimmōzui* in the English and French editions have lost the original tension as a result of the various tracing processes. In the eighteenth century the exotic qualities of those prints, the differences of line and composition and the fact that there are no shadows to define volume, must have been exciting discoveries in themselves, not to mention the strange and fabulous animals represented in these prints.

Among the prints of animals there are a number of pictures of insects that look distinctly different. These are a group of cicadas seen [Pl. 10] from different angles (Plate 10). Drawings were done for Kaempfer in water-colour on bluish paper and signed 'E. Donop pinxit anno 1696' (Painted by E. Donop in 1696).[36] The drawings are executed as a conventional nature study and include all the information that an engraver would need for his work. The accurate translation of this drawing onto an etching plate poses no technical problem. Ferric oxide was applied to the verso of the paper and the drawing was then traced onto the plate. The image was worked up from there and printed. The cicadas on the print are reversed from the original drawing. This would not have been the case had an intermediate drawing been prepared.

4) THE JOURNEY FROM NAGASAKI TO EDO

Kaempfer's written description of this journey has been quoted extensively, but the drawings that accompany it are also remarkable. Three plates illustrate his experience: the procession of travellers (plate 22), the official audience hall (plate 31) and the private audience chamber

145

at Edo castle (plate 32).

The procession of travellers moves in snake-like formation from the lower rim of the picture to the upper part [Pl. 11a, 11b, 11c], changing direction four times. The scene has been drawn carefully.[37] Individual travellers are recognizable from the accompanying legend and are distinct from one another in clothing, deportment and action. In some cases the detail extends to the rendering of faces and to the various insignia (*mon*) on people's clothes. Items such as swords, helmets and sandals are easily recognizable. There is even a humourous touch as traveller number 15 (Kaempfer) shows an interest in how number 14's horse is pushed along. Figure 18 seems to be chatting with the horse and, as with all groups, some members are stragglers. Such detail and the fine quality of the drawing of the original have disappeared or are drastically reduced in the print. The general composition is the same but the wide range of information contained in Kaempfer's work is only partly present in the print.

The compositional form of the snake chosen by Kaempfer to depict the procession is rarely used in Japanese art. In a scroll (*emakimono*) a procession can be represented as a continuous line of people, but Kaempfer chose a form that he was familiar with from Germany: a composition from prints of funeral processions which showed the participants in a similar fashion as here and also included numbers for identification.[38] These prints were regarded as an impressive historical record and souvenir for the participants, which to some degree was also the purpose of Kaempfer's detailed portrayal of the official journey of the Dutch to Edo.

The print of the audience hall is based on a drawing by Kaempfer of the official audience chamber of Edo castle known as the Hall of Thousand Mats (*senjōshiki*). Kaempfer's drawing includes the Dutch delegation and Japanese officials next to the gifts for the shogun as well.[39] The drawing of the room is done competently in a central perspective. The pillars appear to be plain wood [Pl. 12a, 12b]. The floor area has not been divided into mats.

The print looks quite different. Shadows are introduced to emphasize volume and space. The figures have been removed. Instead of relying solely on Kaempfer's original drawing of the official audience chamber, Scheuchzer has introduced features from Kaempfer's drawing of the private audience chamber to supply the missing information. The floor has been divided into mats and the wooden pillars are decorated. Twelve musical instruments have been added in the margin in accordance with the prevailing convention in European art.[40] The atmosphere is more festive, less austere than in the original drawing.

The initial drawing of the private audience chamber where Kaempfer dances in front of the shogun seems to have been in pencil and pen [Pl. 13a, 13b], and and may have been worked up by someone else later.[41] Decorative patterns on the ceiling and on the pillars have been added. Shadows and ornate detail were used here as in the previous plate to make the print more impressive than the original drawing. The figures have lost their original liveliness. The dominating pattern of the mats (*tatami*) is poorly drawn in the etching and the weapons at the margins are more decorative than informative. Nevertheless, this still constitutes a rare and unusual representation of Edo castle that no other foreigner or Japanese had painted or drawn before.

5) MAPS AND PLANTS

As with the other plates in the book, Kaempfer's original maps are richer in detail and more precise than those eventually printed. The first drawing of the map of Ayutthaya (Plate 2) contains houses, pagodas, bridges and boats on the bank of the river.[42] The original in the British Library is an impressive and intriguing work consisting of many small pieces of paper glued together, each with detailed drawings and measurements containing a wealth of information. This is lacking in the print. On the drawing for plate 7 (the Meinam River), houses and settlements are indicated. The words 'rice fields' are added to one of the first intermediate drawings, but then crossed out.[43] I assume that the engraver did not know what rice paddies looked like and therefore decided to settle for a standard landscape, a tree and some grass. The accuracy of the river banks also deteriorates in the various stages of producing the print. The direction and width of the arms of the river have changed to such a degree that the print could never serve as a guide for navigation.

The drawings and prints of plants are much more satisfactory. Here the author, the draftsman and the technician as well as the engraver could all build on an existing mode of representation, enabling them to depict leaves, buds and branches in a net of graphic lines within existing conventions. Kaempfer himself had more time and leisure to draw the plants as the Japanese had no objections to such activity. On the contrary, the governor of Nagasaki complimented him on his work and expressed a keen interest in botany himself.[44]

6) MISCELLANEOUS

This category contains the acupuncture and moxa prints (Plates 43 and 44) and the small print of Deshima in the German edition. Acupuncture had already been illustrated in the *Amoenitates Exoticae*. The preliminary drawing for this was probably done by Brandshagen. I suspect that Kaempfer gave him the box with the needles and explained to him how they were used. The print shows the implements and a baroque female figure with sad facial expressions, the body partly exposed with nine points on the stomach marked for the needles. The figure appears to be wearing a kimono. However, the headdress resembles a helmet. Scheuchzer prepared a new drawing based on the *Amoenitates Exoticae* plate, altering and improving the composition.[45]

A plate to illustrate moxabustion had been used in the *Amoenitates Exoticae*, again done by Brandshagen and was possibly based on a Japanese print or illustrated book [Pl. 14a, 14b, 14c]. The print in *The History of Japan* is quite different from Brandshagen's engraving. The proportions of the figure have been altered

1   The head of 'Laokoon' as represented by a number of artists from the sixteenth to the early nineteenth century.

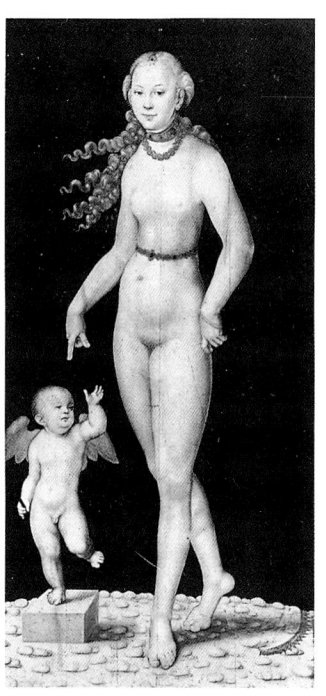

2a   Ganesh, woodcut. From Cartari *Le vere e nove imagini*.
       Padua 1615.

2b   Venus and Cupido. Lucas Cranach d.J.(1515–1586).
       Alte Pinakothek, Munich.

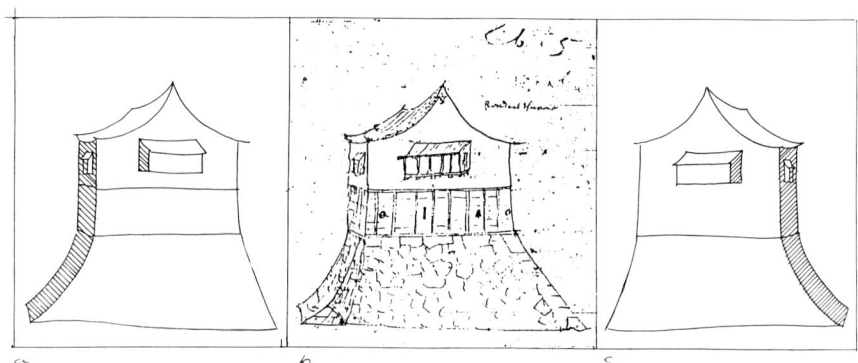

3   Drawings of a house from the front (a. slightly from the left,
       b. the Kaempfer sketch, c. slightly from the right). BL, Sl. 3060,
       fol. 508v.

4a   Berklam's Temple. Sketches of figures. BL, Sl. 3060, fol. 445v.

4b   Berklam's Temple, from *Geschichte und Beschreibung von Japan*, plate V.

 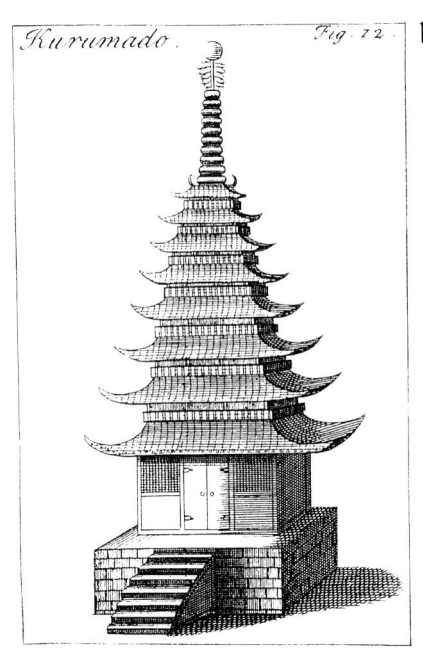

5a   Kurumado. Sketch, BL, Sl. 3060, fol. 526.
5b.   Kurumado from *History of Japan*, plate XXXIII.

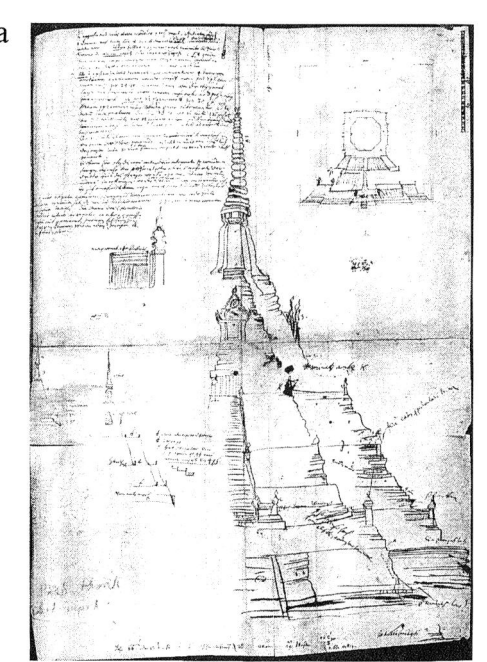 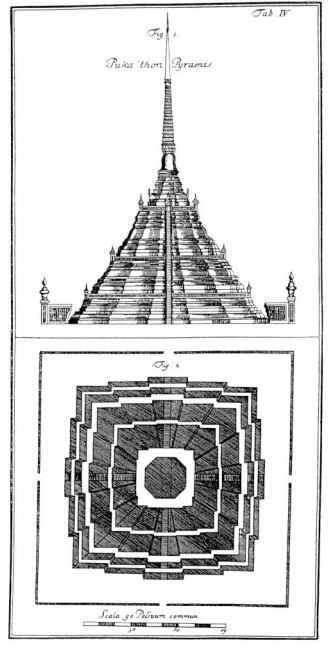

6a   Puka'thon Pagoda, Sketches BL, Sl. 3060, fol. 440.
6b   Puka'thon Pagoda, from *Geschichte und Beschreibung von Japan*. Plate V.

a

Tab. XXXIV

Templum Kiomidsu.

b

7a   Kiyomizu Temple in Kyoto, from *Geschichte und Beschreibung von Japan*. Plate XXXI.

7b   Kiyomizu Temple, aerial photograph.

a

b

c

8a   Hōkōji, Kyoto, brushpainting BL, Sl. 5252, fol. 40.

8b   Hōkōji, Kyoto, Kaempfer's drawing after the original brushpainting, BL, Sl. 3060, fol. 515v.

8c   Hōkōji, from *Geschichte und Beschreibung von Japan*, Plate XXXV.

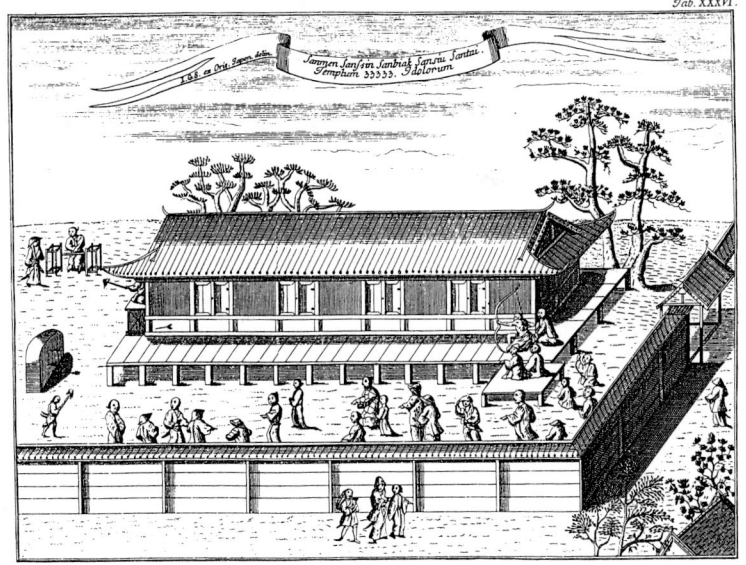

9   Sanjūsangendō, from *Geschichte und Beschreibung von Japan*, Plate XXXVI.

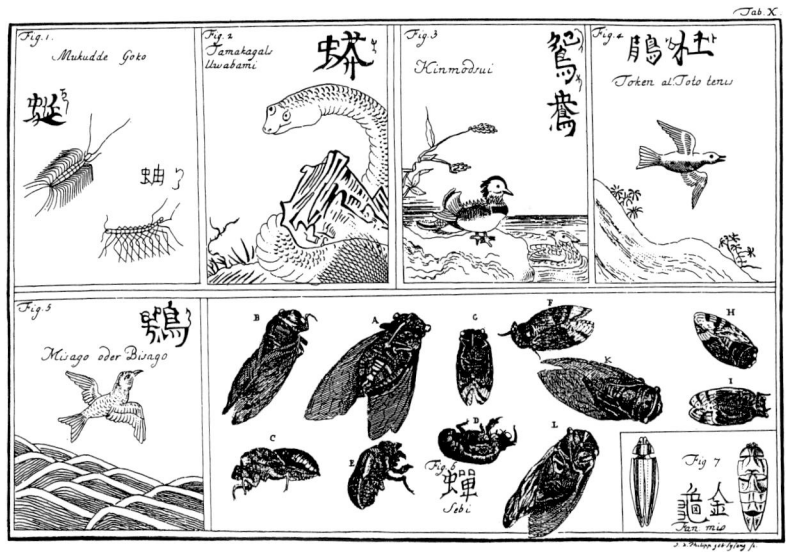

10   Etchings after woodcuts in the *Kimmōzui* and after drawings of Cicadas, *Geschichte und Beschreibung von Japan*, Plate X.

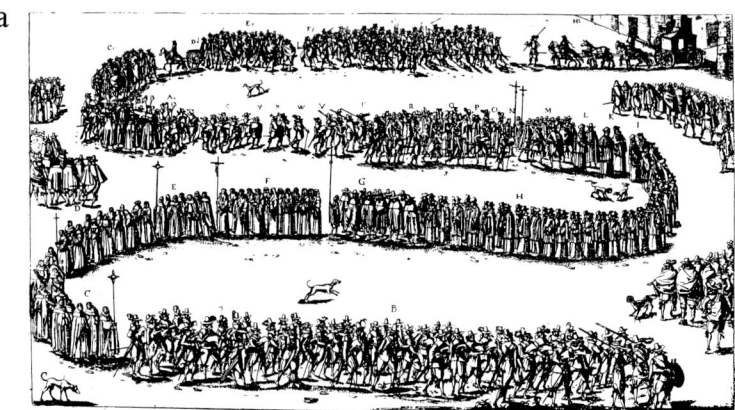

a

b

c

11a Funeral Procession *Zu Ehren von Jacob Bauer von Eiseneck*. 1621. Germanisches Nationalmuseum, Nürnberg. HB 24918, Kapsel 1361.

11b Procession of the Dutch delegation to Edo. Drawing, BL, 3060, fol. 501.

11c Procession of the Dutch delegation to Edo from *Geschichte und Beschreibung von Japan*. Plate XXI.

a

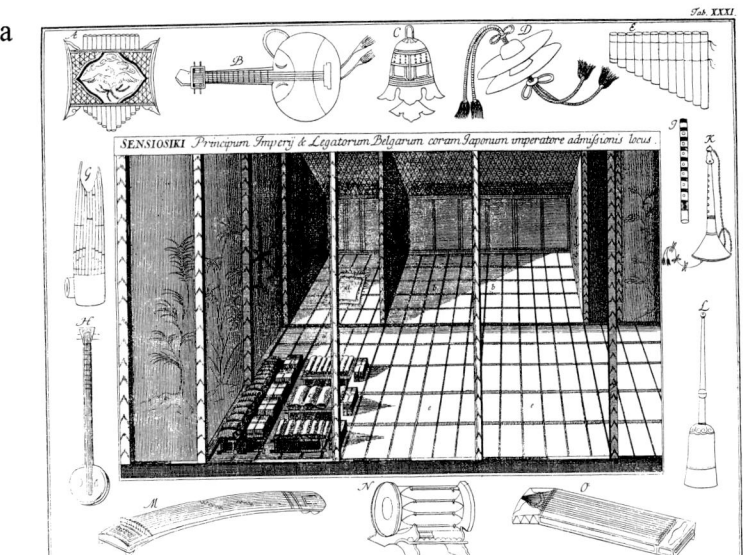

b

12a The official audience chamber from *Geschichte und Beschreibung von Japan*. Plate XXXI.

12b The official audience chamber in the shogun's castle. BL, Sl. 3060, fol. 512.

a

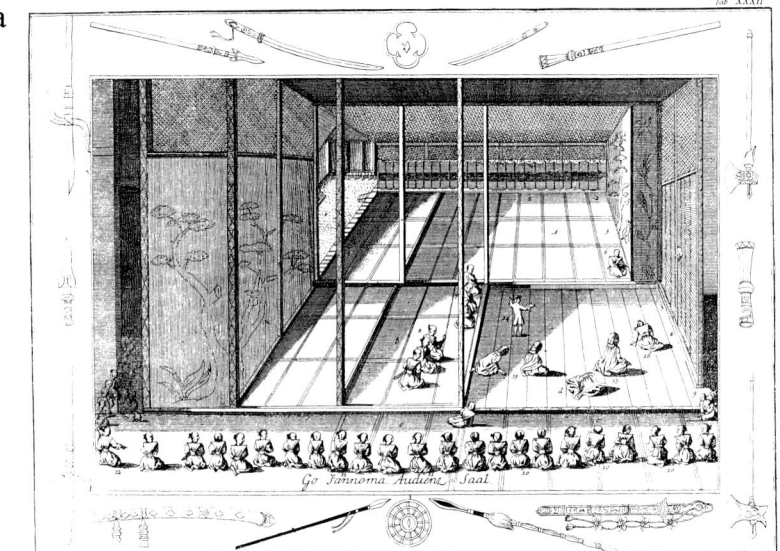

b

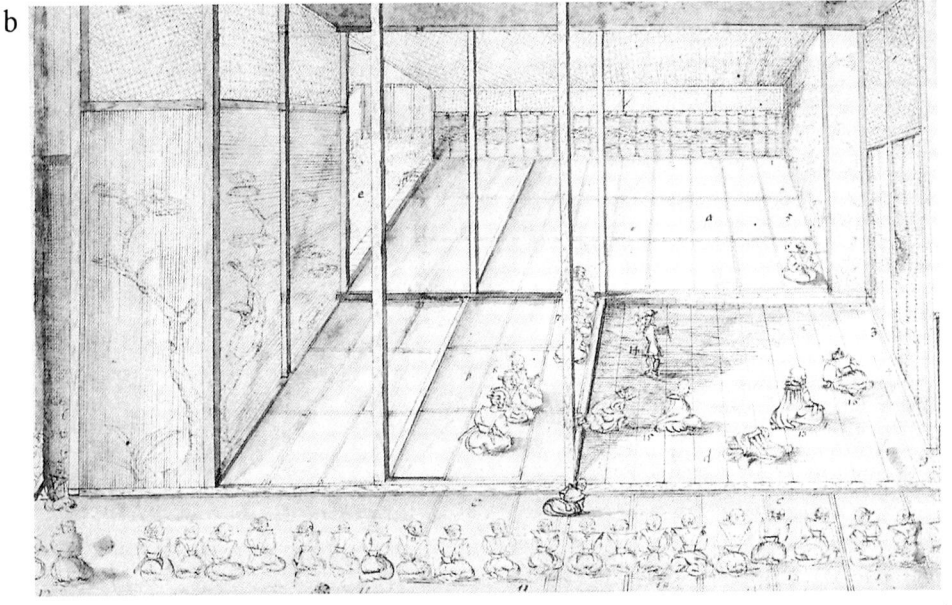

13a The private audience chamber from *Geschichte und Beschreibung von Japan*. Plate XXXII.

13b The private audience chamber. BL, Sl. 3060, fol. 514.

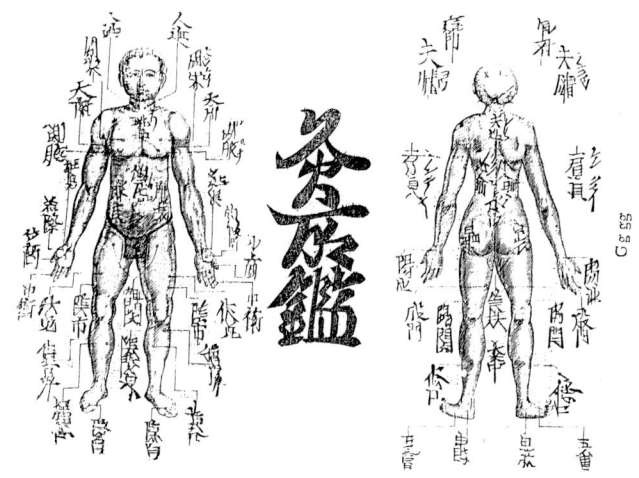

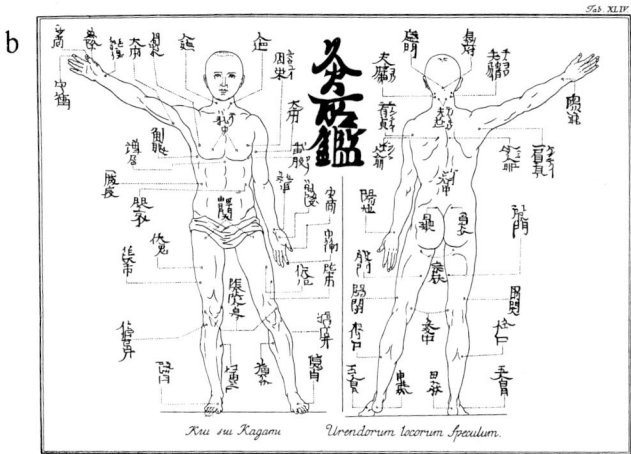

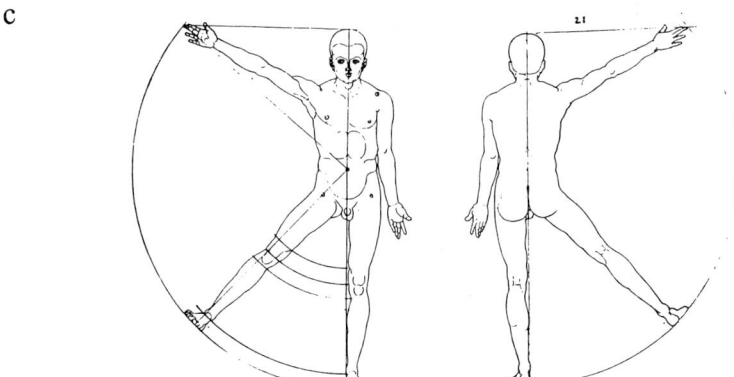

14a   Moxabustion from *Amoenitates. . .* p. 583.

14b   Moxabustion from *Geschichte und Beschreibung von Japan*. Plate XLIV.

14c   'Anatomy Studies', Albrecht Dürer (1471–1528) Sächsische Landesbibliothek, Dresden, 41 Dsdn fol. 112v, 41 Dsdn fol. 113.

a

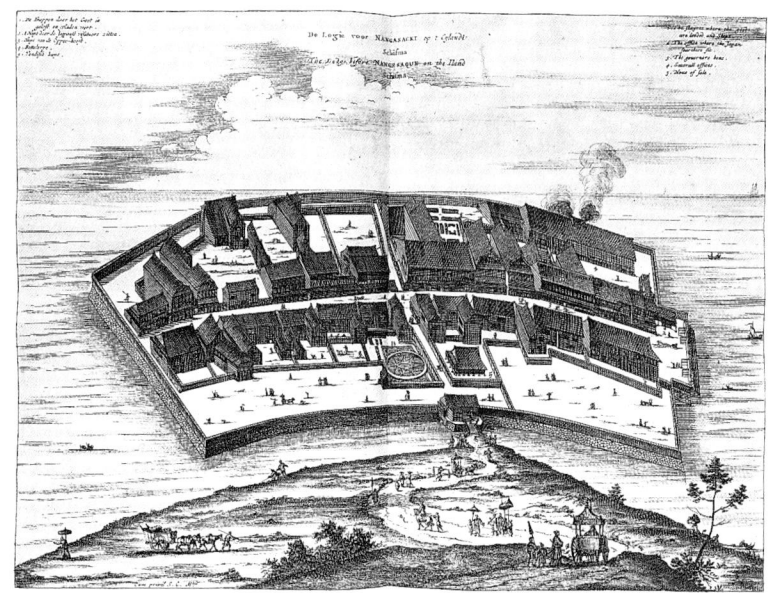

b

D E S I M A.

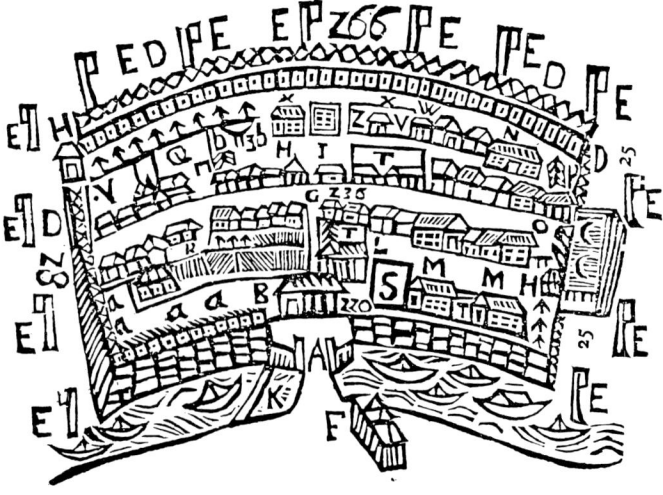

15a Deshima from Arnoldus Montamus, *Atlas Japannensis*, London 1670.

15b Deshima from *Geschichte und Beschreibung von Japan* p.73.

considerably. The figure now shows similarities to Leonardo's studies and Dürer's anatomical research.[46] Presenting Eastern medical practice by means of a Western model made the information more relevant and accessible to the European reader.

The woodblock of Deshima in the German edition was based on a sketch by Kaempfer [Pl. 15a, 15b].[47] It includes the entrance to the island, a row of houses and the direction of the streets, but its informational value is minimal especially when compared with the print published in Montanus.[48]

*   *   *

Save for the French edition, the plates from the English edition were not used in subsequent ones. For the Dutch and German editions new plates were prepared. Some prints bear the engraver's name at the lower right-hand margin of the print. The Nuremberg workshop, Lichtensteger, prepared the plates for the Dohm edition of 1777-79. We know the names of two other engravers who were involved in the work, Johanna Dorothea Sysang and Johann Georg Trautner. Neither was outstanding, a reflection of the general decline in the publishing of art books in Nuremberg by the late eighteenth century. There is some irony in the fact that although those prints were bound into the newly printed volumes of the *Geschichte und Beschreibung von Japan* in Lemgo, Kaempfer's hometown, they differed even more from the original drawings than the prints in Scheuchzer's English edition.

How do these prints compare to similar eighteenth-century publications? In his introduction to *The History*, Scheuchzer mentions Montanus's *Atlas Japannensis*:

> This work does by no means answer neither the expense bestowed on the impression nor the promises made on the very title page, nor does it deserve the favourable reception it has met with. It is full of large digressions, often altogether foreign to the purpose, and what is material, most of the cuts which are the great embellishment as it were, the sole performance of this kind, also greatly deviate from the truth representing things not as

they are, but as the printer fancied them to be.[49] This is harsh criticism for a book held in high esteem at the time. There are important differences between Montanus's manuscript and prints and Kaempfer's material.[50] Montanus used the reports, sketches and visual material of others who had been to Japan with the Dutch East India Company. He was a draftsman of similar ability to Kaempfer. But his way of drawing is more majestic than Kaempfer's and his preliminary sketches cast figures and scenes in a baroque form. The trend continues in the prints. Japan becomes an exotic setting. Baroque concepts of architecture, sculpture and clothing dominate. Yet in technical terms the prints are masterpieces. They have surface texture, subtle greys, velvety blacks and render space and volume credibly, according to the prevailing tastes of the time.

Another major work that was influential in introducing East Asia to the West was *China Illustrata* by Athanasius Kircher. This contained various accounts of China and a large number of illustrations.[51] The artist and engraver of this impressive work are unknown, but the illustrations have influenced Western art and were important for the development of *chinoiserie* in baroque architecture and painting. The book is large and beautifully set, etched and printed. The various forms of visual representation of landscape, architecture, people, space, volume, texture, light and dark, are most impressive, but all are within Western conventions and preconceptions.

When Kaempfer's *History* was published in 1727, the palace of Versailles, the Würzburg Residence and the Dresdner Zwinger had just been completed or were under construction. Handel, Bach and Scarlatti wrote their music and had it performed in London, Leipzig and Rome. In the baroque setting of the time, the prints in Kaempfer's *History* appear dry, unexciting and unassuming especially in comparison with Montanus and Kircher.

Kaempfer saw his drawings not as art works or decorative additions but as visual information about the East Indies, an essential supplement to the text. This was not well understood. His original drawings underwent varying degrees of change on the way to the printer's press. This was due to the incomplete state in which Kaempfer had left many of his drawings and to the limited knowledge and talents of the people who did the intermediate drawings and etchings. This fact and the lack of common reference points, the 'schemata' mentioned above, determined the final form of publication. But in spite of these flaws the illustrations of *The History of Japan* stand out as a unique and relatively reliable source of visual information about Japan in the late seventeenth century.

CHAPTER EIGHT

Epilogue:
Inquisitive and Intelligent Men

Derek Massarella

THE ESSAYS in this volume testify to the enduring value of Kaempfer's achievement and, in particular, to his contribution to our knowledge of early modern Japan. But some loose ends remain to be tied together. Why was there a European interest in Japan? Why was Sir Hans Sloane confident that a work written by a German physician who had travelled to what was then a relatively remote country would command enough interest and be appreciated in the Republic of Letters? The answers are to be found partly in the character and personality of Sloane himself, partly in the intellectual milieu of which he was a product, but principally in the common interest of members of the Republic of Letters in the worlds opened up by colonial settlement across the Atlantic and by commerce in the East Indies. For among European men of science and letters there already was a keen interest in the peoples, cultures and languages of the worlds far beyond Europe's seaboards. With respect to the East Indies, this predated the fascination with China that emerged during the age of the high Enlightenment.

In Chapter 6 mention was made of Sloane's passion for collecting and in an age of collectors and cabinets of curiosities, Sloane, a complex and much underrated individual, stands out preeminently. He cultivated a wide range of contacts not only among the savants of the Republic of Letters but among lesser luminaries, diplomats, travellers and East India Company servants who sent him reports from around the globe and collected examples of natural phenomena from distant places to augment his collection. Towards the end of his life, the collection, which included '...the most precious and remarkable Ornaments used in the Habits of Man from Siberia to the Cape of Good Hope, from Japan to Peru', had became one of the sights of London and, like others before it, a must on the itinerary of visiting VIPs from home and abroad. It had even superseded the Royal Society's own collection, which by the 1730s was in a state of disrepair. But fame spawns detractors and, its scientific value notwithstanding, the collection and its owner became favourite targets for satirists.[1]

But in his lifetime, Sloane's fame in the Republic of Letters was not measured solely by his collection. He was an indefatigable correspondent, one of the most prolific in the Republic, and, one of the most respected. His *Voyage to the Islands of Madeira, Barbadoes, Nieves, St Christopher's and Jamaica* was a substantial contribution to the advancement of natural history.[2]

In the preface to the first volume, Sloane justified his undertaking on the grounds that knowledge of natural history:

...being Observation of Matters of Fact, is more certain than most Others, and in my slender Opinion, less subject to Mistakes than Reasonings, Hypotheses, and Deductions are...These are things we are sure of, so far as our Senses are not fallible, and which, in probability, have been since the Creation, and will remain to the End of the World, in the same condition we now find them.[3]

These assumptions were not original. They were common in Europe immediately before the Enlightenment. Sloane's *Voyage* was one of the most renowned publications in a tradition originating with the *Historia natural y moral de las Indias* (Seville, 1590) by the Spanish Jesuit, José de Acosta. Although written with the

153

purpose of facilitating the conversion of the Indians, the *Historia* is one of the major published works of early ethnology and had a profound influence on subsequent ethnological undertakings.[4] Sloane's *Voyage* contained no prosletysing sub-text and while he believed that natural phenomena reflected God's power, wisdom and purpose in the universe, as did most of his contemporaries, the premise that science should be practical and useful and should contribute, as Francis Bacon had put it, to the advancement of knowledge was central to his undertaking.

There was, of course, considerable leeway for disagreement about exactly how knowledge was to be advanced.[5] Some scientists, notably Newton, considered mathematics essential to scientific research. Others, taking their cue from Descartes, emphasized the value of hypothesis, theory and conjecture. A few, representing an older tradition, fast disappearing and under a fierce barrage of critical attack, believed that the collection of information was a sufficient end in itself. All were influenced to some extent by 'irrational' notions such as the occult or the alchemist's quest, which, like the truths of revelation in the Bible, both Newton and Leibniz took seriously, although it should be remembered that a preoccupation with the 'irrational' could produce rational results.[6] Nevertheless, it is possible to detect a common purpose amidst the diversity of approaches, one that Acosta had emphasized, and one that is fundamental to Kaempfer's own methodology and to the emergence of modern, secular scientific enquiry: the centrality of collecting data and testing hypotheses from 'observed matters of fact', as Sloane had put it. If a hypothesis buckled under the weight of contrary data, then it must be discarded.

The body that aspired to represent England's contribution to experimental philosophy in the Republic of Letters, the Royal Society, in which Sloane was such an influential figure first as editor of the *Philosophical Transactions*, then as secretary, and finally as president, stood at the apex of the English scientific community.

The Society had been established in 1660 with the example of comparable scientific bodies in France and Italy in mind. The founders shared the Baconian aspiration that the Fellows of the Society should work together to seek out and discover new knowledge and to promote its circulation within the Republic of Letters.[7] Part of the programme was spelt out by the Society's first secretary, Henry Oldenburg, who declared (in 1667) that one of the aims of the Royal Society, as set down in its charter:

> ...is ye liberty of entertaining Correspondence in forrin parts, whereby ye observables, Ingenueties, Inventions, & productions both of Art & nature to be mett wth. in ye severall regions of ye World, may by Inquisitive & intellegent men be noted collected & transmitted to the said Society to be by ym. laid up in their storehouse of Nature & Art, yt may serve here after for a Sollid foundation to suprestruct such knowledg upon; as may both inrich ye. understanding indeed &, effectually conduce to ye greater ease & accommodations of Human Life.[8]

If the Society's ambitions to become the equivalent of a modern research centre fell short of attainment,[9] evidence from the surviving correspondence of Fellows testifies that the then secretary's bold declaration was far from being empty rhetoric. So too do the concerns of the Committee for Correspondence, established in March 1664, whose members undertook to peruse 'Books of Voyages...for inquiries' dating from the sixteenth century – the list furnishes a unique guide as to what the members judged to be the major publications – and to consider 'drawing up both general and particular heads of inquiries for all the parts of the world'. The outcome of this activity was Robert Boyle's 'Heads for the Natural History of a Country'.[10]

The members of this short-lived committee agreed that the opportunities provided by England's overseas interests should not remain so pitifully underutilized in the cause of advancing knowledge. So far as Asia was concerned, the East India Company appeared the most obvious and neglected potential conduit for the acquisition and transmission of information. Both Oldenburg, Boyle (who served as a director of the East India Company), and Sir Robert Moray, amongst others, tried hard to engage that great commercial institution in the task of gathering information about the East Indies.[11]

The principle inspiring such a quest was not new. In his essay 'On Travaile', which appeared in 1625, Bacon had already suggested that travellers should record the phenomena they observed on their journeys. The recommendation was restated and amplified by other writers at various times during the course of the seventeenth century.[12]

It was only after the foundation of the Royal Society that practical efforts were made to realize such ambitions. Boyle had been encouraged to draw up his 'Heads' by the 'Answers return'd by Sir Philberto Vernatti resident in Batavia in Java Major, to certain Inquiries sent thither by Order of the Royal Society'. These covered a wide range of natural phenomena which the Society could compare with similar replies sent from the English East India Company's agency at Bantam.[13]

In 1671 the company sent a voyage to Japan to request the reestablishment of direct trade, broken off in 1623 after a ten-year activity when the company withdrew its factory in Hirado. Sensing a unique opportunity, Oldenburg prepared 'Some Directions and Enquiryes concerning Japan recommended to M. Peron and M. del Boe'. These detailed queries covered geography (including the unresolved question of whether or not Jesso, present-day Hokkaido, was a part of the Asian mainland and whether the northeastern coast of Asia, Tartary, fell sharply down towards Japan as some affirmed thereby encouraging hopes of a possible northeastern passage), topography, the language, culture and features of the people and their government, politics and religion. The merchants were also requested 'To sound and make ye depths of coasts & ports'.[14] Oldenburg assumed that the merchants would be able to do this in their spare time.

Two of the company's ships reached Nagasaki in 1673

but the company's request to be readmitted to Japan was rejected by the shogunate on the grounds that Charles II was married to a Portuguese princess.[15] Yet the extent of Engelbert Kaempfer's achievement and the information gathered by subsequent employees of the English company during their stay in the Indies shows that Oldenburg's directions, even if rather overambitious for a single voyage, were not entirely beyond the reach of inquisitive and intelligent men.

That efforts should have been made to involve the company in the pursuit of knowledge appear obvious and logical from a modern perspective. But the institutional contribution of the East India Company, as opposed to the contribution of individual servants, to the advancement of learning in the seventeenth century was negligible. Trade and a healthy return on capital had been the *raison d'être* for the company's founding and remained its central concern. The directors were propelled primarily by business considerations for as long as the company remained solely a commercial enterprise. Priorities would alter only when the company became the agency of British imperial ambitions especially in India. Particularly striking in this respect is the fact that the corpus of information generated by the company's servants in the Indies since its foundation in 1600 was barely utilized by the company itself to further its commercial policies in the seventeenth century.[16] It is not surprising, therefore, to discover that the directors continued to hold that Samuel Purchas's compilation remained the authoritative guide to the lands below the wind. In 1686 they sent the first part of *Purchas His Pilgrimes* (1625) to the company's factory in Bengal recommending them to peruse it 'at all leisure tymes' in order to '...arrive at any maturity of understanding in the affairs of India'.[17]

Such corporate neglect of the pursuit of knowledge is paralleled strikingly by the Dutch company. No less than its English counterpart, the VOC was a commercial institution, not a body devoted to the advance of scholarship. Nicolaas Witsen, burgomaster of Amsterdam and a director of the VOC who corresponded with Oldenburg and Sloane, complained to the Utrecht savant Gisbert Cuper that it was 'only money and not learning from the Indies' that his fellow directors were interested in, 'a lamentable fact', he concluded.[18] The VOC actively discouraged contact between its servants and members of the Republic of Letters, no matter their status, fortunately not with the measure of success it sought.[19]

A man of boundless energy and curiosity, Witsen, like Sloane, was a major figure in the Republic of Letters. He was interested in Asia, including Japan,[20] and although he did not travel there, he wrote an acclaimed study of Tartary, *Noord en Oost Tartarye* (Amsterdam, 1692, 1705). Witsen took his membership of the Republic seriously, particularly the dissemination of information. As has been mentioned, it was through Witsen that the Royal Society received Kaempfer's drawings of Persepolis.[21] Witsen thought highly of Kaempfer, with whom he corresponded, but whom he met only once on the latter's return from the Indies. He described Kaempfer to Cuper as 'a studious man' and recommended him to read Kaempfer's *Amoenitates Exoticae*, which he greatly admired.[22] Witsen also supported Leibniz's strong recommendation that Kaempfer's plans to publish further volumes from his East Indian travels (announced in the *Amoenitates*) should be encouraged.[23]

Witsen made use of a number of protégés who were employees of the VOC to circumvent the company's restrictions. The information and botanical specimens they sent back to Europe contributed greatly to the stock of knowledge about Asia within the Republic of Letters. But even a man of Witsen's position and prestige could not alter the company's Philistine attitude towards the circulation of knowledge or, depending on one's point of view, its jealous, over-protective attitude towards its trade secrets. For example, a Witsen protégé, Herbert de Jager, sent home numerous drawings of East Indian plants and fauna, agricultural implements, and local people and their dwellings. But these were confiscated and put under lock and key in the VOC's Amsterdam offices from which they subsequently vanished.[24]

Two of Kaempfer's fellow Germans in the VOC's employ deserve brief mention in this context, Andreas Cleyer and Georg Everhard Rumpf. Cleyer served as chief surgeon of the VOC in Batavia and then as *opperhoofd* (chief factor) on Deshima during the trading seasons 1682-83 and 1685-86. Through his correspondence and despatch of books from Batavia, he played a key part in Christian Mentzel's plans to further Chinese studies in Berlin, and his compilation *Specimen medicinae Sinicae* (Frankfurt/M, 1682) was a major contribution to the understanding of Chinese medicine. It was also thanks to the personal friendship between the Jesuit Philippe Couplet and Cleyer that the Jesuits were able to convey letters to Europe on VOC ships. The Dutch authorities in Batavia saw this as a *quid pro quo* for Jesuit help in their negotiations in China.[25]

Rumpf, or Rumphius, the name under which he published, lived on Amboina for forty-nine years, from 1653 until his death in 1702, studying the fauna and flora of the region. It is thanks to Governor-General Johannes Camphuis that Rumpf's work has survived. His manuscripts perished en route to Amsterdam; fortunately, Camphuis had made a full copy, which reached Amsterdam safely. Witsen tried to get the VOC, who held on to the papers, to publish the work but the directors agreed to do so only if a subscription could be raised privately. None was. A Table was printed in Leipzig but it was not until the middle of the eighteenth century that Rumpf's *magnum opus* appeared.[26]

The impetus towards observation and the collection of data about the non-European world was, then, a pursuit common to the Republic of Letters, and Japan was by no means excluded from this quest as the activities of the Royal Society and Witsen demonstrate. The private correspondence of the members of the Republic and the articles and notes they contributed to learned journals such as the *Philosophical Transactions* or reviews like the *Journal des Sçavans* testify to the manner and extent of how new information was diffused within the Republic.[27] So too do the books on the East Indies which came off the presses. Regrettably, the achievements of the English company inspired no works on the scale of Hakluyt or Purchas. The company, the privileged monopoly *par excellence* in the public's assessment, was neither a popular institution nor a source of national pride. A few publications were written by company servants: John Ovington's *A Voyage to Suratt in the Year 1689* (London, 1696); John Fryer's *A New Account of East India and Persia* (London, 1698); Daniel Beeckman's *A voyage to and from the Island of Borneo* (London, 1718). Others were written by independent voyagers: the interloper William Dampier's *A New Voyage Round the World* (London, 1697); the private trader Alexander Hamilton's *A new Account of the East Indies* (Edinburgh, 1727). None of these are as ambitious or as comprehensive as Kaempfer's *History*.

The Dutch company has left posterity a far richer legacy of publications, for while it may have discouraged correspondence between Asia and Europe, it was not opposed to having its achievements trumpeted before a public which did take pride in the VOC's achievements. Such publications start with the collection *Begin ende Voortgangh van de Vereenighde Nederlantsche Geoctryeerde Oost-Indische Compagnie* (Amsterdam, 1645). Subsequent publications relevant to Japan and east Asia include François Caron, *Beschrijvinge van het machtigh Coninckrijck Japan* (Amsterdam, 1648),[28] Bernhard Varen, *Descriptio Regni Iaponiae* (Amsterdam, 1649),[29] Johann Nieuhof, *Het Gezantschap der Neerlandtsche O.I. Compagnie aan den grooten Tartarischen Cham den tegenwoordigen keizer van China* (Amsterdam, 1665), Arnoldus Montanus, *Gedenkwaerdige Gesantschappen der Oost-Indische Maetschappy in 't Vereenigde Nederland, aen de Kaisaren van Japan* (Amsterdam, 1669),[30] Olfert Dapper, *Gedenkwaerdig Bedrijf der Nederlandsche O.I.C. op de Kuste en in maastschappij Keizerryik van Taising of Sina* (Amsterdam, 1670).[31] The most comprehensive publication of this genre (it covered all VOC establishments in the East Indies) was François Valentijn's

Oud en Nieuw Oost-Indien (8 vols, Dordrecht, 1724-1726).[32]

Sloane, who was said to be of the 'opinion, that modern Travels are very behoefull towards forming the mind and Inlarging the thoughts of the Curious part of mankind',[33] occupies a central place within this larger European context. Like Witsen, a man of curiosity in the best sense of that word, his interests ranged far and wide. Of the countries of the Indies, first China then Japan seized his imagination. In 1703, the Scots botanist James Cunninghame, who had sailed to China as a surgeon in the service of the East India Company, sent Sloane botanical specimens, shells, meteorological observations, a chart of Chusan and the surrounding islands, which Cunninghame noted, showed that Martinus Martini's *Atlas* needed amendment, sketches, some done by a Jesuit priest at Ning-po, and printed books, including a prayer book translated into Chinese by a member of the Jesuit mission.[34] Other East Indies-bound individuals offered their services to Sloane, for example, Alex Stuart who was going to China as a surgeon.[35] The French Jesuit Jean de Fontaney, a veteran of the China mission, who had visited London in 1704 and been treated generously by Sloane, endeavoured to repay the hospitality and friendship by helping Sloane establish a correspondence with the Jesuits in China.[36]

It was from Cunninghame's correspondence, however, that Sloane became familiar with Japan where, no matter the rebuff in 1673, the East India Company continued to entertain notions of a restoration of direct trade. Cunninghame hoped to be dispatched to Japan and if so promised to send Sloane specimens from there.[37] Cunninghame's references to Japan are not as extensive as those of his colleague James Pound, a chaplain in the company's service, and a Fellow of the Royal Society. Pound served in the Indies from 1699-1706 and during his tour of duty he visited Chusan and Batavia where he picked up and noted down more detailed information about Japan from VOC employees who had been there. Pound's notes are a good, humorous and, on the whole, accurate summary of the Dutch-Japanese relationship.[38] Thus Sloane was not deficient in information about the East Indies. Nor was his interest in Engelbert Kaempfer's work a flash in the pan inspired by his mania for collecting and another manifestation of his supposed dilettanteism.

Sloane first became acquainted with Kaempfer's scholarly writings through the *Amoenitates Exoticae*, although before then Kaempfer's name had become known in England. In his *Voyage to Surat in the Year 1689*, John Ovington refers to discussions he enjoyed with Kaempfer in India calling him 'an Ingenious Traveller, and German physician'.[39] The full story of how the manuscript of *The History* came into his collection has been discussed above.[40] What can be added here is that Sloane's acquisition of the manuscript and other Kaempfer materials and his supervision of the publication of the English translation coincided with the publication of the delayed second volume of his *Voyage* in 1725, like the first lavishly illustrated with copious copper-plate engravings.

In the new introduction, he apologized for the eighteen-year gap between the two volumes saying that his energies had been absorbed in his medical practice, and in the task of classifying, arranging and procuring books and specimens for his vast collection. He still hoped to complete his revision of Georg Abraham Mercklein's *Lindenius renovatus, sive Joannes Antonides van der Linden de scriptis medicis* (1686), a project he had been collaborating on with Claude Bourdelin until war and the latter's death in 1699 cut this short, together with a bibliographical up-date listing recent books on travel and voyages. No matter the time and expense, he assured his readers, he remained committed to 'the propagating useful knowledge'.[41] This project remained unfulfilled, however. In 1725 Sloane was sixty-five, his productive years of original scholarship over. Instead, he diverted his energies into supervising Scheuchzer's translation of *The History of Japan*. Written by a fellow physician and kindred spirit, based on fieldwork in Japan, and crafted according to the same principles that underlay Sloane's own work, it was a worthy companion piece to his *Voyage*. Like the *Voyage*, Kaempfer's *History* was completely in tune with the agenda and aspirations of the Royal Society, which through his editorship of the *Philosophical Transactions* and finally his presidency, Sloane had helped further.

Alas, the same could not be said of an earlier pioneering work of scholarship, Thomas Hyde's *Historia Religionis Veterum Persiarum*. The foolhardy Hyde, professor of Arabic and Hebrew in Oxford and librarian of the Bodleian, went ahead with the printing of his *magnum opus*, which was based upon Arabic, and what Hyde believed to be ancient Persian sources, only to discover, when the book was a quarter of the way through the press, that he faced an acute liquidity crisis, and needed to raise a subscription. He sought the intervention of influential advocates, including Sloane and Thomas Smith, to campaign on his behalf, but even they were unable to find backers. The fellows of the Royal Society found the work old-fashioned, '. . .not so agreeable to the studies of experimental philosophy, mathematicks, and natural history which they are pursuing'. References from well-connected patrons failed to convince potential subscribers to unlock their purses and support Hyde's enterprise. Eventually his *Historia* was published (Oxford, 1700) and became an influential work, but the poor doctor was said to have been so despondent about its appalling sales that he '. . .boil'd his Tea kettle with the greatest part of the Impression which made it so scarce that the original price of 10/- is now 2 guineas which even at that price is cheap concerning its real value'.[42]

But precisely because Kaempfer had been to the places he was writing about, unlike Hyde who, figuratively speaking at least, had never left his study, his work was felt to chime exactly with the pursuits of the Royal Society and its admirers at home and abroad. It had the cachet of authenticity, was a worthy scholarly achievement, and was a viable publishing undertaking. It remains an impressive achievement. The shrewd Sir Hans had got it right and it is thanks to his efforts that Kaempfer's work was saved from oblivion and achieved fame as the most important book about Japan, shaping European perceptions of the island empire until well into the modern age.

References

CHAPTER ONE

1. E. Kaempfer, *The History of Japan*, Scheuchzer, trans., London 1727. Elsewhere I have shown that neither the English translation nor the German edition of C.G. Dohm (*Geschichte und Beschreibung von Japan*, Lemgo, 1777/9) conform to Kaempfer's manuscript *Heutiges Japan*. ('Kaempfer Restor'd', *Monumenta Nipponica*, 43:1, 1988, pp. 2-33.) However, for convenience's sake the work is referred to throughout this book as *The History*.

2. For publication details see 'Internationale Kaempfer-Bibliographie', in Hans Hüls and Hans Hoppe, eds, *Engelbert Kaempfer zum 330. Geburtstag*, Lippische Studien Band 9, Lemgo, 1982, pp. 229-31.

3. F.M.A. de Voltaire, *Essai sur les moeurs*, Éditions Garnier Frères, Paris, 1963, 2:315, 795.

4. Perry cited Kaempfer twice in his journal: R. Pineau ed., *The Personal Journal of Commodore Matthew C. Perry*, Washington, 1968, pp. 75, 78; see also S.E. Morrison, *'Old Bruin' Commodore Matthew C. Perry 1794-1858*, Oxford, 1968, p. 276.

5. T. Yokoyama, *Japan in the Victorian Mind*, London, 1987, pp. 3-4.

6. H. Hoppe, 'Engelbert Kaempfers Stellung in der Gesellschaft seiner Zeit' in *Engelbert Kaempfer zum 330. Geburtstag*, p. 134.

7. A. Olearius, *Vermehrte Newe Beschreibung der Muskowitischen und Persischen Reyse...*, Schleswig, 1656, reprint Tübingen, 1971.

8. For a more detailed account see B.M. Bodart-Bailey, *Kenperu to Tokugawa Tsunayoshi*, Tokyo, 1994; *Ein Lied für den Shogun*, forthcoming.

9. K. Meier-Lemgo, *Engelbert Kaempfer, der erste deutsche Forschungsreisende, 1651-1716*, Stuttgart, 1937, p. 3; H. Hoppe, 'Engelbert Kaempfers Stellung in der Gesellschaft seiner Zeit', *Engelbert Kaempfer zum 330. Geburtstag*, p. 136-7.

10. 'Meier-Lemgo, 1937, p. 3.

11. *Amoenitates Exoticae*, p. 490.

12. Meier-Lemgo, 1937, p. 4. Some towns, however, burnt greater numbers of women relative to their population figures. See: W. Niess, *Hexenprozesse in der Grafschaft Buedingen*, Buedingen, 1982, pp. 177-79, 302-3.

13. K. Meier-Lemgo, *Engelbert Kämpfer erforscht das seltsame Asien*, Hamburg, 1960, pp. 9-10.

14. *De Majestatis Divisione*, Danzig, 1673, translated into German by R. Mueller-Koenig, *Engelbert Kaempfer zum 330. Geburtstag*, pp. 18-29.

15. E. Kaempfer, 'Das Stammbuch Engelbert Kaempfers,' Meier-Lemgo, ed., *Mitteilungen aus der lippischen Geschichte und Landeskunde*, 21, 1952 p. 164.
16. *Amoenitates Exoticae*, p. 502.
17. See B.M. Bodart-Bailey, 'Tokugawa Tsunayoshi (1646-1709), A Weberian Analysis', *Asiatische Studien/Etudes Asiatiques*, XLIII:1,1989, pp. 5-27.
18. H. Hüls, 'Zur Geschichte des Drucks von Kaempfers "Geschichte und Beschreibung von Japan" und zur sozialökonomischen Struktur von Kaempfers Lesepublikum im 18. Jahrhundert', in *Engelbert Kaempfer zum 330. Geburtstag*, p. 196.
19. Meier-Lemgo, 1960, p. 7.
20. 'Stammbuch', pp. 148-161.
21. Sl. 3060, f. 3; *The History*, first unnumbered page of the introduction.
22. Sl. 3063, f. 41.
23. 'Stammbuch', p. 163.
24. *Meyers Enzyklopädisches Lexikon*, Mannheim, 1981, XX:424; *The New Encyclopaedia Britannica*, Chicago, 1989, VIII:738, XXVII:13.
25. This is the interpretation proposed by Meier-Lemgo, 'Stammbuch', p. 163. A variety of other interpretations are possible.
26. 'Stammbuch', p. 163.
27. 'Stammbuch', p. 164. Again a number of interpretations are possible; I follow that suggested by Meier-Lemgo.
28. Sl. 2923, f. 116; E. Kaempfer, *Die Reisetagebücher Engelbert Kaempfers*, Meier-Lemgo ed., Wiesbaden 1968, contains a rather free transcription of this text.
29. Sl. 2923, f. 117.
30. Sl. 2923, f. 118.
31. Sl. 2923, f. 119.
32. Sl. 2923, f. 119v.
33. Letter to Herbert de Jager of 3.9.1684, in Meier-Lemgo, ed., *Die Briefe Engelbert Kaempfers*, Abhandlungen der mathematisch-naturwissenschaftlichen Klasse, Akademie der Wissenschaften und der Literatur, Jg. 1965, Nr. 6, Mainz, 1965, p. 14.
34. Sl. 2923, f. 124.
35. Sl. 2923, f. 147.
36. E. Kaempfer, *Geschichte und Beschreibung von Japan*, Dohm, ed., Lemgo, 1777-79, I: XXVIII, letter to Joachim Kaempfer, dated 'Nagasacki in Japan 1688'. From the contents of the letter and the location one may assume that the date is a misprint for 1690.
37. *Reisetagebücher*, pp. 14-37.
38. *Reisetagebücher*, pp. 31-36.
39. 'Stammbuch', p. 127, Meier-Lemgo, 1960, p. 25.

References

40. *Amoenitates Exoticae*, pp. 253-62.
41. *Mundus Subterraneus in XII Libros Digestus,* Amsterdam, 1668. See H. Hüls and R. Müller-König, 'Medizinische Dissertation über zehn fremdländische Beobachtungen', *Engelbert Kaempfer zum 330. Geburtstag,* pp. 36-8; *Amoenitates Exoticae,* p. 253-5.
42. *Amoenitates Exoticae*, pp. 262-8.
43. *Amoenitates Exoticae*, pp. 271-86.
44. Sl. 3063, ff. 115v-117; *Amoenitates Exoticae,* p. 60.
45. *Amoenitates Exoticae*, opposite p. 162.
46. *Estat de la Perse*, 1660; Meier-Lemgo, 1960, p. 42.
47. Sl. 3063, ff. 131v-132v. For the grammar see: Sl. 2924.
48. Sl. 2917; Meier-Lemgo, 1960, p. 42.
49. *Amoenitates Exoticae*, p. 57; Meier-Lemgo, 1960, p. 54.
50. Sl. 3060, f. 3; *The History,* first unnumbered page of the introduction.
51. Sl. 3063, ff. 129-30, letter dated 3.9.1684. Also *Briefe,* pp. 278-9.
52. Letters to G. Weyer and M. Tunkelfeld, 1.10.1685: Sl. 3063, ff.60- 61; *Briefe,* pp. 279-80.
53. Sl. 2912, f. 69v.
54. For fuller treatment of this topic see *Ein Lied für den Shogun.*
55. Letter to Joachim Kaempfer, dated 25.11.1687, Dohm, I:XXIII.
56. *Amoenitates Exoticae*, Book IV, pp. 660-764; also in M.B. Valentini, *Museum Museorum,* Frankfurt/Main 1716, pp. 545-75, translated into German by W. Muntschick, *Phoenix persicus – Die Geschichte der Dattelpalme,* Marburg, 1987.
57. *Philosophical Transactions,* No. 210, May 1694, pp. 117-8.
58. *Amoenitates Exoticae*, pp. 297-381.
59. *Amoenitates Exoticae*, pp. 565-73; *Reisetagebücher,* pp. 153-4.
60. Sl. 3060, f. 3v.
61. Sl. 3060, f. 4v; *The History,* I:iv.

CHAPTER TWO
1. See chapter 1, n. 1.
2. J.W. Spalding, *The Japan Expedition, Japan and Around the World,* New York, 1855, footnote p. 133.
3. J. Numata et.al, eds., *Yōgakushi jiten* (Dictionary of the History of Western Learning), Tokyo, 1984, p. 461.
4. Onno Zwier van Haren, *Proeve, op de leevens-beschryvingen der nederlandsche doorlugtige mannen: behelzende het leeven van Joannes Camphuis, haarlemmer,* Tezwolle, 1772.
5. 'dat dezelve minder het werk van dezen Duitscher is . . . dan wel van den Gouverneur-Generaal Camphuis', (Hendrik Doef, *Herinneringen uit Japan,* Haarlem, 1833, p. 5.)
6. The whole biography consists only of 66 pages of small format (21.5 × 13 cm).

7. Van Haren, *Proeve*, pp. 63-64.
8. Ibid., p. 64.
9. Sl. 3063, ff. 71-71v. I would like to thank Professor Mark Elvin, Research School of Pacific Studies, Australian National University, Canberra, for his help in reading the Latin text.
10. Kaempfer addresses also other patrons as Maecenas, for example, he calls Adrian van Reede tot Drakensteen '*Magne Aesculapiadum Maecenas*' (letter of 10 June, 1689, K. Meier-Lemgo, ed., *Die Briefe Engelbert Kaempfers*, Abhandlungen der mathematisch-naturwissenschaftlichen Klasse, Akademie der Wissenschaften und der Literatur, Jg. 1965, Nr. 6, Mainz, 1965, p. 287). Aesculapius is the patron god of medicine.
11. François Valentyn, *Oud en Nieuw Oost-Indien*, Dordrecht, Amsterdam, 1726, IV, p. 316.
12. Van Haren, p. 1.
13. *Oud en Nieuw Oost-Indien*, IV, pp. 421-91.
14. Sl. 3060, f. 259.
15. Sl. 3063, f. 71.
16. *Oud en Nieuw Oost-Indien*, IV, p. 322.
17. Sl. 2910, ff. 219, 254.
18. Sl. 3063, f. 65v-66; *Briefe*, p. 288.
19. See *Ein Lied für den Shogun*, forthcoming.
20. Sl. 3060, f. 255v-256.
21. Sl. 3060, f. 340v.
22. Sl. 3063, f. 71.
23. Sl. 3060, f. 55.
24. Sl. 3061, ff. 90-99v.
25. For instance, Daniel Six's report notes the amount of coins distributed as 130 thaels, Kaempfer as over 100. Kaempfer further checks and refines the mileage (7 1/2 miles instead of 7) and improves upon the spelling of names. (Sl. 3061, f. 90; Sl. 3060, ff. 303v-304).
26. Sl. 3062, f. 92.
27. Sl. 3061, f. 97; Sl. 3060, f. 354.
28. *Gedenkwaerdige Gesantschappen der Oost-Indische Maetschappy in't Vereenigde Nederland, aen de Kaisaren van Japan*, Amsterdam, 1669.
29. Sl. 2910, ff. 277-78v.
30. Sl. 2910 ff. 267-76.
31. For the dates of directors on Deshima, the listing in *Yōgakushi jiten*, pp. 60-65 has been consulted. These are also contained in M.P.H. Rossingh, *The Dutch Factory in Japan*, The Hague, 1964.
32. Sl. 3061, ff. 121-26v.
33. Sl. 3061, ff. 119-19v.
34. Sl. 3061, ff. 115-18. See also Kanai Madoka, *Nichiran kōshōshi*

no kenkyū (A study of the history of Japanese-Dutch relations), Kyoto, 1986, p. 45.

35. Sl. 3061, f. 118.

36. Sl. 2910, ff. 177-98v.

37. After Kaempfer had died the document in question was mistakenly described as being dated 1613. See Derek Massarella and Izumi K. Tytler, 'The Japonian Charters: The English and Dutch *Shuinjō*', *Monumenta Nipponica*, 45:2, 1990, pp. 204-5.

38. Sl. 2910, ff. 199-203v; *Oud en Nieuw Oost-Indien*, IV, pp.310-15.

39. Van Haren, p. 63.

40. Sl. 2910, f. 297.

41. Sl. 3060, f. 232.

42. Sl. 2910, ff. 267-74v.

43. Sl. 3061, ff. 125v-26v; Sl. 3060, f. 260. Neither in the manuscript text nor that published by Dohm (II:114) does Kaempfer accuse Cleyer of smuggling, as has been suggested in Eva Kraft, *Andreas Cleyer, Tagebuch des Kontors zu Nagasaki auf der Insel Deshima*, vol. 6 of *Bonner Zeitschrift für Japanologie*, Bonn 1985, p. 52.

44. On this subject see also Imai Tadashi, 'Engelbert Kaempfer und seine Quellen', *Engelbert Kaempfer zum 330. Geburtstag*, H. Hüls and H. Hoppe, eds., Lemgo, 1982, pp. 63-81.

45. Sl. 3061, ff. 84-89v.

46. Sl. 3061, ff. 69-83.

47. I.e., *Edo Dōchūki*, Sl. 3062, ff. 222-51.

48. Sl. 3061, ff. 24-43.

49. Sl. 3060, f. 237.

50. *Estat de la Perse*, 1660. Engelbert Kaempfer, 'Das Stammbuch Engelbert Kaempfers', Meier-Lemgo, ed., *Mitteilungen aus der lippischen Geschichte und Landeskunde*, 21, 1952, p. 179.

51. *Die Reisetagebücher Engelbert Kaempfers*, Meier-Lemgo, ed., Wiesbaden, 1968, p. 152.

52. Sl. 2921, f. 25v; Sl. 3060, f. 29.

53. *Amoenitates Exoticae*, pp. 201-3.

54. 'Stammbuch', p. 177.

55. *Amoenitates Exoticae*, p. 243.

56. See Larry Sternstein, 'Kaempfer as Mapper' in D. Haberland, ed., *Engelbert Kaempfer: Werk und Wirkung*, Stuttgart, 1993, pp. 383-93.

57. MSS in Algemeen Rijksarchief, The Hague, 01.04.21, Het archief van de Nederlandse factorij in Japan, 1609-1860, 104, October 1690.

58. E.g. Sl. 3063, ff. 71-78v.

59. Sl. 2915, f. 24.

60. Sl. 2915, f. 88v.

61. Sl. 2915, f. 24.

62. Sl. 2910, f. 294. I thank Prof. Kasaya Kazuhiko of the International Research Center for Japanese Studies, Kyoto, for this information.
63. Sl. 3062, ff. 366, 372v.
64. Sl. 3062, f. 365v.
65. Sl. 3062, f. 365.
66. Sl. 3060, f. 404.
67. Sl. 3060, ff. 3v-4.
68. Sl. 3060, f. 385: 'Heute vernahm ich von beyden Tollmetschen ...'. Dohm's version (vol. II, p. 327) differs slightly.
69. Sl. 3061, f. 2.
70. Sl. 3061, ff. 141-159.
71. See Chapter 3.
72. Sl. 3060, f. 4v: 'Diesem schlauen Kopfe habe ich in dem ersten jahre die Holländische Sprache (ohne welche ich mit ihm nicht hette fort kommen mögen) Grammatice beÿgebracht, ...'. Scheuchzer (vol. I, p. xxxii) translates this as: 'As I could not well have obtain'd my end without giving him a competent knowledge of the Dutch language, I instructed him therein with so much success, ...'.
73. Imamura Akitsune, *Rangaku no sō Imamura Eisei*, Tokyo, 1942, p. 24.
74. Sl. 3060, f. 4v.
75. See chapter 5.
76. Sl. 3060, ff. 272-3.
77. Sl. 3060, ff. 557, 558v.
78. Sl. 3060, f. 340v.
79. Montanus, pp. 100-3; Sl. 3060, f. 340v.
80. Sl. 3061, f. 95v.
81. Sl. 3061, f. 108.
82. Sl. 3060, ff. 340-340v.
83. British Library, Or. 75. f. 3 and Or. 75. f. 4. Notes: Sl. 3062, ff. 222-51v.
84. Sl. 3060, f. 340v. The first phrase re-appears with only minor alterations in Kaempfer's description of the second journey in 1692 (Sl. 3060, f. 396).
85. Sl. 3062, f. 226.
86. Sl. 3062, ff. 225-225v.
87. Sl. 3060, f. 341. Notes: SL. 3062, f. 225v. Moreover, the passage is written in the margin and might have been inserted at a later date.
88. Sl. 3062, ff. 244-45.
89. Sl. 3060, f. 339v.

CHAPTER THREE
1. Sl. 3060, ff. 4-4v. I am most grateful to Dr Beatrice Bodart-Bailey for supplying me with this and other translations from this manuscript.

References

2. Imamura Akitsune, *Rangaku no sō Imamura Eisei*, Tokyo, 1942. Again, I am indebted to Dr Bodart-Bailey for this and other references to Imamura Akitsune's work.

3. See also P.G.E.I.J. van der Velde, 'Deshima, mon amour. The publishing of the marginals of the Deshima Diaries, 1641-1860', in Y.Y. Brown (ed.), *Japanese Studies*, British Library Occasional Papers, 11, London, 1990, pp. 102-112.

4. Imamura, *Rangaku no sō*, pp. 5, 11. For interpreters who moved from Hirado to Nagasaki see Katagiri Kazuo, *Oranda tsūji no kenkyū* (A Study of the Dutch Interpreters), Tokyo, 1985, p.10. I am indebted to Dr Bodart-Bailey for this information.

5. Sl. 3060, f 248v. Kaempfer uses the word 'teütsch' for both German and Dutch, a word that formerly included Dutch ('neder Duyts') among its meanings. Nowadays 'deutsch' applies only to German.

6. Imamura, *Rangaku no sō*, p. 5.

7. Ibid., p. 24.

8. Sl. 3060, f 210v.

9. See B.M. Bodart-Bailey, 'Kyoto Three Hundred Years Ago', in *Nichibunken Newsletter*, 9, 1991, pp. 4-12; idem, 'The Most Magnificent Monastery and Other Famous Sights: The Japanese Paintings of Engelbert Kaempfer', in *Japan Review*, 3, 1992 pp. 25-44.

10. For the importance of the Deshima Diaries as a source for the history of Tokugawa Japan see J. L. Blussé, 'A Glimpse behind the Screens: Some Remarks on the Significance of the Deshima Dagregisters for the Study of Tokugawa Japan', in P. van der Velde and R. Bachofner (eds), *The Deshima Diaries Marginalia 1700-1740*, Tokyo, 1992, p. xv-xxiii.

11. NFJ, 108 (1695), p. 290.

12. Ibid., p. 297.

13. Numata Jirō, 'Engelbert Kaempfer in Japan und sein Einfluß auf Japan', in OAG (ed.), *Engelbert Kaempfer (1651–1716) Philipp Franz von Siebold (1796-1866) Gedenkschrift*, Tokyo, 1966, pp. 27-41.

14. NFJ 110 (1696), pp. 307-8; NFJ 110 (1697), p. 211.

15. NFJ 110 (1696), p. 308.

16. Ibid., loc. cit.

17. Ibid., p. 78.

18. Ibid., loc. cit.

19. Sl. 3060, f. 4v; Scheuchzer, 1, p. xxxii.

20. NFJ 111 (1698), p. 242.

21. Ibid., loc. cit.

22. ARA/VOC, 01.04.01, 1935, f. 2146.

23. Grant K. Goodman, *Japan: The Dutch Experience*, London, 1986, p. 46.

24. Ibid, p. 61.
25. NFJ 121 (1710), p. 5.
26. Ibid., loc. cit.
27. Ibid., p. 79.
28. Goodman, *Japan*, p. 46.
29. NFJ 134 (1724), p. 36.
30. NFJ 133 (1723), p. 80.
31. NFJ 122 (1711), p. 8.
32. Ibid., pp. 22-23.
33. NFJ 123 (1712), pp. 128-139.
34. Ibid., pp. 157-8.
35. Ibid., p. 158.
36. NFJ 126 (1716), p. 117.
37. NFJ 125 (1714), pp. 93-4.
38. Ibid., pp. 86-92.
39. See Kate Wildman Nakai, *Shogunal Politics: Arai Hakuseki and the Premises of Tokugawa Rule*, Cambridge, Mass, 1988, pp. 106-14.
40. J. Feenstra Kuiper, *Japan en de Buitenwereld in de achttiende eeuw*, The Hague, 1921, pp. 101-2.
41. NFJ 126 (1716), pp. 4-6.
42. Ibid., p. 35.
43. Ibid., p. 71.
44. Ibid., pp. 136, 141.
45. Ibid., p. 71.
46. Ibid., p. 74. See also A. Bogaert, *De ondergang van den Arion*, Amsterdam, 1724.
47. NFJ 127 (1717), pp. 126-144.
48. NFJ 129 (1719), pp. 74.
49. NFJ 136 (1726) p. 51.
50. See Goodman, *Japan*, pp. 41, 55.
51. NFJ 135 (1725), p. 144.
52. Ibid., pp. 180-2. Johan Georg Keijserling of Hamburg has frequently been mistaken as Hans Jürgen Keijserling of Hildesheim. In two wills (ARA/VOC, 6048, dated 19 May 1734 and NFJ 1573, dated 5 February 1735) Johan Georg Keijserling of Hamburg bequeathes all his possessions to his wife Jacoba Helena Ka. See also Goodman, *Japan*, p. 57.
53. NFJ 139 (1729), pp. 66-7.
54. Ibid., pp. 381-2.
55. Osamu Katsuyama, 'The Result of an Attempt to find the Source of an old Japanese Book on Equine Medicine', *Argos Bulletin van het Veterinair Historisch Genootschap*, 8, 1993, pp. 253-57.
56. See Iwao Seiichi, *Meiji izen yoba no yunyū to zō shoku* (Import and proliferation of horseback riding in the pre-Meiji period), Tokyo, 1990, which contains an appendix on horse keeping, compiled by

Genemon from Dutch sources in 1729. See also Goodman, *Japan*, p. 58.
57. NFJ 146 (1736), p. 166.

CHAPTER FOUR
1. Scheuchzer, I, pp. 261-2. Dr. Bodart-Bailey has kindly translated this passage for me from the German manuscript. The Scheuchzer translation has not materially affected the meaning, save that the 'crown' is more accurately rendered as 'Imperial cap'.
2. W. G. Aston, *Shinto: the Way of the Gods*, London, 1905, pp. 36, 41.
3. W. G. Aston, 'Kaempfer as an Authority on Shinto', *Man*, vol 2, 1902, pp. 182-4.
4. J. G. Frazer, *Taboo and the Perils of the Soul: The Golden Bough*, part 2, 3rd edition, 1911, pp. 1-4.
5. Ibid., pp. 6, 131-7, 265.
6. Michael Cooper, *They Came to Japan: an Anthology of European Reports on Japan, 1543-1640*, London, 1965, p. 86.
7. F. Caron and J. Schouter, *A True Description of the Mightie Kingdoms of Japan and Siam*, edited by C. R. Boxer, London, 1935, pp. 24-25.
8. Cooper, *They Came to Japan*, pp. 87-8.
9. Ibid., p. 86.
10. *Tankai, maki 3, Nihon shōmin seikatsu shiryō shūsei*, vol. 8, Tokyo, 1969, p. 55.
11. Ibid., pp. 55-6.
12. Ibid., p.56.
13. Frazer, *Taboo and Perils*, pp. 226-30, 258-62.
14. Miyata Noboru, *Ikigami shinkō*, Tokyo, 1970, pp. 104-5, 76-92. See also his *Minzoku shūkyō no kadai*, Tokyo 1977, pp. 31-4. I am deeply grateful to Professor Miyata for drawing my attention to these works and to *Tankai*.
15. Henry Yule (ed.), *The Book of Ser Marco Polo*, London, 1875, vol. 2, pp 236-7, 240-2.
16. See my *Catalpa Bow, A Study of Shamanistic Practices in Japan*, London, 1975, 1986, p. 302 for a description of the *aragyō*. The long hair sometimes turns prematurely white with the strain.
17. The two *matsuhijiri* begin their *gyō* on 24 September so that the hundred-day period is completed by 31 December. They then demonstrate their holy powers by *genkurabe* or contests in the magic art. See Miyake Hitoshi, *Shugendō jiten*, Tokyo, 1986, p. 211.
18. For a full account of the career of Tokuhon Gyōja see A. M. Bouchy, *Tokuhon Ascète du Nembutsu*, Paris, 1983. For Tansei and Chōzen, Gorai Shigeru has written extensively in the series 'Shugendō no shisō' in the journal *Agama*. See, for example, vol.

38, June 1984, 'Tansei no sokushin-jōbutsu no shisō', and vol. 17, January 1982, 'Chozen oshō no mokujiki'.
19. Harada Toshiaki, 'Matsuri no soshiki to shisaisha', in *Nihon minzokugaku taikei*, vol. 8, Tokyo, 1962, pp. 270-4.
20. Dr I. J. McMullen has suggested to me that the strange passage about the emperor sitting immobile on the throne for several hours a day might possibly find a dim origin in the passage of the *Analects*, XV, i. Here Confucius declares that Shun, the ancient sage king, was able to govern efficiently without exerting any effort (*wu- wei*). What did he do? He did nothing except with due reverence sit on the royal seat facing south. Admittedly, there is no mention in the *Analects* of Shun wearing a cap or crown, and there is no mention in Kaempfer about the emperor facing south. But the figure of the king as immobile, inactive, exerting magical protective power by simply being, is similar.

CHAPTER FIVE
1. Translated by Beatrice M. Bodart-Bailey. Dr Bodart-Bailey wishes to thank Dr C. Behm, Faculty of Science, Australian National University and Mr R.O. Makinson, Curator of the Herbarium of the Australian National Botanic Gardens, Canberra for their help with the more technical aspects of this translation.
2. E. Winckler, *Geschichte der Botanik*, Frankfurt/M., 1854; E. H. F. Meyer, *Geschichte der Botanik*, vol. 4, Königsberg, 1857; J. Sachs, *Geschichte der Botanik vom 16. Jahrhundert bis 1860*, Munich, 1860; K. Mägdefrau, *Geschichte der Botanik*, Stuttgart, 1973.
3. *Pharmazie und der gemeine Mann*, catalogue nr. 36, Herzog August Bibliothek, Wolfenbüttel, 1982.
4. P. Schiller, *Der botanische Garten in Padua*, Venice, 1987.
5. W. T. Stearn, 'An Introduction to the Species Plantarum and Cognate Botanical Works of Carl Linnaeus' in C. Linnaeus, *Species plantarum* (1753), repr. London, 1957.
6. J. Heniger, *Hendrik Adriaan van Reede tot Drakenstein (1636-1691) and Hortus Malabaricus*, Rotterdam, 1986, p. 95, writes: 'Hortus Malabaricus may be considered as the first publication on the flora of a definite district in Asia'. See also D. H. Nicolson, C. R. Suresk, and K. S. Manilal, *An Interpretation of van Rheede's Hortus Malabaricus*, Königstein, 1988 (vol. 119 of *Regnum Vegetabile*).
7. See the correspondence between Kaempfer and van Rheede in *Die Briefe Engelbert Kaempfers*, K. Meier-Lemgo (ed.), Abhandlungen der mathematisch-naturwissenschaftlichen Klasse, Akademie der Wissenschaften und der Literatur, Nr. 6, Mainz, 1965 p. 287.
8. E. Kaempfer, *Phoenix persicus – Die Geschichte der Dattelpalme*, translated and edited by W. Muntschick, Marburg, 1987, p. 19.
9. M. J. Sirks, 'Rumphius, the blind seer of Amboina', in P. Honig and F. Verdoorn, eds, *Science and Scientists in the Netherlands*

References

Indies, New York, 1945, pp. 295-308; H. C. D. de Wit, *Rumphius Memorial Volume*, Baarn, 1959.

10. J. and R. Gicklhorn, *Georg Josef Kamel S.J. (1661-1706): Apotheker, Botaniker, Arzt und Naturforscher der Philippinen*, Eutin, 1954.

11. J. Douglas, *Lilium Sarniense*, London, 1725.

12. G. Koidzumi, 'Nihon shokubutsu kenkyū shiryaku', *Acta phytotaxonomica et geobotanica*, 1, 1932, pp. 1-10; F. Berger and W. Bonsack (eds), *George Meister: der Orientalisch-Indianische Kunst- und Lustgärtner*, Weimar, 1972; P. W. van der Pas, 'The earliest European descriptions of Japan's flora', *Janus*, 61,1974, pp. 281-95; E. S. Kraft, 'Andreas Cleyer', *Festschrift zum 86. Deutschen Ärztetag*, Kassel, 1983, pp. 25-40; W. Muntschick, 'Ein Manuskript von Georg Meister, dem Kunst- und Lustgärtner, in der British Library', *Medizinhistorisches Journal*, 19, 1984, pp. 225-32; Deutsches Institut für Japanstudien (ed.), *Kenperu ten*, Tokyo, 1990, pp. 68-73, 132-7.

13. J. Beckmann, *Litteratur der älteren Reisebeschreibungen*, Göttingen, 1808, 1:4, p. 692.

14. Kaempfer's *Flora Japonica* is contained in *Amoenitates Exoticae*. For a partial translation and reproduction see W. Muntschick, *Engelbert Kaempfer: Flora Japonica (1712)*, Wiesbaden, 1983.

15. C. P. Thunberg, *Flora Japonica*, Leipzig, 1784.

16. H. Goerke, *Carl von Linné: Arzt, Naturforscher, Systematiker*, second edition, Stuttgart, 1989, p. 181.

17. J. G. Zuccarini in *Gelehrte Anzeigen*, 13, Munich, 1841, p. 251.

18. P. F. von Siebold and J. G. Zuccarini, *Flora Japonica*, Leiden, 1835-1870. See also G. Schmid, 'Über Ph. Fr. v. Siebolds Reise nach Japan. Mit Briefen aus den Jahren 1822 bis 1827', *Botanisches Archiv*, 43, 1942, pp. 487-530; J. Kimura, *Shiiboruto to nihon no shokubutsu* (Siebold and Japanese plants), Tokyo, 1981.

19. P. F. von Siebold, 'Einige Worte über den Zustand der Botanik auf Iapan', *Nova Acta Academiae Caes. Leopold.-Carolinae*, 14, 1829, pp. 675-78.

20. These words are contained in the title of Kaempfer's work. See also the reproduction contained in Muntschick, *Engelbert Kaempfer: Flora Japonica (1712)*, p. 38.

21. Ibid; *Amoenitates Exoticae*, p. 769.

22. Page numbers in brackets refer to *Amoenitates Exoticae*; also in Muntschick, *Flora Japaonica*.

23. British Library, Or.ff.1. See S. Kitamura, 'Kaempfer no nihon shokubutsu-ki ni tsuite' (Kaempfer's description of Japanese plants), *Journal of History of Science*, Japan, 26, 1953, pp. 19-24.

24. Y. Kimura, 'Nakamura Tekisai no kimmōzui ni tsuite' (The

kimmō-zui of Nakamura Tekisai), *Journal of the Department of Liberal Arts*, University of Tokyo, 5, 1972, pp. 105-31.

25. E. Kaempfer, *Geschichte und Beschreibung von Japan*, Dohm, (ed.), Lemgo 1777-79, II:174.

26. Ibid., p. 372; Muntschick, *Engelbert Kaempfer: Flora Japonica (1712)*, p. 176ff.

27. *Geschichte und Beschreibung*, II:9, 125; B. Matsubayashi, *Nagasaki shokubutsu no rekishi* (The history of plants at Nagasaki), Tokyo, 1981, p. 37.

28. T. Shimizu, *Nihon yakugaku-shi* (The history of Japanese pharmacy), Tokyo, 1949, p. 258.

29. Linnaeus, nr. 154.

30. Y. Kimura, 'Kaempfer, Thunberg and Siebold', *Japanese Studies in the History of Science*, 15, 1976, p 4.

31. J. Ōi (Ohwi), *Nihon shokubutsu-shi* (The history of Japanese plants), Tokyo, 1975, p. 22.

32. Sl. 2914 and 2915 contain Kaempfer's sketches; Sl. 211, his herbarium; Sl. 74, his catalogue of Japanese plants.

33. Nakamura Tekisai, *Kimmōzui*, Kobayashi, (ed.), Tokyo, 1976, p. 895.

34. According to the rules of the *International Codes of Botanical Nomenclature* only works published after 1753 are relevant for the determination of scientific names of plants.

35. J. Breyne, *Exoticarum aliarumque minus cognitarum plantarum centuria prima*, Danzig, 1678, p. 11 ff.

36. J. Breyne, *Prodromus rariorum plantarum II*, Danzig, 1689, p. 16.

37. J. F. Gronovius, *Camphorae historia*, Leiden, 1715.

38. J. Banks (ed.), *Icones selectae plantarum, quas in Japonia collegit et delineavit Engelbertus Kaempferus*, London, 1791.

39. H. Hara, 'Nomenclatural notes on some Asiatic plants with special reference to Kaempfer's Amoenitatum exoticarum', *Taxon*, 26, 1977, pp. 584-87. See also ibid., vol. 30, pp. 455-56 and vol. 36, p. 75.

CHAPTER SIX

1. Scheuchzer, 1, p. xlviii.

2. See chapter 8 below.

3. Sl. 4047, f. 12v. All dates are given old style unless new style (NS) is indicated.

4. Ibid., ff. 23-24v.

5. Royal Society, Council Minutes, vol. 2, 1682-1727, p. 342. Zollman spent most of his adult life in England, where he died in 1748, and he was known by the English version of his German name, Philip Heinrich Zollmann. I have written about Zollman more fully in 'Philip Henry Zollman, the Royal Society's First Assistant Secretary

for Foreign Correspondence', *Notes and Records of the Royal Society London*, 46:2, 1992, pp. 219-34.

6. Royal Society, Council Minutes, vol. 2, 1682-1727, p. 341; Sl. 4047, f. 31.

7. Sl. 4047, f. 31; Add. 4289, f. 13; *Zedlers Universal Lexicon*, 63, col. 299. Zollman's plan for a history of Russia was never fulfilled.

8. Bodl. Rawlinson MS D 871, f. 42. Scheuchzer's redrawing of Kaempfer's map of Japan for the preparation of the copperplate included the provenance of the Kamchatka map but this identification was dropped from the printed version (Add. 5232, f. 161).

9. This list did not represent a full inventory of Engelbert Kaempfer's collection. Johann Hermann preferred to tease prospective purchasers with partial revelations about the extent of the material, hoping to drive up prices. It was a tactic that failed miserably when tried on the canny Sloane.

10. Sl. 4061, f. 109; Sl. 4047, f. 43v-44.

11. Sl. 4289, f. 12v.

12. Sl. 4047, ff. 36v-37; Sl. 4061, f. 109.

13. 2 vols, London, 1707, 1725, esp. vol. 2, p. i.

14. Sl. 4047, f. 43v.

15. Bodl. Rawlinson MS D 871, ff. 45-46v.

16. On the new first chapter of Book One, written by Scheuchzer, see Beatrice Bodart-Bailey, 'Preliminary Report on the manuscripts of Engelbert Kaempfer in the British Library', in Yu-Ying Brown (ed.), *Japanese Studies*, British Library Occasional Papers, 11, London, 1990, pp. 30-32. Scheuchzer based his new chapter on two Kaempfer manuscripts. In the manuscript catalogue of Sloane's library these are entitled 'Diarium Itineris Eng Kempferi Batavia Siamum indeque Iaponiam' and 'Miscellanea varia Siamensium Regni Historiam Naturalem ac politicam spectantia ab eodem' (Sl. 3972b f. 249). There are other minor differences between Zollman's heads and the printed translation, for example, Zollman changed his mind about some translations crossing out 'Idolotary' and substituting 'Worship' in chapter 2 of the third book (the term used in the printed version), and 'exterminated' instead of 'extirpated' in chapter 5 of the fourth book, which was altered to 'banish'd' in the printed version.

17. Hüls, 'Zur Geschichte', p. 191.

18. Sl. 4047, f. 100. Figures for the exchange rate between sterling and thalers vary according to writer and time, but Steigerthal gives the sterling equivalent for the first purchase (450 thalers) as £82 which makes 1 thaler equal to 18.22p (Sl. 4047, f. 104). This figure is supported by some calculations at the end of Scheuchzer's translation of Kaempfer's letter of 18 February 1724 (NS) (Sl. 4065, f.316v).

19. Sl. 4047, ff. 59, 93, 104. Steigerthal had hoped to reduce the cost to Sloane even further by sending the curiosities as part of George I's baggage. It is not clear whether the delay in concluding an agreement with Kaempfer aborted this plan in which case the curiosities would have been shipped at Sloane's cost (ibid., f.77v.).
20. Sl. 4061, f. 116; ibid., 4047, ff. 74, 77v, 84v; Bodl. Rawlinson MS D 871, f 52a.
21. Sl. 3064, ff. 69-70; Bodl. Rawlinson MS D 871, ff. 53, 55.
22. Sl. 4061, ff. 558-559; Beatrice Bodart-Bailey, 'Warum noch einmal Kaempfer?', *Lippische Mitteilungen aus Geschichte und Landeskunde*, 57, 1988, p.156.
23. Christian Wilhelm von Dohm, *Nachricht die Urschrift der Kämpferischen Beschreibung von Japan betreffend*, Lemgo, 1774, p. 13.
24. The standard quota of free copies given to an author at this time was twenty-five. The clause means that Kaempfer was to receive his twenty-five plus another twenty-five printed on lower quality paper to cut costs.
25. A subseqent letter of Kaempfer to Steigerthal confirms that a contract with Zollman was signed and sealed and that Kaempfer retained a copy of the manuscript in Lemgo. The existence of the contract is beyond doubt, even if no copy has survived. Kaempfer is specific (Sl. 3064, ff. 69-70), Steigerthal refers to one (Sl. 4048, f. 56). Zollman records only four clauses (Bodl. Rawlinson MS D 871, f. 55) but he noted these down almost a decade after the contract was signed at a time when he was concerned to recall his obligation, not the exact wording of the contract itself, the copy of which he had clearly lost by then.
26. Sl. 4047, ff. 100-101.
27. Bodl. Rawlinson MS D 871, f. 52a. On the range of publishing options available to authors at this time, see James Hepburn, *The Author's Empty Purse and the Rise of the Literary Agent*, Oxford, 1968, pp. 9-14.
28. Bodl. Rawlinson MS D 871, ff. 57-57v. Twenty-eight copper plates had been used in the *Amoenitates*. They were indeed of poor quality. Sloane acquired 217 (Sl. 2914; Meier-Lemgo, 'Wie kam der handschriftliche Nachlaß. . .?' p. 98). Cornelis de Bruyn criticised the poor quality of the drawings of the ruins of Persepolis in the *Amoenitates Exoticae*, but refused to accept Kaempfer's explanation that this was the fault of poor printing reproduction. Unfairly, he blamed Kaempfer's draughtsmanship (*Journal des Sçavans*, February 1719, p. 88). See chapter 7 for a full discussion of the plates.
29. Sl. 4065, ff. 315-315v.
30. Ibid., ff. 315-316v; Bodl. Rawlinson MS D 871, f. 57.
31. Sl. 4065, ff.315v-316; Bodl. Rawlinson MS D 871, f. 57.

32. Ibid., ff. 50-50v, 60-61; Bodl. MS Autogr. d 4, f. 76.
33. Sl. 4069, ff. 214-214v. For a list of the extant Japanese works originally belonging to Kaempfer in the British Library see Bonn, 'Der wissenschaftliche Nachlaß...', p. 99ff.
34. Sl. 4065, f. 316v. As this is a translation of Kaempfer's original German into French it is possible that 'marqué' is a slip for 'manqué' and that the items had not been packed because of some oversight.
35. Sl. 2907, f. 1.
36. Bodl. Rawlinson MS D 871, ff. 47-47v.
37. Ibid., f. 48.
38. Bodl. MS Autogr. d 4, f. 76.
39. Sl. 4047, ff. 182, 184v, 188-188v, 193.
40. Ibid., f. 193v.
41. Bodl. Rawlinson MS D 871, f. 48.
42. Sloane's payment to Zollman is mentioned in a letter by Steigerthal (Sl. 4047, f. 304).
43. Ibid.
44. Ibid., ff. 161, 304-305v.
45. Zentralbibliothek Zürich MS H 293, pp. 34, 39-40.
46. Ibid., pp. 13-14, inaccurately transcribed by G. R. De Beer, 'Johann Gaspar Scheuchzer, F.R.S. 1702-1729', *Notes & Records of the Royal Society*, 6, 1948-49, pp. 63- 64. Sloane was overstating the worth of a licence from the College of Physicians. The College continued to promote unlicensed physicians (George Clark, A *History of the Royal College of Physicians*, vol. 2, Oxford, 1966, pp. 512-13). But otherwise Sloane was true to his word in furthering the young Scheuchzer's career. Johann Gaspar was made a Fellow of the Royal Society in 1724 at the tender age of 22 (three years before Zollman) and in 1728 he recieved the degree of doctor of medicine at Cambridge (De Beer, 'Johann Gaspar Scheuchzer', p. 64).
47. Bodl. Rawlinson MS D 871, f. 7.
48. Ibid., f. 19.
49. Ibid. , f. 99v; Sl. 4048, f. 50.
50. Ibid., ff. 92-93v; Scheuchzer, 1, p. lxxxii.
51. Sl. 4048, ff. 21v-22, 38v-39.
52. Sl. 3064, ff. 69-72v; Sl. 4065, f. 338ff.
53. No copy of Zollman's original contract has survived among Sloane's papers and it is unlikely that one was ever made.
54. Sl. 4048, ff. 56, 75, 76; Sl. 4065, ff. 343-343v; Bodl. Rawlinson MS D 871, f. 19.
55. Sl. 4048, ff. 76, 82, 96, 99. Negotiations over the Kaempfer legacy were of minor importance for both Sloane and Steigerthal at this time. On Sloane's instructions Steigerthal was buying up books at a major auction held in Hanover in late November (NS) (Sl. 4048, f. 96).
56. Sloane valued the small manuscripts which Steigerthal had been

given as a present by Kaempfer at 10 guineas (Sl. 4047, f. 304). It is highly likely that Sloane paid Zollman some other out-of-pocket expenses for the History but there is no record of this.
57. Bodl. Rawlinson MS D 871, ff. 21v-22.
58. Sl. 3972c, vol. vii, f. 228.
59. *Journal des Sçavans*, October 1726, p. 646; ibid., February 1727, p. 119. The journeys to the imperial (*sic*) court were not added by Scheuchzer. They were part of Kaempfer's manuscript.
60. See Sl. 3060.
61. Sl. 1968, f. 221. As has been mentioned, Zollman's 'Heads of M. Kaempfer's Manuscript relating to Japan', which he drew up in 1723, also shows that Kaempfer's intended first chapter was the description of Siam (Bodl. Rawlinson MS D 871, f. 45).
62. Royal Society, Journal Book, 13, 1726-1731, pp. 75, 89. In his introduction to the English edition Scheuchzer records that he asked various friends 'to correct' things they found 'amiss' (Scheuchzer, 1, p. xc). A comparison between the only extant fragments of the working draft of Scheuchzer's translation (Sl. 4026) and the published edition shows that changes were indeed made. I am grateful to Dr Bodart-Bailey for drawing my attention to these fragments.
63. Add. 4289, f. 12v.
64. See Massarella, 'Philip Henry Zollman', p. 223.
65. *Journal des Sçavans*, September 1727, pp. 570-71.
66. *Histoire du Japon*, The Hague, 1729. The Bibliothèque Nationale's general catalogue gives the French translator as François Naude but besides the *Journal des Sçavans*, references among Sloane's catalogues and Des Maizeaux's papers confirm that Des Maizeaux was indeed the translator (Sl. 3972c vol. 7, f.178; Add. 4289, f.356 which gives two references to the translation, the second being 14 October, suggesting that Des Maizeaux had been oiling the publicity machine of the Republic of Letters before completing his translation). It is certain that Des Maizeaux would have secured Sloane's permission before embarking on his translation.
67. Bodl. Rawlinson MS D871, f. 22.
68. Sl. 4049, ff., 13-13v.
69. Sl. 4066, f.15-15v.
70. Sl. 4051, ff. 118-119.
71. Ibid., f. 138.
72. Bodl. Rawlinson MS D 871, f. 53. Kaempfer wrongly stated that the Dutch edition had appeared in 1728 and that the French one was forthcoming. In fact the French and Dutch editions both appeared in 1729. The Dutch edition was also published by Goffe and Neaume, Des Maizeaux's publishers. The identity of the Dutch translator is unknown, probably someone under contract to the publisher. It was

clearly through the publicity and call for subscriptions for Des Maizeaux's translation that the Lemgo publisher, Meier, found out about the translations. The news, somewhat garbled, was passed on to Johann Hermann.

73. Ibid., ff. 53v-54.
74. Ibid., ff. 54-54v.
75. Ibid., f. 56.
76. Ibid., f. 56v.
77. Ibid., ff. 52-52v.
78. Ibid., f. 58.
79. For example, *Eduard Ives Reisen nach Indien und Persien, in einer freien Übersetzung aus dem englischen Original*, 2 vols, Leipzig, 1774/1775; *Geschichte der Engländer und Französen im östlichen Indien*, Leipzig, 1776.
80. Dohm, *Nachricht die Urschrift*.
81. Ibid., p. 28.
82. Ibid., pp. 14-17; Dohm, 1, pp. XL-XLI. His initial zeal led him to speculate that the Lemgo manuscripts were the only surviving ones and that the Sloane one had been lost, a suggestion he withdrew in the introduction to the German edition (Dohm, *Nachricht die Urschrift*, p. 18; Dohm, 1, p. XL).
83. Dohm, a critic of Colbert's failed Compagnie des Indies, was an admirer of the English East India Company's success which he judged the most appropriate model for future Prussian involvement in the Indies. His suggestions were dismissed in Berlin, Frederick the Great noting that for Prussia a regiment of soldiers was more important than a man-of war (Ilsegret Dambacher, *Christian Wilhelm von Dohm*, Frankfurt/M, 1974, pp. 118-24).
84. Meier-Lemgo, 'Wie kam der handschriftliche Nachlaß... ?', p. 96; Hüls, 'Zur Geschichte des Drucks', pp. 193-94.
85. Doubts about the authenticity of the Sloane manuscript were raised by a reviewer of Dohm's edition in the *Monthly Review* (61, 1779, pp. 145-46) who claimed to have compared the writing in the manuscript with examples of Kaempfer's writing in the then British Museum and judged it not to be the doctor's. A copy of Scheuchzer's edition in the Bodleian Library (Douce K 138) records the doubts.
86. For a discussion of the handwriting in the British Library manuscript see Bodart-Bailey, 'Preliminary Report', p. 27ff. Zollman's difficulties with the handwriting in the manuscript and his mention of a hand other than Engelbert Kaempfer and his nephew (see above) supports Dr Bodart-Bailey's argument.
87. Ibid., p. 33.
88. Dohm, 1, p. XLI.
89. The 9 has been changed into a 10 to allow for the subdivision of chapter 7 (Sl. 3060, f. 267v.).

90. For a full discussion of the missing chapter see Bodart-Bailey, 'Preliminary Report', pp. 34-36.
91. Sl. 4060, f. 239; Dohm, 2, p. 73.
92. Dohm says much about the efforts he and Büsching expended to determine the authenticity of the uncle's manuscript; nothing about Johann Hermann's writing.
93. The doubts voiced by the anonymous *Monthly Review*'s critic in 1779 were repeated by one of the *Edinburgh Review*'s contributors who contended that Scheuchzer's translation 'is very incomplete'. He cited the English edition of Johann Beckmann's *A History of Inventions and Discoveries* which noted that Dohm included a reference to the Japanese use of matches or links not included in the French translation of Scheuchzer (*Monthly Magazine*, 16, 1804, pp. 503-504; ibid., 17, 1804, p. 5; John Beckmann, *A History of Inventions and Discoveries*, vol. 3, London, 1797, p. 440n.).
94. Dohm, 1, pp. LV-LVI.
95. Ibid., p. XLIX.
96. The notice appeared in the September number of the *Journal* on p. 565, not the November one.
97. Sl. 3972c vol 7, f. 228.
98. *Journal des Sçavans*, June 1734, pp. 367-68. The index volume to the *Journal*, published in 1756, provided this reference but wrongly states that the edition was indeed published (*Journal des Sçavans: Table Générale des Matières*, vol. 6, Paris, 1756, p. 171).
99. Royal Society Letter Book Copy, 26, p. 90. See also Wolfgang Muntschick, 'Nachlese zur Kaempfer-Forschung', *Lippische Mitteilungen*, 54, 1985, pp. 196-98.

CHAPTER SEVEN
1. The suggestion to research Kaempfer's drawings and published prints came from Dr Beatrice Bodart-Bailey who has been most supportive during all stages of the work and generous in sharing her knowledge with me. I would also like to thank Dr John Clark, Dr Christian Dittrich, Professor Roger Goepper, Antony Griffiths, Dr Christian von Heusinger, Guy Hutsebaut, Dr Rüdiger Joppien, Professor Hans Kuhn, Professor Derek Massarella, Dr Rudolf Mayer, Dr Rainer Schoch, Dr Lothar Weiß and the participants of the the Tokyo symposium on Kaempfer.
2. On the rediscovery see B. M. Bodart-Bailey, 'Kaempfer Restor'd', *Monumenta Nipponica*, 43:1, 1988, pp. 27-33.
3. Dohm, 2, p. 73; Sl. 3060, f. 239.
4. See Abraham Bosse, *Die Kunst in Kupfer zu stechen*, Dresden, 1765, p. 86.
5. *Amoenitates Exoticae*, introduction.
6. Niedersächsische Landesbibliotek, Hanover, Leibniz Briefe 1007,

References

Leibniz to Witsen, Hanover, 12 October 1708; Witsen to Leibniz, 29 November 1712. I am most grateful to Derek Massarella for this information and for these references.

7. See John Gabriel Stedman, *Narrative of a Five Years Expedition against the Revolted Negroes of Surinam*, edited by Richard and Sally Price, Baltimore, 1988, pp. xxxviii- xlviii. Again, I wish to thank Derek Massarella for this reference.

8. Antony Griffith, 'The Art and Hand of the Printmaker' in Skira Rizzoli (ed.), *Prints*, Geneva, 1981, p. 163.

9. Quoted in James A. Michener, *The Hokusai Sketchbooks*, Rutland, Vt, 1958, pp. 32-33.

10. William M. Iving, Jr, *Prints and Visual Communication*, Cambridge, Mass., 1969, p. 89.

11. Partha Mitter, *Much Maligned Monsters*, Oxford, 1977, p. 5ff.

12. John Nieuhoff, *An Embassy sent by the East India Company of the United Provinces to the Grand Cham or Emperor of China*, second edition, London, 1673.

13. Sl. 3060, f. 508v.

14. Ibid., f. 501.

15. Bodart-Bailey, 'Kaempfer Restor'd', pp. 21, 28.

16. Ibid., p. 15ff.

17. See chapter 6.

18. Nakamura Tekisai, *Kimmōzui*, 1688.

19. Scheuchzer, 1, p. xc.

20. Preparatory drawings for this plate are in Sl. 3060, ff. 445, 447; Sl. 5232, ff. 157-60.

21. Sl. 3060, f. 445.

22. On the mistaken name for this pagoda see B. M. Bodart-Bailey, 'Kyoto Three Hundred Years Ago', *Nichibunken Newsletter*, 9, May 1991, p. 8-9.

23. Sl. 3060, f. 526.

24. For example, the plate 'T Keysers Hof van binnen' in Johann Nieuhof, *Die Gesantschaft...an den Tartarischen Cham*, Amsterdam, 1669.

25. Sl. 3060, f. 440.

26. Sl. 5232, ff. 154, 155.

27. Or.75, f.16.

28. Sl. 5232. See B.M. Bodart-Bailey, 'The Most Magnificent Monastery and Other Famous Sights: The Japanese Paintings of Engelbert Kaempfer', *Japan Review*, 3, 1992, pp. 25-44.

29. Sl. 3060, f. 515.

30. See Bodart-Bailey, 'Kaempfer Restor'd', p. 28.

31. Sl. 5232, f. 39.

32. Sl. 3060, f. 523.

33. Sl. 5232, f. 15.

34. Or.75. f.1*.
35. Sl. 3060 contains a number of drawings by Kaempfer copied from *Kimmōzui*. The same images appear in Sl. 5232 and may be the preparatory tracings that Scheuchzer did for the etchings in *The History*.
36. Sl. 3060, f. 457ff.
37. Ibid., f. 501.
38. For example, the funeral procession '...zu Ehren von Jacob Bauer von Eiseneck', 1621, Germanisches Nationalmuseum Nürnberg, H.B. 24918, Kapsel 1361.
39. Sl. 3060, f. 512.
40. E.g. Hogarth's 'Analysis of Beauty'.
41. Sl. 3060, f. 514.
42. Ibid., f. 429.
43. Sl. 5232, f. 162.
44. Bodart-Bailey, 'Kaempfer Restor'd', pp. 5, 11.
45. Sl. 5232, f. 169.
46. Albrecht Dürer, Sächsische Landesbibliothek, Dresden, 41 Dsdn, ff. 112v, 113.
47. Dohm, 2, p. 7; Sl. 3060, f. 239.
48. Arnoldus Montanus, *Atlas Japannensis*, London, 1670.
49. Scheuchzer, 1, pp. lxxix-lxxx.
50. Facsimile Series: Classica Japonica, Tenri Central Library, Tokyo, Section 3/4, Montanus, *Description de l'empire du Japon*, 1973.
51. *Anthanasii Kircheri e Soc Jesu China monumentis qua sacris qua profanis*, Amsterdam, 1667.

CHAPTER EIGHT
1. Bodl. MS Gen Top. c 27/1, ff. 5, 7; Bodl. MS Rawlinson Letters 124, f. 41; E. St John Brooks, *Sir Hans Sloane: The Great Collector and his Circle*, London, 1954, pp. 191, 193, 198-200; Christine G. Thomas, 'Sir Hans Sloane and the Russian Academy of Sciences', *British Library Journal*, 14:1, 1988, p. 24; Maarten Ultee, 'Sir Hans Sloane, Scientist', ibid., pp. 8, 9; 'A Contemporary Opinion from the Commonplace Book of Dr William Stukeley 1687-1765', *British Museum Quarterly*, 18, 1953, p. 2; Anon, 'Sir Hans Sloane and the British Museum', *British Museum Quarterly*, 18, 1953, p. 2ff; Richard D. Altick, *The Shows of London*, Cambridge, Massachusetts, 1978, pp. 15-16; Michael Hunter, *Establishing the New Science: The Experience of the Early Royal Society*, Woodbridge, 1989, pp. 123, 129, 154-55. Joseph M. Levine's dismissal of Sloane (*Dr. Woodward's Shield*, Ithaca, 1977, p. 88) is based on James Woodward, hardly an impartial authority.
2. London, 2 vols, 1707, 1725.
3. Ibid, vol. 1, preface.

References

4.   The *Historia* was translated into Italian, French, Dutch, German, English and Latin. Other early works of ethnology by missionaries in the New World were not published at the time. An English translation was published by the Hakluyt Society, *The Natural and Moral History of the Indies*, edited by Clements Markham, London, 1858. For a discussion and assessment of Acosta see Anthony Pagden, *The Fall of Natural Man*, Cambridge, 1986, chapter 7. See also J. H. Elliot, *The Old World And the New 1492-1650*, Cambridge, 1992 edition, pp. 35, 38.

5.   For what follows see especially Barbara Shapiro, 'History and Natural History in Sixteenth and Seventeenth Century England' in Barbara Shapiro and Robert G. Frank Jr, *English Scientific Virtuosi in the 16th and 17th Centuries*, Los Angeles, 1979; idem, *Probability and Certainty in Seventeenth Century England*, Princeton, 1983; Michael Hunter, *Science and Society in Restoration England*, Cambridge, 1981; Elliot, *The Old World and the New*, pp. 34-35; Pagden, *Fall of Natural Man*, pp. 146, 152; Krzysztof Pomian, *Collectors and Curiosities*, Cambridge, 1990, pp. 60-64.

6.   Allison P. Coudret, 'Forgotten Ways of Knowing: The Kabbalah, Language, and Science in the Seventeenth Century' in D. R. Kelley and R. H. Popkin (eds.), *The Shapes of Knowledge from the Renaissance to the Enlightenment*, Amsterdam, 1991, pp. 83-99. Stephen Jay Gould, *Time's Arrow, Time's Cycle*, Harmondsworth, 1988, esp. pp. 21-41, shows crisply and clearly how belief in revelation far from inhibiting scientific enquiry encouraged it, at least in England.

7.   Hunter, *Science and Society*, pp. 35-36.

8.   Oldenburg to Sir George Oxenden in A. Rupert Hall and Marie Boas Hall (eds), *The Correspondence of Henry Oldenburg*, vol.3, Madison, 1966, pp. 384-85. On the Society's concern to act as an agent for the dissemination of knowledge and information see Marie Boas Hall, 'The Royal Society's Role in the diffusion of Information in the Seventeenth Century', *Notes and Records of the Royal Society*, 29:2, 1975, pp. 173-92; Hunter, *Establishing the New Science*, pp. 245-60. It should be emphasized that the Royal Society had no monopoly over such activities. Individuals outside the Society were also engaged in the business of correspondence within the Republic of Letters (Hunter, Science and Society, p. 14).

9.   Hunter, *Science and Society*, chapter 2, passim.

10. Hunter, *Establishing the New Science*, pp. 93-94 and esp. pp. 118-21; *Philosophical Transactions*, 11, April 1666, pp. 186-89, later published as *General Heads for the Natural History of a Country. . .for the Use of Travellers and Navigators*, London, 1692.

11. See Hall and Hall (eds), *Correspondence of Henry Oldenburg*, vol. 2, Madison, 1966, pp. 310-11; ibid., vol. 3, Madison, 1966, p. 58;

ibid., vol. 4, Madison, 1967, p. 207; ibid., vol. 10, London, 1975, pp. 197-98.

12. John Woodward, *Brief Instructions for Making Observations in all Parts of the World*, London, 1696; P. J. Marshall and Glyndwr Williams, *The Great Map of Mankind*, London, 1982, pp. 45-46; Shapiro, *Probability and Certainty*, pp. 126-27.

13. Thomas Sprat, *History of the Royal Society*, repr., St Louis, MO, 1958, pp. 158-72; Thomas Birch, *The History of the Royal Society of London*, repr., New York, 1968, vol. 1, pp. 317-19, 454. Louys Philibert Vernatti served as the VOC's fiscal of the Indies (J. A. van der Chijs [ed.], *Dagh-Register gehouden int Casteel Batavia. . .Anno 1670-1671*, Batavia, 1898, p. 46).

14. Royal Society, Classified Papers, XIX.72. The individuals to whom the directions, dated 14 August 1671, were addressed are Samuel Baron and Simon Delboe, both members of the Company's voyage.

15. See Derek Massarella, *A World Elsewhere: Europe's Encounter with Japan in the Sixteenth and Seventeenth Centuries*, New Haven, 1990, chapter 8.

16. See Derek Massarella. '"The Loudest Lies": Knowledge of Japan in Seventeenth Century England', *Itinerario*, 11:2, 1987, pp. 52-71.

17. IOR E/3/91, f. 24.

18. J. F. Gebhard, *Het Leven van Mr Nicolaas Cornelisz. Witsen (1641-1717)*, 2 vols, Utrecht, 1882, 2, p. 347.

19. Rolf Winau, 'Christian Mentzel, die Leopoldina und der ferne Osten', *Medizinhistorisches Journal*, 11:1/2, 1976, pp. 87-88.

20. Marion Peters, 'Nicholaes Witsen and Gijsbert Cuper', *Lias*, 16, 1989, pp. 112-13.

21. See above, p. 13.

22. Niedersächsische Landesbibliothek, Hanover, Leibniz Briefe 1007, Leibniz to Witsen, Hanover, 12 October 1708; ibid., Witsen to Leibniz, Amsterdam, 29 November 1712; Gebhard, *Het Leven van Mr Nicolaas Cornelisz. Witsen*, 2, p. 347. At their meeting, Kaempfer presented Witsen with some books of plants and herbs and several maps of Japanese cities and castles (Leibniz Briefe 1007, Witsen to Leibniz, Amsterdam, 29 November 1712).

23. Ibid. Professor Rietbergen's assertion that Witsen tried to have the *Amoenitates* published in Amsterdam is wrong (P. J. A. N. Rietbergen, 'Witsen's World: Nicolaas Witsen [1641-1717] Between the Dutch East India Company and the Republic of Letters' in Robert Ross and George D. Winius [eds], *All of One Company: The VOC in Biographical Perspective*, Utrecht, 1986, p. 130).

24. Peters, 'Nicholaes Witsen and Gijsbert Cuper', p. 113. On Witsen and de Jager see also P. F. Kornicki, 'European Japanology at the End of the Seventeenth Century', *Bulletin of the School of Oriental and*

References

African Studies, 56, 1993, pp. 502-24.

25. Winau, 'Christian Mentzel', esp. pp. 87-88; Eva Kraft, 'Christian Mentzel, Philippe Couplet, Andreas Cleyer und die Chinesische Medizin' in *Fernöstliche Kultur, Wolf Haenisch zugeeignet*, Marburg, 1975, pp. 158-96; idem, 'Frühe chinesische Studien in Berlin', *Medizinhistorisches Journal*, 11:1/2, 1976, pp. 116-22; Paul Demaerel, 'Couplet and the Dutch' in Jerome Heyndrickx (ed.), *Philippe Couplet, S.J. (1623-1693)*, Nettetal, 1990, pp. 87-120. Cleyer published *Curieuse Aenmerckingen Der bysonderste Oost en West-Indische Verwonderenswaer Dingen* (Utrecht, 1682). His 'Flora Japonica', which he had sent to Berlin after his first tour of duty in Japan, remained unpublished despite Mentzel's hopes (Kraft, 'Frühe chinesische Studien in Berlin', p. 120).

26. Rumphius, *Herbarium Amboinense*, Amsterdam, 1741-50; Niedersächsische Landesbibliothek, Hanover, Leibniz Briefe 1007, Leibniz to Witsen, Hanover, 12 October 1708; Witsen to Leibniz, 29 November 1712; F. W. Stapel, *Geschiednis van Nederlandsch Indië*, 5 vols, Amsterdam, 1938-40, 3, pp. 482-3.

27. See Paul Dibon, 'Communication in the Republica Literaria of the 17th Century', in *Res Publica Literarum: Studies in the Classical Tradition*, 1, 1978, pp. 43-55; Marteen Ultee, 'The Republic of Letters and Learned Correspondence, 1680-1720', *The Seventeenth Century*, 2:1, 1987, pp. 95-112.

28. This was translated into English, along with Joust Schouten's account of Siam, as *A True Description of the Mighty Kingdoms of Japan and Siam*, London, 1663. Caron had lived in Japan in the service of the VOC for twenty-two years from 1619-1641. See the inroduction to the modern edition of the *True Description* edited by C. R. Boxer (London, 1935).

29. This is based on Caron and published Jesuit sources.

30. This compilation was translated into English by John Ogilby as *Atlas Japannensis: Being Remarkable Addresses by way of Embassy from the East-India Company of the United Provinces, to the Emperor of Japan*, London, 1670.

31. Translated into English by Ogilby as *Atlas Chinensis: Being a Second Part of Relation of Remarkable Passages, in Two Embassies from the East India Company of the United Provinces, to the...Emperor of China and East Tartary*, London, 1671, and wrongly attributed to Montanus.

32. For a discussion of seventeenth-century printed works on Japan see Donald F. Lach and Edwin van Kley, *Asia in the Making of Europe*, vol. 3, book 4, Chicago, 1993, chapter 23.

33. Anthony Henley to Jonathan Swift, July 1709 in Harold Williams (ed.), *The Correspondence of Jonathan Swift, vol. 1, 1690-1713*, Oxford, 1963, p. 147.

34. Sl. 4039, ff. 81, 85, 92. Cunninghame was sending similar material to the apothecary James Petiver, a Sloane protégé, whose collection Sloane was eventually to acquire (ibid., ff. 89, 112; Ultee, 'Sir Hans Sloane, Scientist', pp. 4, 15, 17 n. 12) and to the botanists John Ray and Leonard Plukenet (*Dictionary of National Biography*, sub Cunninghame). Two of Cunninghame's letters (Sl. 3321, ff. 52, 92-93) were printed with minor omissions in *Philosophical Transactions*, 280, July-August 1702, pp. 1201-9). The second letter refers to Cleyer's *Specimen medicinae Sinicae* (ibid., p. 1209).
35. Sl. 4161, f. 142.
36. Sl. 4040, ff. 41v, 55, 81v, 99; ibid., 4041, f. 50.
37. Sl. 4039, ff. 17-17v, 85v. The company soon switched its attention decisively to China. See Derek Massarella, 'Chinese, Tartars and Thea or a Tale of Two Companies: The English East India Company and Taiwan in the later Seventeenth Century', *Journal of the Royal Asiatic Society*, third series, 3:3, 1993, pp. 393-426.
38. Bodl. MS Bodley 24, pp. 35-39, 40. Had circumstances allowed him to visit Japan, Pound would have produced a first-rate account of the country. There is no evidence to confirm that Sloane saw these notes but the probability that he discussed Pound's travels with him is extremely high.
39. Ibid. pp. 49, 252.
40. Chapter 6 above.
41. Vol 2, pp. iii-iv. Sloane gives the wrong date for publication of *Lindenius renovatus*, 1687 instead of 1686.
42. The sad but fascinating saga of Dr Hyde's travails can be followed in Sl. 4037, ff. 100, 254, 269; Sl. 4038, ff. 43, 75, 89, 292; G. Sharpe (ed.), *Syntagma Dissertationum...Thos. Hyde*, 2 vols, Oxford, 1767, 2, pp. 487-90, 493-94; J. Harris, *Navigautium atque Itinerantium Bibliotheca*, London, 1748 edition, vol. 2, p. 890. See also Marshall and Williams, *Great Map of Mankind*, pp. 12, 92.

Bibliography

I. MANUSCRIPTS

Bodleian Library, Oxford
Gen Top. c 27/1; Rawlinson Letters 124; Rawlinson D 871;Bodley
24; Autogr. d4.
British Library, London
Additional MSS 4289, 5232.Sloane MSS 74, 211, 1968, 2907, 2910,
2912, 2914, 2915, 2917, 2921, 2923, 3060, 3061, 3062, 3063, 3064,
3321,3972b, 3972c vol. vii, 4026, 4037, 4038, 4039, 4040, 4041,
4047, 4048, 4049, 4051, 4061, 4065, 4066, 4069, 4161.
Oriental Collections: Or.75.f.
Royal Society, London
Classified Papers, XIX.72; Journal Book, 13, 1726-1731; Letter Book
Copy, 26; Council Minutes, vol. 2, 1682-1727.
India Office Library and Records, London
E/3/91.
Algemeen Rijksarchief, The Hague
01.04.21, Het Archief van de Nederlandse factorij in Japan, 1609-
1860: 108, 110, 111, 121, 122, 123, 125, 126, 127, 129, 133, 134,
135, 136, 139, 146, 1573
01.04.01, Het Archief van de Vereenigde Oostindische Compagnie,
1602-1860: 1935, 6048.
Zentralbibliothek, Zürich
MS H 293.
Niedersächsische Landesbibliothek, Hanover
Leibniz Briefe 1007.

II. PRINTED WORKS

'A Contemporary Opinion from the Commonplace Book of Dr
William Stukeley 1687-1765', *British Museum Quarterly*, 18,
1953.
Altick, Richard D., *The Shows of London*, Cambridge, Massachusetts,
1978.
Anon, 'Sir Hans Sloane and the British Museum', *British Museum
Quarterly*, 18, 1953.
Aston, W. G., 'Kaempfer as an Authority on Shinto', *Man*, vol 2,
1902.
Aston, W. G., *Shinto: the Way of the Gods*, London, 1905.
Banks, Joseph (tr), *Icones selectae plantarum, quas in Japonia*

collegit et delineavit Engelbertus Kaempferus, London, 1791.

Beckmann, J., *Litteratur der älteren Reisebeschreibungen*, Göttingen, 1808.

Beckmann, John, *A History of Inventions and Discoveries*, vol. 3, London, 1797.

Berger, F. and Bonsack, W. (eds), *George Meister: Der Orientalisch-Indianische Kunst- und Lustgärtner*, Weimar, 1972.

Birch, Thomas, *The History of the Royal Society of London*, repr., New York, 1968.

Blacker, Carmen, *The Catalpa Bow: A Study of Shamanistic Practices in Japan*, London, 1986.

Blussé, J. L., 'A Glimpse behind the Screens: Some remarks on the Significance of the Deshima Dagregisters for the Study of Tokugawa Japan' in Paul van der Velde and Rudolf Bachofner (eds), *The Deshima Diaries Marginalia 1700-1740*, Tokyo, 1992.

Bodart-Bailey, Beatrice M., 'Warum noch einmal Kaempfer?', *Lippische Mitteilungen aus Geschichte und Landeskunde*, 57, 1988.

Bodart-Bailey, Beatrice M., 'Kaempfer Restor'd', *Monumenta Nipponica*, 43:1, 1988.

Bodart-Bailey, Beatrice M., 'Kyoto Three Hundred Years Ago', *Nichibunken Newsletter*, 9, 1991.

Bodart-Bailey, Beatrice M., 'Preliminary Report on the Manuscripts of Engelbert Kaempfer in the British Library', in Yu-Ying Brown (ed.), *Japanese Studies*, British Library Occasional Papers, 11, London, 1990.

Bodart-Bailey, Beatrice M., 'The Most Magnificent Monastery and Other Famous Sights: The Japanese Paintings of Engelbert Kaempfer', *Japan Review*, 3, 1992.

Bodart-Bailey, Beatrice M., 'Tokugawa Tsunayoshi (1646- 1709): A Weberian Analysis', *Asiatische Studien/Études Asiatiques*, 43:1, 1989.

Bodart-Bailey, Beatrice M., *Kenperu to Tokugawa Tsunayoshi* (Kaempfer and Tokugawa Tsunayoshi), Tokyo, 1994.

Bogaert, A., *De onderfgang van den Arion*, Amsterdam, 1724.

Bonn, Gerhard, 'Der wissenschaftliche Nachlaß des Lippischen Forschungsreisenden Engelbert Kaempfer im Britischen Museum', *Lippische Mitteilungen aus Geschichte und Landeskunde*, 48, 1979.

Bosse, Abraham, *Die Kunst in Kupfer zu stechen*, Dresden, 1765.

Bouchy, A.M., *Tokuhon Ascète du Nembutsu*, Paris, 1983.

Boyle, Robert, *General Heads for the Natural History of a Country. . .for the Use of Travellers and Navigators*, London, 1692.

Bibliography

Breyne, J., *Exoticarum aliarumque minus cognitarum plantarum centuria prima*, Danzig, 1678.

Breyne, J., *Prodromus fasciuli rariorum plantarum*, Danzig, 1680, 1689.

Brooks, E. St. John, *Sir Hans Sloane: The Great Collector and his Circle*, London, 1954.

Caron, François and Schouten, Joust, *A True Description of the Mightie Kingdoms of Japan and Siam*, reprinted from the English edition of 1663 and with introduction, notes and appendixes by C. R. Boxer, London, 1935.

Chijs, J. A. van der (ed.), *Dagh-Register gehouden int Casteel Batavia...Anno 1670-1671*, Batavia, 1898.

Clark, George, *A History of the Royal College of Physicians*, vol. 2, Oxford, 1966.

Cleyer, Andreas, *Curieuse Aenmerckingen der bysonderste Oost en West-Indische Verwonderenswaerdige Dingen*, Utrecht, 1682.

Cooper, Michael (ed.), *They Came to Japan: An Anthology of European Reports on Japan, 1543-1640*, London, 1965.

Coudret, Allison P., 'Forgotten Ways of Knowing: The Kabbalah, Language, and Science in the Seventeenth Century' in D. R. Kelley and R. H. Popkin (eds.), *The Shapes of Knowledge from the Renaissance to the Enlightenment*, Amsterdam, 1991.

Dambacher, Ilsegret, *Christian Wilhelm von Dohm*, Frankfurt/M, 1974.

De Beer, G. R., 'Johann Gaspar Scheuchzer, F.R.S. 1702- 1729', *Notes & Records of the Royal Society*, 6, 1948-49, pp. 63-64.

Demaerel, Paul, 'Couplet and the Dutch' in Jerome Heyndrickx (ed.), *Philippe Couplet, S.J. (1623-1693)*, Nettetal, 1990.

Dibon, Paul, 'Communication in the Respublica Literaria of the 17th Century', in *Res Publica Literarum: Studies in the Classical Tradition*, 1, 1978.

Dictionary of National Biography.

Doeff, Hendrick, *Herinneringen uit Japan*, Haarlem, 1833.

Dohm, Christian Wilhelm von, *Nachricht die Urschrift der Kämpferischen Beschreibung von Japan betreffend*, Lemgo, 1774.

Douglas, J., *Lilium Sariense*, London, 1725.

Du Mans, R., *Estat de la Persie en 1660*, Paris, 1890.

Feenstra, Kuiper, J., *Japan en de Buitenwereld in de achttiende eeuw*, The Hague, 1921.

Frazer, J. G., *Taboo and the Perils of the Soul:The Golden Bough, part II*, 3rd edition, 1911.

Gebhard, J. F., *Het Leven van Mr Nicolaas Cornelisz. Witsen (1641-1717)*, 2 vols, Utrecht, 1882.

Gicklhorn, J. and Gicklhorn R., *Georg Josef Kamel, S.J. (1661-1706):*

Apotheker, Botaniker, Arzt und Naturforscher der Philippinen, Eutin, 1954.

Goerke, H., *Carl von Linné: Arzt, Naturforscher, Systematiker*, second edition, Stuttgart, 1989.

Goodman, Grant K., *Japan: The Dutch Experience*, London, 1986.

Gorai Shigeru, 'Chozen Oshō no mokujiki', *Agama*, 17, January 1982.

Gorai Shigeru, 'Tansen no sokushin-jiobutsu ni shisō', *Agama*, 38, June 1984.

Griffith, Anthony, 'The Art and Hand of the Printmaker', in Skira Rizzoli (ed.), *Prints*, Geneva, 1981.

Gronovius, J. F., *Camphorae historia*, Leiden, 1715.

Hall, A. Rupert and Hall, Marie Boas (eds), *The Correspondence of Henry Oldenburg*, vols 2, 3, Madison, 1966; vol 4, Madison, 1967; vol 10, London, 1975.

Hall, Marie Boas, 'The Royal Society's Role in the Diffusion of Information in the Seventeenth Century', *Notes and Records of the Royal Society*, 29:2, 1975.

Hara, H., 'Nomenclatural notes on some Asiatic Plants with Special Reference to Kaempfer's Amoenitatum Exoticarum, *Taxon*, 25, 1977.

Harada Toshiaki, 'Matsuri no soshiki to shisaisha', in *Nihon minzokugaku taikei*, vol. 8, Tokyo, 1962.

Haren, Onno Zwier van, *Proeve, op de leevens- beschryvingen der nederlandsche doorlugtige mannen: behelzende het leeven van Joannes Camphuis*, Tezwolle, 1772.

Harris, J., *Navigautium atque Itinerantium Bibliotheca*, London, 1748.

Heniger, J., *Hendrik Adriaan van Reede tot Drakenstein (1636-1691) and Hortus Malabaricus*, Rotterdam, 1986.

Hepburn, James, *The Author's Empty Purse and the Rise of the Literary Agent*, Oxford, 1968.

Hoppe, Hans, 'Engelbert Kaempfers Stellung in der Gesellschaft seiner Zeit', in Hans Hüls and Hans Hoppe (eds), *Engelbert Kaempfer: Zum 330. Geburtstag*, Lippische Studien Band, 9, Lemgo, 1982.

Hüls, Hans, 'Zur Geschichte des Drucks von Kaempfers "Geschichte und Beschreibung von Japan" und zur sozialökonomischen Struktur von Kaempfers Lesepublikum im 18. Jahrhundert', in *Engelbert Kaempfers Geschichte und Beschreibung von Japan: Beiträge und Kommentar*, Berlin, 1980.

Hüls, Hans and Hoppe, Hans (eds), *Engelbert Kaempfer: Zum 330. Geburtstag*, Lippische Studien Band, 9, Lemgo, 1982.

Hüls, Hans and Müller-König, R., 'Medizinische Dissertation über zehn fremdländische Beobachtungen', in *Engelbert Kaempfer:*

Zum 330. Geburtstag, Lippische Studien Band, 9, Lemgo, 1982.

Hunter, Michael, *Science and Society in Restoration England*, Cambridge, 1981.

Hunter, Michael, *Establishing the New Science: The Experience of the Early Royal Society*, Woodbridge, 1989.

Imai Tadashi, 'Engelbert Kaempfer und seine Quellen', in *Engelbert Kaempfer: Zum 330. Geburtstag*, Lippische Studien Band, 9, Lemgo, 1982.

Imamura Akitsune, *Rangaku no sō Imamura Eisei* (The founder of Dutch studies, Imamura Eisei), Tokyo, 1942.

Iving, Wiliam M., Jr, *Prints and Visual Communication*, Cambridge, Ms, 1969.

Iwao Seiichi, *Meiji izen yoba no yunyū to zōshoku* (Import and proliferation of horseback riding in the pre-Meiji period), Tokyo, 1990.

Journal des Sçavans, February 1719; June 1734; October 1726; February 1727; September 1727.

Journal des Sçavans: Table Générale des Matières, vol. 6, Paris, 1756.

Kaempfer, Engelbert, *Amoenitatum exoticarum politico-physico-medicarum fasciculi V, . . .*, Lemgo, 1712.

Kaempfer, Engelbert, 'Das Stammbuch Engelbert Kaempfers', edited by Karl Meier-Lemgo, *Mitteilungen aus der Lippischen Geschichte und Landeskunde*, 21, 1952.

Kaempfer, Engelbert, 'De Majestatis Divisione', translated by R. Müller-König, in *Engelbert Kaempfer: Zum 330. Geburtstag*, Lippische Studien Band, 9, Lemgo, 1982.

Kaempfer, Engelbert, *Die Briefe Engelbert Kaempfers*, edited by Karl Meier-Lemgo, Wiesbaden, 1965.

Kaempfer, Engelbert, *Die Reisetagebücher Engelbert Kaempfers*, edited by Karl Meier-Lemgo, Wiesbaden, 1968.

Kaempfer, Engelbert, *Flora Japonica*, edited and translated by Wolfgang Muntschick, Wiesbaden, 1983.

Kaempfer, Engelbert, *Geschichte und Beschreibung von Japan*, edited by Christian Wilhelm von Dohm, 2 vols, Lemgo, 1777-79, reprint F.A. Brockhaus, Stuttgart, 1964.

Kaempfer, Engelbert, *Phoenix persicus: Die Geschichte der Dattelpalme*, translated by Wolfgang Muntschick, Marburg, 1987.

Kaempfer, Engelbert, *The History of Japan*, translated by Johann Gaspar Scheuchzer, 2 vols, London, 1727.

Kaempfer, Engelbert, *The History of Japan, together with a Description of the Kingdom of Siam*, translated by Johann Gaspar Scheuchzer, 3 vols, Glasgow, 1906, reprint London, 1993.

Kanai Madoka, *Nichiran kōshōshi no kenkyū* (A study of the history of Japanese-Dutch relations), Kyoto, 1986.

Katagiri Kazuo, *Oranda tsūji no kenkyū* (A Study of the Dutch Interpreters), Tokyo, 1985.

Katsuyama, Osamu, 'The Result of an Attempt to find the Source of an Old Japanese Book on Equine Medicine', *Argos Bulletin van het Veterinair Historisch Genootschap*, 8, 1993.

Kimura Yōjirō, *Shiiboruto to nihon no shokubutsu* (Siebold and Japanese plants), Tokyo, 1981.

Kimura Yōjirō, '*Kaempfer, Thunberg and Siebold*', *Japanese Studies of the History of Science*, 15, 1976.

Kircher, Anthanasius, *Anthanasaii Kircheri e Soc Jesu China monumentis qua sacris qua profanis*, Amsterdam, 1667.

Kitamura Shirō, 'Kaempfer no Nihon shokubutsu-ki ni tsuite (On Kaempfer's notes on Japanese plants), *Journal of the Department of Liberal Arts*, University of Tokyo, no. 5, 1953.

Koidzumi Gen'ichi, 'Nihon shokubutsu kenkyū shiryaku' (A short history of the study of Japanese plants), *Acta Phytotaxonomica et Geobotanica*, 1, 1932.

Kornicki, P. F., 'European Japanology at the End of the Seventeenth Century', *Bulletin of the School of Oriental and African Studies*, 56, 1993.

Kraft, Eva (ed.), *Andreas Cleyer, Tagebuch des Kontors zu Nagasaki auf der Insel Deshima*, Bonn, 1985.

Kraft, Eva, 'Andreas Cleyer', in *Festschrift zum 86. Deutschen Ärztetag*, Kassel, 1983.

Kraft, Eva, 'Christian Mentzel, Philippe Couplet, Andreas Cleyer und die chinesische Medizin' in *Fernöstliche Kultur, Wolf Haenisch zugeeignet*, Marburg, 1975.

Kraft, Eva, 'Frühe chinesische Studien in Berlin', *Medizinhistorisches Journal*, 11:1/2, 1976.

Lach, Donald F. and van Kley, Edwin, *Asia in the Making of Europe*, vol. 3, book 4, Chicago, 1993.

Levine, Joseph M., *Dr. Woodward's Shield*, Ithaca, 1977.

Mägdefrau, K., *Geschichte der Botanik*, Stuttgart, 1973.

Marshall, P. J. and Williams, Glyndwr, *The Great Map of Mankind*, London, 1982.

Massarella, Derek, 'Chinese, Tartars and Thea or a Tale of Two Companies: The English East India Company and Taiwan in the later Seventeenth Century', *Journal of the Royal Asiatic Society*, third series, 3:3, 1993.

Massarella, Derek, 'Philip Henry Zollman, the Royal Society's First Assistant Secretary for Foreign Correspondence', *Notes and Records of the Royal Society London*, 46:2, 1992.

Massarella, Derek, *A World Elsewhere: Europe's Encounter with Japan in the Sixteenth and Seventeenth Centuries*, New Haven, 1990.

Bibliography

Massarella, Derek, '"The Loudest Lies": Knowledge of Japan in Seventeenth Century England', *Itinerario*, 11:2, 1987.

Massarella, Derek and Tytler, Izumi K., 'The Japonian charters: The English and Dutch Shuinjō', *Monumenta Nipponica*, 45:2, 1990.

Matsubayashi Bunsaku, *Nagasaki shokubutsu no rekishi* (A history of the plants of Nagasaki), Tokyo, 1981.

Meier-Lemgo, Karl, 'Wie kam der handschriftliche Nachlaß Engelbert Kaempfers nach England?', *Sinologica*, 5, 1958.

Meier-Lemgo, Karl, *Engelbert Kaempfer erforscht das seltsame Asien*, second edition, Hamburg, 1960.

Meier-Lemgo, Karl, *Engelbert Kaempfer, der erste deutsche Forschungsreisende*, 1651-1716, Stuttgart, 1937.

Meyer, E. H. F., *Geschichte der Botanik, Königsberg*, 1857.

Michener, James A., *The Hokusai Sketchbooks*, Rutland, Vt, 1958.

Mitter, Partha, *Much Maligned Monsters: A History of European Reactions to Indian Art*, Oxford, 1977.

Miyake Hitoshi, *Shugendō jiten* (Dictionary of shugendō), Tokyo, 1986.

Miyata Noboru, *Ikigami shinkō*, Tokyo, 1970.

Miyata Noboru, *Minzoku shūkyō no kadai*, Tokyo 1977.

Montanus, Arnoldus, *Atlas Japannensis: being Remarkable Addresses by way of Embassy from the East-India Company of the United Provinces to the Emperor of Japan*, London, 1670.

Montanus, Arnoldus, *Description de l'empire du Japon*, Tokyo, 1973.

Montanus, Arnoldus, *Gedenkwaerdige gesantschappen der Oost-Indische Maetschappy in't Vereenigde Nederland, aen de Kaisaren van Japan*, Amsterdam, 1669.

Monthly Magazine, 16, 1804; 17, 1804.

Monthly Review, 61, 1779.

Morrison, S. E., *'Old Bruin': Commodore Matthew C. Perry 1794-1858*, Oxford, 1968.

Muntschick, Wolfgang, 'Ein Manuskript von Georg Meister, dem Kunst- und Lustgärtner, in der British Library', *Medizinhistorisches Journal*, 19, 1984.

Muntschick, Wolfgang, 'Nachlese zur Kaempfer-Forschung', *Lippische Mitteilungen*, 54, 1985.

Nakai, Kate Wildman, *Shogunal Politics: Arai Hakuseki and the Premises of Tokugawa Rule*, Cambridge, Mass, 1988.

Nakamura Tekisai, *Kimmōzui*, 1688.

Nakamura Tekisai, *Kimmōzui*, edited by Kobayashi Shōjiro, Tokyo, 1976.

Nicolson, D. H., Suresk, C. R. and Manilal, K. S., *An Interpretation of van Rheede's Hortus Malabaricus*, Königstein, 1988.

Niess, W., *Hexenprozesse in der Grafschaft Buedingen*, Rastatt, 1982.

Nieuhof, Johann, *Die Gesantschaft der Ost-Indischen Geselschaft in den Vereinigten Niederländern an den tartarischen Cham den tegenwoordigen keizer van China*, Amsterdam, 1669.

Nieuhof, John, *An Embassy sent from the East India Company of the United Provinces to the Grand Cham or Emperor of China*, London, 1673.

Numata Jirō et al. (eds), *Yōgakushi jiten* (A Dictionary of the history of Western learning), Tokyo, 1984.

Numata Jirō, 'Engelbert Kaempfer in Japan und sein Einfluß auf Japan', in OAG (ed.), *Engelbert Kaempfer (1651-1716) Philipp Franz von Siebold (1796-1866) Gedenkschrift*, Tokyo, 1966.

Ōi (Ohwi) Jisaburō, *Nihon shokubutsu-shi* (A history of Japanese flora), Tokyo, 1975.

Pas, P. W. van der, 'The earliest European Descriptions of Japan's Flora', *Janus*, 61, 1974.

Peters, Marion, 'Nicholaes Witsen and Gijsbert Cuper', *Lias*, 16, 1989.

Pharmazie und der gemeine Mann, Catalogue nr. 36, Herzog August Bibliothek, Wolfenbüttel, 1982.

Philosophical Transactions, 11 April 1666.

Pineau R. (ed.), *The Personal Journal of Commodore Matthew C. Perry*, Washington, 1968.

Rietbergen, P. J. A. N., 'Witsen's World: Nicolaas Witsen (1641-1717) Between the Dutch East India Company and the Republic of Letters' in Robert Ross and George D. Winius (eds), *All of One Company: The VOC in Biographical Perspective*, Utrecht, 1986.

Rossingh, M. P. H., *The Dutch Factory in Japan*, The Hague, 1964.

Rumphius, *Herbarium Amboinense*, Amsterdam, 1741-50.

Sachs, J., *Geschichte der Botanik vom 16. Jahrhundert bis 1860*, Munich, 1860.

Schiller, P., *Der botanische Garten in Padua*, Venice, 1987.

Schmid, G., 'Über Ph. Fr. v. Siebolds Reise nach Japan. Mit Briefen aus den Jahren 1822 bis 1827', *Botanisches Archiv*, 43, 1942.

Shapiro, Barbara, 'History and Natural History in Sixteenth and Seventeenth Century England' in Barbara Shapiro and Robert G. Frank Jr, *English Scientific Virtuosi in the 16th and 17th Centuries*, Los Angeles, 1979.

Shapiro, Barbara, *Probability and Certainty in Seventeenth Century England*, Princeton, 1983.

Sharpe, G. (ed.), *Syntagma Dissertationum...Thos. Hyde*, 2 vols, Oxford, 1767.

Shimizu Tōtarō, Nihon yakugaku-shi, (History of Japanese Pharmacy), Tokyo, 1949.

Siebold, Philipp Franz von and Zuccarini, J. G., *Flora Japonica*, Leiden, 1835-1870.

Bibliography

Siebold, Philipp Franz von, 'Einige Worte über den Zustand der Botanik auf Japan', *Nova Acta Academicae Caes. Leopold.-Caroline*, 14, 1829.

Sirks, M. J., 'Rumphius, the Blind Seer of Amboina', in P. Honig and F. Verdoorn (eds), *Science and Society in the Netherlands Indies*, New York, 1945.

Sloane, Hans, *Voyage to the Islands of Madeira, Barbadoes, Nieves, St Christopher's and Jamaica*, 2 vols, London, 1707, 1725.

Spalding, J. W., *The Japan Expedition*, New York, 1855.

Sprat, Thomas, *History of the Royal Society*, repr., St Louis, 1958.

Stapel, F. W., *Geschiednis van Nederlandsch Indie*, 5 vols, Amsterdam, 1938-40, vol. 3.

Stearn, W. T., 'An Introduction to the Species Plantarum and Cognate Botanical Works of Carl Linnaeus' in Carl Linnaeus, *Species plantarum*, repr., London, 1957.

Stedman, John Gabriel, *Narrative of a Five Years Expedition against the Revolted Negroes of Surinam*, edited by Richard and Sally Price, Baltimore, 1988.

Sternstein, Larry, 'Kaempfer as Mapper', in Detlef Haberland (ed.), *Engelbert Kaempfer: Werk und Wirkung*, Stuttgart, 1993.

Tankai, maki 3, Nihon shōmin seikatsu shiryō shusei (A collection of material of the life of the commoners in Japan), vol. 8, Tokyo, 1969.

Thomas, Christine G., 'Sir Hans Sloane and the Russian Academy of Sciences', *British Library Journal*, 14:1, 1988.

Thunberg, C. P., *Flora Japonica*, Leipzig, 1784.

Ultee, Marteen, 'Sir Hans Sloane, Scientist', *British Library Journal*, 14:1, 1988.

Ultee, Marteen, 'The Republic of Letters and Learned Correspondence, 1680-1720', *The Seventeenth Century*, 2:1, 1987.

Valentijn, François, *Oud en Nieuw Oost-Indien*, 8 vols, Dordrecht, 1724-1726.

Velde, P. G. E. I. J. van der, 'Deshima, mon amour. The publishing of the Marginals of the Deshima Diaries, 1641-1860' in Y.Y. Brown (ed.), *Japanese Studies*, British Library Occasional Papers, 11, London, 1990.

Voltaire, François-Marie Arouet de, *Essai sur les moeurs*, Paris, 1963.

Williams, Harold (ed.), *The Correspondence of Jonathan Swift*, vol. 1, *1690-1713*, Oxford, 1963.

Winau, Rolf, 'Christian Mentzel, die Leopoldina und der ferne Osten', *Medizinhistorisches Journal*, 11:1/2, 1976.

Winckler, T., *Geschichte der Botanik*, Frankfurt/M, 1854.

Wit, H. C. D. de, *Rumphius Memorial Volume*, Baarn, 1959.

Woodward, John, *Brief Instructions for Making Observations in all Parts of the World*, London, 1696.

Yokoyama, Toshio, *Japan and the Victorian Mind*, London, 1987.

Yule, Henry (ed.), *The Book of Ser Marco Polo*, London, 1875, vol. 2.

Zedlers Universal Lexicon.

Zuccarini, J. G., 'Bericht über die japanische Flora und ihre Erforschung', *Gelehrte Anzeigen*, 13, 1841.

Index